THE BACKPACKING
WOMAN

Lynn Thomas is a free-lance writer who has been a monthly contributor to *Camping Journal* magazine for the past five years. She has also written for *Backpacking Journal, San Francisco* and *Adventure Travel.*

THE BACKPACKING WOMAN

LYNN THOMAS

ANCHOR BOOKS

Anchor Press / Doubleday
Garden City, New York   1980

The Anchor Books edition is the first publication of *The Backpacking Woman*.
Anchor Books edition: 1980

ISBN: 0-385-15303-1
Library of Congress Catalog Card Number: 79-6890
Copyright © 1980 by Lynn Thomas
All Rights Reserved
Printed in the United States of America
First Edition

For Chet, with love

ACKNOWLEDGMENTS

If this book inspires some to move into a new realm, it is because of sensitive contributions made by many. Besides the women and men herein who speak to all, I also thank those special people who spoke personally to me before and during the process of creating this book.

Thanks go first to my parents for rarely saying no when I asked to go outdoors; to Ellen Matthews for going along; to spry Will and Bill Shephard, who guided my first steps; to Miriam Parker who, by example, taught me how much wilderness gives; to Andrew Carra, for encouragement and the opportunity to write; to Phil Ward for sharing the blisters, giggles and wilderness miles.

For helping shape the book, while also keeping me in shape, I thank Bruce Maxwell for being astute, outrageous—and caring; Lynn Ferrin, for gentleness and guidance when I needed some; Michael Rogers and Jan Hopson for generous helpings of champagne, streamers and sound advice; Jean Shinoda Bolen for her unwavering belief in what is possible; Lynne Neall, for being a friend and showing it in all-night work sessions in a wood-stove-warmed country cottage; Phil Arnot and Myra Harris for sharing my vision and passion for wilderness; Jim Owens for knowledge and constant kindness; Delores and Pete DeVasto for simplifying the task. For general lovingness, for reaching out, I thank Virginia Davidson, Gail and Peter Holland, the dear Tomlinsons—Frank, Irene, and Mayre—Jeanne Walsh and Rich Ward.

Finally, thanks go to the two women who offered the chance to transform thoughts and feelings into a book: Mary Evans, who first saw the promise, and Angela Iadavia Cox, who whittled it into shape.

—Forest Knolls, California
April, 1980

Contents

Perspectives

There is a lingering impression—some twenty-five hundred years old—that women don't belong outdoors. It is poppycock, pure and simple. It springs not from what history says, but from what it fails to say. One survey of written history completed in Europe in 1910 showed that the women deemed worthy of historic note were mostly queens, French salon women of the seventeenth century, mothers, mistresses, martyrs, religious leaders and women important only through marriage. Not an outdoor woman was among them.

Throughout history wilderness heroines have always been conspicuously absent. How many can you name? Two, maybe three? What do these women tell you about your capabilities or place in the world? The two on my list were Pocahontas—a tired cliché at best—and Calamity Jane, a sharpshooter with a cute name. In my formative years, neither of these women seemed real to me; neither assisted me in my sometimes solitary attempt to remain active outdoors.

Yet women have always been active outdoors. Consider America during these past two hundred years. When white men were pushing the frontiers of the United States from east coast to west, Sacajawea, a daughter of the Shoshone tribe, was there. By guiding Meriwether Lewis, William Clark and thirty-two other men on their epic journey from Missouri to the Pacific Ocean and back, by saving explorers' scalps from tribal tomahawks, Sacajawea played a crucial role in opening the west. While the achievement speaks for itself, the journals of Lewis and Clark provide no notion of the frustrations, elation or sense of triumph this fifteen-year-old must have known. Nor do they show how the journey changed her philosophies, her attitude, her life. What a different perception women might have of themselves today had Sacajawea known how to write!

Native American women spent entire lifetimes outdoors. Actually, they gave rise to backpacking centuries ago. The "pack" in those days was called a travois. From birch trees two crude poles, six to twelve feet long, were carved. Between these two parallel poles buffalo hide was stretched taut, then secured to the poles by leather thongs. The poles were then placed on either side of the woman's waist, and held in position by the strength of her arms and by leather thongs tied about her waist. On moving days— which happened seasonally—once the family's tepee and possessions were secured, the women were left to drag the travois, while the men rode ahead on their horses.

For sheer spunk, though, pioneer women were unsurpassed. Three- to five-thousand-mile junkets seem nothing compared to the conditions they endured. Food consisted of salt pork, jerked beef and flour—and when those ran out, buffalo tongues and humps. When wagons broke down, or too many oxen died, they walked. In high-heeled, high-top boots, they walked. In corsets and dresses which would be considered formal today, they walked: fifteen to twenty-five miles a day. It was seldom an unencumbered march. Usually they carried children. Frequently they herded cattle. To give birth they were grudgingly granted a one-day halt. But weakness after birth was no cause to stop. Historians' scant notes on women in those days assumed a tone of disbelief, for despite hunger, emotional hardship and physical trials of the most enervating sort, many times women were the only ones who survived.

First women crossed a continent; next they discovered mountains as a source of challenge and sport. They lacked the sophisticated equipment of today—ice axes, crampons, jumars and lightweight climbing rope—but they went anyway. In 1894, thirty-eight women reached the 11,245-foot summit of Mount Hood. In high-necked blouses and long skirts they slid fearlessly down thousand-foot snowfields in tin washbasins. It was, according to one journalist, a sign of ladies' "timid entry into sports."

Outdoor woman, circa 1916.

On early Sierra Club trips, starting in 1896, women usually out-
numbered men, and morals committees were formed to protect
their virtue. The result: single women slept upstream, single men
slept down, while married couples slept between. If integrity was
preserved by these rules, sleep was not, for tents were nonexistent
then, while "sleeping bags" consisted of wool blankets or light
comforters filled with eiderdown. Cold mountain mornings found

women rolled in blankets and every stitch of clothing—including picture hats and high-top boots.

Unlike the wilderness of today—with trailheads, pit toilets, stone hutches and direction signs—wilderness then was a trackless domain ruled by black flies, rattlesnakes, buffalo and grizzly bears. That didn't stop the women of those days. Equipment was home-made, and crude at best. Clothes were confining and cumbersome. *That* didn't stop them. If, given these conditions, our foremothers found value and fun in wilderness, so can women of today.

What is the best way for a woman to know the pleasure wilderness holds? In my opinion, it is with a backpack. The backpack is an entry point for many wilderness sports, for rock and mountain climbing, cross-country skiing, for studying birds, plants, insects, or stars. More than this, it is a ticket to independence and freedom. It offers the chance to explore ways of thinking and being that seldom present themselves in the regimented byways of city life.

Every time a woman takes up a pack she learns a little more about nature, about the value of self-determination and about the satisfaction that comes from setting a goal and achieving it. She opens herself to the energy in nature, energy available only to those who abandon roofs and walls. But, in backpacking there are also blisters, sore muscles and scraped knees. There is thirst, coldness, sleepless nights. There is, midway up most hills, a desire to be somewhere else. These are not bad things, really, for they reconnect a woman to her body, to the invigorating sense of being alive.

Why should a woman backpack? She shouldn't—unless and until she has the urge. When that happens she will find reason enough on her own. For those women who seek additional reason or urge the following pages may help.

This book is intended to keep women from feeling as I did when I began—alone and somehow wrong for preferring wilderness to dress shops and beauty salons. It results from eight years of backpacking, and the musings that sprang from that. It results from written or personal interchanges with more than a hundred and fifty vital women whose lives have been meaningfully shaped by wilderness.

It is designed as a primer for the beginner, as a source of education or motivation for the intermediate to experienced woman backpacker—but it does not stand on its own. Technical skills involved in backpacking are diverse and complex. To instruct on each in the confines of a single book would, because of the need for brevity, do an injustice both to the skill and to the reader. Fortunately, books exist that teach specific skills. For example, one entire book has been devoted to map and compass reading. Such books, as well as invaluable nature guides, appear in the Recommended Reading list. Skills also can be developed or refined by joining night school or college courses, or by participating in organized trips. National organizations that sponsor backpacking trips are listed in the Appendix.

Because history has steadfastly denied women outdoor role models, one is introduced at the start of three sections of this book. Each of these women became active outdoors for different reasons. Each grew from her experience in different ways. Through their lives and quality of thought each has much to teach.

Mostly this book is an inspiration expanded. It is an invitation from myself and every woman herein to join in celebrating the lessons and joys wilderness holds. If you accept the invitation only one thing is asked—that when you walk in wilderness you do so with care. In return for all wilderness gives women, that is the very least we can do.

Section One
FIRST STEPS

CHAPTER 1

Starting Off—
For Better or for Worse

The subject of backpacking—and the backpack itself—edge their way into women's awareness and life in different ways, for different reasons. Usually introductions are made by some man—a father, boyfriend or mate—eager for a little company, or for the chance to share the enjoyment they have known. Other women, motivated by deeper stirrings, don't wait for a man to ask. They pack up and head out in the company of other women or, in Lynne Neall's case, entirely on their own. As most quickly discover, first trips seldom go as smoothly as planned.

In Sun Valley, Idaho, in the Sixties, Lynne and seven friends decided to celebrate Labor Day with a backpack trip. As the date approached, all seven backed out, one by one. This left Lynne and her faithful dog, Jacques—neither of whom had backpacked before. Lynne decided to go anyway. Into an ancient frameless Army pack, which some sympathetic soul had passed on, she began stuffing supplies: one ragged sleeping bag, canned dog food, canned tuna and bottled mayonnaise to mix it with, bread, eggs, a can opener, a few beers. She packed, she admits today, as if she were going on a picnic in the backyard. At the appointed hour she drove to the designated trailhead, parked and headed out. Two hours later, after going only a few miles, physical pain forced her to stop. The pack had pierced a hole in her back. She rested awhile, padded the wound with sweaters, then pushed on in a stooped shuffle reminiscent of the Hunchback of Notre Dame.

She camped that first night near the shores of a lake. After dark, bears and night critters came out. No one had warned her that she would be afraid when alone in wilderness at night, but she was. After she finally slipped into uneasy sleep, a boulder field on the opposite shore took the opportunity to avalanche. Lynne mistook the bombastic rumble for a bear, and instantly began bargaining with God: if God got her out of this alive she would go home immediately and would never do anything bad the rest of her life. Sunshine the next morning found her reneging on at least part of the bargain—she decided to continue on. In three days alone she saw and spoke to no one except her ragged-mop Jacques. Jacques, also footsore and body weary, had little to say in return. When finally they stumbled back to the car, Lynne picked up the first hitchhikers she passed, for companionship and the chance to use her voice.

Her reaction to backpacking following the first trip was entirely typical: she hated it. Furthermore, she never intended to do it again. One year later she reversed her stand. Since then, though scars from her first pack remain, she has backpacked in the Sierra, the Rockies, in Canada and Alaska, and she has trekked in Nepal. From backpacking, an interest in climbing was born. After training in Yosemite, she joined climbs in the Grand Tetons, the Rockies and the Minarets.

Diane Strachan is another case in point. Except for two weekend trips the preceding year, she and companion Jeff Christiansen approached their first official backpack trip as quintessential greenhorns. Their goal? To cover California on foot! They knew where they wanted to go; they just weren't sure how—or even if—they were going to get there.

High hopes accompanied them during their first days out. So did sore feet. To compound foot problems caused by the sweltering Mojave desert floor, Diane hiked in boots a half size too small. When she purchased the boots neither she nor the salesman knew that she should simultaneously try on a full pack, to flatten and spread her feet to the dimensions they would assume on the trail. "I liked the boots, right? So I bought them," Diane says. "My whole feet, *both* feet, were blisters . . . all the way around, blisters. I had to walk a hundred miles in those boots. One day we walked eight miles, then stopped. I couldn't walk anymore. I couldn't feel my feet either. It was two days before I could walk again. We spent the time watching hawks nesting. We learned a lot about hawks."

Most backpackers harbor some sort of weight fetish. Diane's concern was not how much her pack weighed, but how little her body would weigh by the end of the trip. To encourage weight loss she packed the minimum amount of food needed to survive. In no time at all the plan worked. "We lost fifteen pounds in twenty days of walking eight miles a day," Diane recalls. In addition, they lost their humor, their strength and most of their inspiration.

On their eighth day out they reached the foot of their first mountain just as a storm hit. Diane was in no shape for either. It was the first day of her period. She had skipped breakfast, and was putting out more energy than she had put into her body in days. To compound her problems, she was soaked to the skin when her Sears plastic rain suit shredded with the first whip of wind. When uncontrollable shivers began halfway up the mountain, Jeff set up the tent and sleeping bags and coaxed her to crawl in. By then her responses were minimal: she didn't care, she just wanted to sleep. Such profound character change caused Jeff to react. He pulled her from the bag, assembled the gear and began pushing her up the mountain in hopes of locating more suitable shelter. At the summit he found a motel cabin renting for $12—exactly what he had in his jeans. He splurged remaining loose change on a candy bar, bundled Diane into cabin and bed, turned the heat on full, then sat back to hope for some return to normalcy. They didn't learn until years later, when studying first aid, that Diane was suffering from hypothermia, labelled "the killer of the unprepared." By his instinctive actions Jeff had saved her life.

Despite this near miss, dietary skimping continued. By the time they reached their second resupply point, a few hundred miles north, Jeff's naturally lanky body had been reduced to the sorry dimensions of a stick figure. When, to protect himself from gape-jawed stares, Jeff refused to unzip his down parka, though it was 90 degrees in the shade, they both agreed that it was time to eat more. To supplement their protein intake, which had been limited until then to beef jerky, they began buying fresh eggs along the way. At each resupply point they stocked up with as many high-calorie goodies as they could carry. The effect of increased food intake was negligible where Diane was concerned. By the time she reached the Oregon border she weighed thirty pounds less than when she had begun.

One unanticipated problem in covering those long miles was boredom. "You go to sleep, you wake up and you walk. And walk. And walk," Diane recalls. At first they walked eight miles a day. Once in condition they increased daily mileage, covering at times as much as twenty-five miles a day. Some days they'd walk five miles before breakfast, eat, then walk five miles before lunch, eat, then walk five to ten miles before dinner: Diane recalls falling asleep once walking a thirty-mile straight line through the desert. "People think how neat, how adventurous," she says. "But, really, a month goes by, another month goes by and you're still walking north."

One basis of boredom, she recognizes now, was her lack of involvement in trip logistics. "On that walk I did what I think a lot of women might do," Diane says. "I handed the responsibility for figuring out where we were, for reading the map, for making sure everything was okay to Jeff. When I was done walking the length of California I still didn't know how to read a compass!"

To hardships and blisters, hard-earned lessons and boredom, one prized quality was added: intimacy. Six months in wilderness alone gave this couple a sense of one another such as few couples ever know. While at times they might gladly have pushed one another off the nearest cliff, during these months together they discovered shared values and sensitivities, one vital basis of love.

Today, Diane and Jeff are together still. They share a cottage on a hilltop sanctuary. Both attend Sonoma State College, pursuing degrees and future careers in environmental studies. Both sustain active hobbies: Jeff carpentry and woodwork, Diane running and mountaineering.

She walked an unconventional route to earn the right to live as she chooses. A six-month journey with backpack gave new direction to her life, offering insights and opportunities rare to so young a woman.

As first trips go, Lynne's ranks pretty near the norm. Diane's is beyond a beginner's norm and is recounted only to show what is possible, not advisable.

For perfectly understandable reasons, few backpackers ever experience love-at-first-trip. There simply are too many discomforts, inconveniences and unknowns for that. Usually the body is not accustomed to exercise or to the humbling experience of carrying a pack. The senses are not attuned to the splendors and subtleties that wilderness holds. All that most women know on their first outing is that everyone else is having a grand time—and they're not.

This thought accompanies them home, and lingers until sore muscles are forgotten and blisters disappear. Then, for some, new feelings emerge. They remember how good it felt, after a long day's walk, to dip in the crystal waters of an icy lake. They recall the dapple of morning dew on some fragile leaf, the pungent odor of wood smoke or how many wishes they made on shooting stars. They bask in the joy of stepping out of a rut and achieving something new.

At this point, usually, a woman decides whether the backpack is for her. Either the remembered pleasures of wilderness and physical exertion entice her, like the mythical siren Ceres on a rocky shoal, or they do not. Those who respond to the silent call are those who will endure those first awkward steps—and trips. Likely, they have within them the makings of an outdoor woman. For them, for the rest of their lives, thoughts of wilderness will dance in their soul.

But the trick is bridging the gap; it is bringing yourself to and through your first trip so that your sense of wilderness, whether you become further involved or not, will be a positive one. This is not hard to do. On your part it takes awareness, a little reading, a lot of planning. And it takes heeding the advice of others who have gone before.

The object here is to supply that advice, to help reduce the negatives and uncertainties of those first trips. Advice comes from women such as myself who lived to laugh and tell about their first fumbling steps—and the things they wish some woman had told them.

CHAPTER 2

Shaping Up

Ever since the advent of male dominance, of Hollywood and ladies' magazines, women have been getting two messages about their bodies. One, they should be shapely and cosmetically perfect. Two, they should be not very strong.

By holding to these messages, since Victorian times, women have developed a negative orientation toward their bodies. They think of them not in terms of the miracles they perform, but in terms of how visually imperfect they are. Beyond that, many women disdain any exercise that might make them strong. When pressed on the subject many reply, almost defensively, how much energy goes into keeping the house clean and the family fed and clothed, or how hard they work at developing their careers. But, as sports medicine specialist Dr. Evalyn Gendel recognizes, physical work is a far different animal from physical fitness.

Dr. Gendel has studied the value of physical fitness for women, both professionally and in her personal life. Her own fitness regime began at age three with ballet lessons. In high school she was a sprint and relay runner. She commuted to college and medical school by bike—twenty-five miles a day. While maintaining a busy family practice in Kansas she swam a mile a day. At night, while doing laundry for her five children, she worked out in the laundry room on her ballet *bierre*. Now, as a program director at the University of California Medical Center, she runs four miles a day, or she manages a few rounds on the office stairs—all seven flights of them. "If you ever have trouble finding me," she once told her secretary, "try the stairs."

Professionally, Dr. Gendel has conducted two separate studies to examine the effects of exercise on women. In one she discovered that the common denominator for women who had difficulty resuming normal functions after pregnancy was a lifetime of inactivity. In another, with 150 college freshmen as her sample, she learned that those women who suffered least from allergies, headaches or menstrual cramps were those who exercised most. Dr. Gendel subsequently concluded that it is a myth to consider housework physically beneficial. "Woman's work," that age-old exercise, has left women weak in arms and upper bodies, knees, ankles and cardiovascular systems. Legs, which statisticians claim carry us an average of 60,000 miles in our lifetime, are considered a woman's strongest attribute. Yet even they lack strength and tone.

Now, however, we are entering a more energetic age. Doctors tell us that regular daily exercise enhances not only our body, but also our brain. We are encouraged to grow strong, to undertake physical conditioning. Backpacking is a gentle way of doing both, but before backpacking some preliminary conditioning is advised.

The ideal conditioning program involves two forms of exercise: aerobics and weight training. Aerobic exercise conditions the cardiovascular system—the heart, lungs, arteries and capillaries—which processes oxygen and blood. Weight training increases muscle tone, strength and endurance, without building muscles.

With aerobic exercise almost everyone has a natural preference —choosing either to swim, bicycle, jog, walk or dance. Because it takes only twenty minutes a day and the track is as near as my front door, I opt to jog. Important as jogging is in strengthening calves and thighs, other backpackers prefer to swim. "Swimmers are often better backpackers," Dr. Gendel says, "because they have strengthened their arms and shoulders."

To become aerobically fit you should exercise at least four times a week, covering increasingly longer distances in relatively shorter times. Your age and condition when you start the program makes a difference. To determine your present cardiovascular condition, administer the pulse test. Using a clock or watch with a second hand, begin by sitting quietly for five minutes. Locate your pulse at your wrist and measure it by counting the number of beats for thirty seconds. Multiply by two to determine how many times your heart beats per minute. While many doctors consider a pulse rate between 72 and 80 normal, other doctors, advocates of physical conditioning, contend that "normal" and "fit" are two different states. To them a pulse over 60 indicates a lack of physical fitness.

The pulse can be lowered and the body can achieve fitness by systematic exercise, but it is no overnight affair. As Dr. Kenneth Cooper, America's leading expert on aerobics, says, "If it has taken you ten years to get out of shape, plan to spend ten months getting back into shape."

The key to success in any fitness program is starting slowly. The jog-walk test is an excellent way to begin. First, pick a flat route or athletic track, the mileage of which you know. Start by jogging at a pace that is comfortable for you. If that becomes difficult, slow to a walk until your body feels ready to jog again. If in twelve minutes you cover more than a mile and a half, you are in excellent condition; if a mile and a quarter, your condition is good; if a mile or less, you are in poor shape.

Once you have determined your current condition you will find carefully diagrammed, age-coded conditioning programs for all forms of aerobic exercises in Dr. Kenneth Cooper's *The New Aerobics* and in *Aerobics for Women* by Mildred Cooper.

Aerobic exercise is long on rewards—including weight loss, physical toning, bowel regularity, improved sex lives, clear complexions and enhanced self-esteem. There also is intrinsic pleasure in watching your body realize its potential, in gradually developing the strength and stamina to travel four miles in the time it once took to travel two.

Weight training, the second form of recommended exercise, has a notoriously bad name among women. Many confuse it with weight *lifting,* a competitive sport, or body building, an esthetic exercise. Having no desire to resemble Arnold Schwarzenegger (of *Pumping Iron* fame), I, for one, dodged it for years. Then I met Jane Dickerson.

Jane was a typical physical lightweight until she fell in love with mountain climbing. Within two years, with guided instruction, she climbed Washington's Mount Rainier twice, plus Mount Orizaba in Mexico. We met while she was training for a six-week traverse of Alaska's Mount McKinley. In a group of thirteen she was to be the only woman. Her goal on climbs is "not necessarily to be first, but certainly not to be last." To sustain that, Jane has practiced weight training for two years. She could have fooled me.

The woman answering the door had the look of a delicately wrought figurine. She was dressed simply, in a long-sleeved peasant blouse, slacks and strap sandals. Chestnut hair, casually barretted back, fell to her waist. There wasn't a muscle in sight, yet she was strong. When asked how much her strength had increased by weight training, she demonstrated by getting down on the living room carpet and completing fifteen full push-ups—the type that men do. "Two years ago," she beamed, "I couldn't have managed more than one of those." She isn't the only one. Kathryn Lance, prime advocate of weight training for women, maintains that if you can complete even one full push-up, you are stronger than most American women.

Clearly, Jane achieved all the bonuses of weight training with none of the bulges. Here is why. Because of the effects of female hormones, there is a limit to the size a woman's muscles can grow. This is proven by medical studies. In a ten-week weight training program one exercise physiologist discovered that when men and women of the same size followed the same program, the percentage of increased strength was the same for both sexes, but women generally developed only one-tenth the muscle mass.

Weight training is accomplished selectively and gradually, beginning with the muscles you use most. In backpacking this includes arms and upper body, lower back, legs and knees. A weight training program is managed best either by joining a local gym, as Jane did, or by following the tailored-to-backpacking guidelines which follow.

There is one other way to condition, and that is to backpack. Such conditioning can begin long before the journey. One seasoned hiker starts four months early by carrying groceries home from the store, or stuffing her pack with books and taking day hikes. Or, for the exceptionally busy woman, it can begin at the outset of the trip. But this latter approach is acceptable only if you are thirty or under, if the terrain is easy and the trip short, or if, on a longer trip, you start slowly and travel no farther than six miles a day for the first week. If this is not feasible, you will be courting discomfort and potential injury from the unaccustomed strain the pack imposes.

Teddi Boston, a forty-nine-year-old mother of four who solo-hiked the 2,600-mile Pacific Crest Trail, conditions with a back-pack. Months before her epic journey, she hiked 25 miles each weekend under the weight of a fully loaded pack. Teddi acknowledges that the speed at which conditioning occurs relates directly to age. "Every year it takes me one day longer on the trail to get in condition," she says. She advises women to expect to spend one day on the trail conditioning for every year they are over thirty. Given this formula, the thirty-eight-year-old should not push to perform at her peak level until after the eighth day of the trip.

Too few of us have such luxury of time on the trail. Therefore, some form of preconditioning is essential.

Because both aerobics and weight training place mild stress on the heart and lungs, physicians recommend that women over thirty have a checkup within the three months prior to the start of a conditioning program, including an electrocardiogram (ECG) taken at rest. If you are over forty, the ECG should be taken while you are exercising. Women over sixty should be examined immediately before embarking on any exercise program.

GUIDE TO GETTING FIT

To strengthen the areas backpacking stresses most, when preparing for any trip longer or more physically demanding than a relaxed weekend outing, the following preconditioning exercises are recommended.

For Overall Conditioning

● JOGGING, SWIMMING

While each aerobic exercise is beneficial, those that serve the backpacker best are jogging and swimming. With jogging, as the cardiovascular system is being conditioned, the thighs, calves and lower back are being strengthened. The ideal conditioning pro-

gram would include jogging two miles a day for one month before
the trip. If you prefer swimming, which develops strength in the
arms and shoulders as well as in the legs, plan to cover one-half to
one mile a day four times a week for one month before the trip.

For Abdomen and Lower Back

- SIT-UPS

If your abdominal muscles are weak, start with a half sit-up.
Lie flat on the floor with knees bent and arms at your side. Slowly
raise your head, shoulders and chest off the floor, keeping your

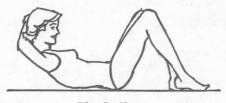

Fig. 2. Sit-up.

lower back flat. Return slowly to starting position. This is a half
sit-up. When abdominal muscles have developed, advance to the
full sit-up. In this, hands should be clasped behind your head and
you should raise all the way up. To develop abdominal strength,
do 10 bent-legged sit-ups a day for one month before the trip.

For Arms, Shoulders and Upper Body

- PUSH-UPS

If you are to lift a heavy pack without straining yourself, your
upper body muscles must be developed. The push-up is considered the best overall strengthening exercise for the upper body.
Because few women can perform a full push-up, begin the conditioning process with the negative push-up. Begin in the upper position of the standard push-up—palms under shoulders, arms
straight, trunk and legs straight. Slowly lower yourself to the floor
while keeping your trunk straight. Relax. Start with 5 negative
push-ups; build to 20. Once arms develop, graduate to the full

Fig. 3. Full push-up.

push-up, in which you both lower and raise your body with the strength of your arms. Work up to 10 full push-ups each day for one month before your trip.

For Upper Back

● SHOULDER SHRUG

To avoid cramping in upper back muscles from the unaccustomed weight of the pack, you should strengthen the trapezius

Fig. 4. Shoulder shrug.

muscles, those triangular-shaped muscles covering your upper back. The best exercise for this is the shoulder shrug. Holding one five-pound weight in each hand (books, bricks or two filled paint cans will do), slowly raise your shoulders to your ears, if you can, then lower them slowly, rolling your shoulders backward. Start with two sets of 6 shoulder shrugs. When you can manage this with ease, increase the number of shrugs to 8, 10 and eventually 12. Next increase weights to eight pounds, and return to two sets of 6 shoulder shrugs, building eventually to 12. The shoulder-shrug series should be performed once a day for at least one month before the trip.

For Knees and Ankles

Knees and ankles generate the highest incidence of injuries among women backpackers. To avoid such problems, incorporate two exercises into your preconditioning program.

Fig. 5. Knee lift.

● KNEE LIFTS

Sit on a surface high enough to keep your feet from touching
the floor. Suspend a three- to five-pound weight from your foot—a
small sand bag, say, or a paint can filled with sand. Slowly raise
your lower leg until it is parallel to the floor. Hold for three seconds, then lower slowly. Perform this exercise 12 times with each
leg. As thighs strengthen, gradually increase the number of knee
lifts, eventually working up to 25 with each leg.

● ANKLE LIFTS

Remain seated on the same surface as for the above exercise.
Drape the three- to five-pound weight across the toes. Slowly ele-
vate the foot from the ankle. Hold for three to five seconds, then
lower. Do this with each foot. Begin with 12 lifts. As your ankles
adjust to the weight and exercise, gradually increase the number of
lifts you perform. Your goal should be 25 with each foot.

For one who has never tried it, conditioning may seem more
struggle than fun, but the long-term benefits make it worthwhile.
When, if, incentive begins to wane, simply remember this: the
stronger you feel before you go, the better you'll feel as you go.
That applies not just to backpacking, but to all areas of your life.

✕✖✕✖✕✖✕✖✕✖✕✖✕✖✕✖✕✖✕✖✕✖✕✖✕✖✕✖✕✖✕✖✕✖✕

CHAPTER 3

Equipment

The trick to backpacking is implied in the name. You must carry on your back, in a pack, whatever you will need to survive comfortably and safely outdoors. It amounts to an entire household, and it must be compressed into a mere 3,300 cubic inches or less, without exceeding the comfort limit, which is set at roughly one-third your body weight. Into your pack, your temporary home, you must stuff shelter from the elements, a working kitchen, food, the makings of a comfortable bed, imperative toiletries, a versatile wardrobe, tools—for pathfinding, for repair, for construction—and any favorite books or games.

Impossible though this task may seem, fortunately modern technology has come to our aid. One generation of equipment designers, with their helpmates—nylon, polyester, aluminum, natural and synthetic insulators—have gifted us with the broadest, most sophisticated selection of outdoor equipment in history. We should be grateful. Instead, many of us are merely confused. With so much to choose from, it is difficult to distinguish what among the vast assortment is best for us—and why.

The easy solution would be to compose a list of recommended brand names and send you on your way. But, your local equipment outlet might not stock these brands, which would leave you none the wiser or better equipped. Or it could leave you shopping by mail—the worst possible way to acquire equipment. The alternative is to provide enough information on equipment function and features to permit you to make educated choices from brands which are available. But, first, it is important to examine the history of equipment.

Since its conception, the equipment world has been dominated by men. They have designed, manufactured, advertised and sold equipment. Outdoor women were in short supply, and because manufacturers believed that men were the only equipment users, equipment was designed and marketed accordingly.

As the number of outdoor women has grown, gradually a few manufacturers have begun acknowledging women's unique needs. If your retail outlet does not carry a line designed to accommodate women, or carries one that does not feel comfortable to you, ask them to carry more. The word should filter back to manufacturers and inspire change. As one manufacturer insists, "We rely on consumer input."

It is hardly news that equipment prices are soaring. Nylon and polyester are oil derivatives. Every time OPEC raises its prices, the cost of fabric jumps, as does the cost of equipment. In response to the law of supply and demand, the price of prime goose down also is climbing. In 1977, one pound of down jumped from $11.50 to $22! Despite this inflationary trend, select the most well-made equipment you can afford, for as you quickly learn, there is no such thing as a bargain when your cut-rate tent begins to leak in a downpour. When seasonal demand for equipment dips, so does price. To stretch your equipment budget, shop after Labor Day or Christmas.

Equipment acquisition should be a gradual process prefaced by experience on the trail with borrowed or rented equipment. At a fraction of the purchase price, renting allows you to experiment, to discover which equipment works best for you and why. If you don't like it, return it. If you do, in some stores you can apply the price of rental toward purchase.

There are a few rules to heed while shopping. One, mountaineering shops usually offer a higher grade of equipment than sporting goods stores. Two, always comparison-shop. It is the best way to learn about equipment, and the only way to assure that you get the best buy. Three, always shop first for an experienced salesperson before you shop for equipment.

Most retail clerks are people with good intentions who strive to be well instructed. Quite understandably, however, many men are not sensitive to women's requirements. Recently, in Berkeley's most popular mountaineering shop, I asked a salesman which pack he recommended for women. "The same pack I recommend for men," he replied. "Women don't have any special needs." Most outdoor women vehemently disagree. To avoid such bias, seek out a sales*woman* who loves to backpack. If the salespeople are men only, ask many questions to determine their knowledge and their sensitivity to women's needs. According to outdoor leader Nancy Skinner, who conducted her own shopping survey, "The best equipment salespeople are owners or co-owners of smaller stores. They will take time with you because they see you as a potential future customer. Few salespeople have the same perspective."

When selecting equipment, color is an important consideration. With wilderness shrinking, with more people occupying what wilderness remains, we must be conscious of the visual impact we are making. To minimize that impact, to remain inconspicuous, choose browns, blues, rusts and greens. However, there is another factor to be considered: safety. When trigger-happy hunters are about, or in the midst of a paralyzing storm, for her own protection, a backpacker must be seen. Under such conditions red, orange and yellow are effective attention-getters. Still, there are other times when, for her own safety, a woman should strive not to be seen—particularly when camping alone. Perhaps the best way to minimize visual impact while also remaining safe is to select major equipment—pack, parka and tent—in colors that blend in with your surroundings. To this should be added one bright accent, such as a large red poncho, which can be worn or stored in the pack depending on the desire to be seen.

We expect equipment to take care of us, yet few of us know how to take care of it. While working in an equipment outlet, one woman was assigned to repair stoves. She would dismantle them, wash the parts in white gas and reassemble them. This took fifteen minutes and cost the customer $10. How many could manage that task on the trail where it is needed? To avoid untimely breakdowns, familiarize yourself with your equipment before traveling with it. Where possible, dismantle it and learn the function of each part. Such knowledge will serve you and your equipment well.

One other way to gain a thorough understanding of equipment is to make your own. A number of manufacturers specialize in supplying components for do-it-yourself packs, sleeping bags, tents and outdoor clothing. The advantages are two. You may realize up to a 50 per cent savings, and you have absolute quality control. You can take time to double-stitch seams, to seal nylon edges against fraying, to build in extra strength where needed.

Frostline, the pioneer kit maker, has been in business since 1966. Because the company was started by a man, equipment is designed for men. Clothes are unisex, or, as product development manager Carol Moon admits, "sort of baggy"—but quality is excellent. Designs are borrowed from other top-of-the-line equipment, while fabric and filler are the same as used by other quality manufacturers. Carol Moon, who describes herself as "a basic home ec major, not a tent maker," has made two tents and all of Frostline's jackets from the kits. "The people we have the most trouble with," Carol says, "are professional sewers. They don't follow the instructions." Other kit makers include EMSKIT, from Eastern Mountain Sports of Boston, Altra Kits and Holubar Kits (Boulder, Colorado), Mountain Adventure Kits (Whittier, California), Sun Down (Burnsville, Minnesota).

Finally, when shopping, if you have the choice, support those manufacturers who have made some specific effort in their equipment lines to welcome women outdoors. These include Caribou Mountaineering, Hine/Snowbridge and Lowe Alpine Systems. If you cannot locate these manufacturers' products in your equipment outlet, their addresses are listed in the Appendix. Write to them to obtain the address of the nearest outlet which stocks their products.

THE PACK

Thirty years ago, when selecting a backpack, you had your choice of a heavyweight wood-and-canvas affair known as the Trapper Nelson. Today, in a resolute thrust in the opposite direction, four different styles of packs are manufactured by many companies in every conceivable color, weight, range of quality and price.

The four pack designs include the external frame, the internal frame, the frameless or soft backpack, and the day pack. Both the frameless pack and the day pack take their shape from the con-

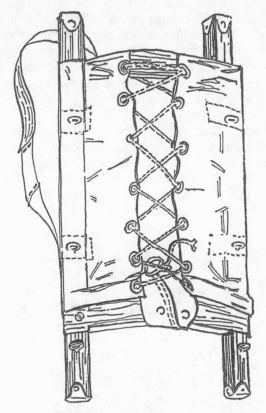

Fig. 6. Trapper Nelson, the early model pack frame.

tents. But there the similarity ends, for the day pack features a
limited carrying capacity (a standard load is 15 pounds), and
shoulder straps only, which places all weight on the shoulders. Because of this the day pack is best suited for day hikes or climbing.
The frameless pack, on the other hand, features a larger pack bag
which accommodates loads up to 50 pounds, and a wraparound
belt which permits weight to be supported by the hips.

Actually this belt, known as the hip belt, helped revolutionize
backpacking. Early European and American packs, up to and including the Trapper Nelson, featured shoulder straps or a tump
line which wound around the head. With these, the entire weight
of the pack was borne by the neck or shoulders. Because women

are traditionally weak in their upper bodies, most of them were automatically excluded from backpacking. The introduction of the hip belt in 1959 by equipment designer George Rudolf enabled weight to be transferred to the hips, the heaviest, strongest part of the body, and its central balance point. This, plus the development of the lightweight aluminum frame, served as the unofficial invitation for women to get involved.

The external frame pack, the first product of this mini-revolution, is a three-part system featuring a contoured frame of aluminum tubing, a lightweight nylon pack bag, and a harness system which includes padded shoulder straps and hip belt. This pack is designed so that between 80 and 90 per cent of the weight is supported by the hips. Because of its larger carrying capacity, the ex-

Fig. 7. External frame pack.

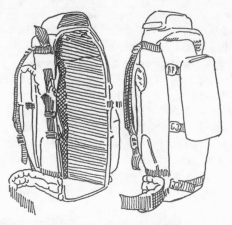

Fig. 8. Cross-section of an external frame pack.

ternal frame pack works best when you are carrying heavy loads or walking long distances.

The internal frame pack, the newest addition to the pack line, is a compromise between the frameless and external frame pack. It offers certain advantages for women. First, most internal frames are flexible, which means they can be bent with a knee to fit a woman's body. The frame is usually narrower than the external

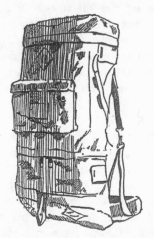

Fig. 9. Internal frame pack.

frame, which suits a woman's narrower back. Besides this, in some packs the span between waist and shoulders can be adjusted to conform with a woman's shorter torso. Because it fits more closely to the body, it will not throw you off balance when you are climbing or cross-country skiing. With its protected frame, this pack suffers less damage during airplane travel. Unfortunately, the internal frame pack does have its drawbacks. The pack bag capacity is generally smaller than that of external frame packs, which limits how much you can carry and, as a result, how far you can go. This pack is designed so that 25 per cent of the weight is carried on the shoulders. Finally, because nothing separates pack from back, perspiration accumulates, leaving you with a wet back and/or pack.

When choosing a pack, women face the same problem they do with most outdoor equipment. While manufacturers claim that the packs with small and medium-size frames are sized for women, actually they, like the large and expedition-size packs, are designed for the male anatomy. Thus, most frame packs bend in where women traditionally bend out—or vice versa.

Classic problem areas for women are frame, shoulder straps, chest straps and hip belts—in other words, everything but the pack bag. Too-tall frames force the head forward, which produces stiff necks and cramped upper-back muscles. Too-broad frames produce bruised upper arms on narrow-shouldered women. Broad, untapered shoulder straps tend to cut into breasts. Too-low sternum straps constrict breasts and breathing. Finally, because women's pelvic bones are more pointed and splayed than men's, inadequately padded hip belts produce blisters and bruises. Fortunately, on most packs such drawbacks are limited to only one or two of the above, or women backpackers would number among the vanishing species.

Because most women have never experienced a truly comfortable pack, they do not know what to ask for or expect when buying a pack. Equipment salespeople, mostly men, compound the problem because they simply do not understand a woman's physiological needs. So, many women buy a poorly fitting pack, endure the resulting discomfort for a time, then quickly lose interest in the sport. To avoid this, where possible always rent before you buy. Under ideal conditions you should trail-test both the exter-

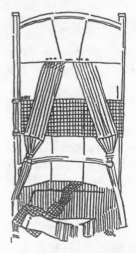 

Fig. 10. Diagram of frame and harness system (left) and pack
bag (right) of external frame pack.

nal and internal frame pack to see which you prefer. If rental
packs are not available, beg, borrow or steal, but never buy until
you locate *the* pack that offers maximum comfort. The following
guidelines may help.

ON FITTING THE PACK

Critical considerations in selecting a pack are capacity and
comfort: does it hold as much as you will realistically need? Does
it conform comfortably to the contours of your body?

The appropriate frame size is determined by the distance between your hips and shoulders. The rule of thumb is: the smaller
the torso, the smaller the pack frame should be. When trying on
the pack, position it first so that the hip belt rides just above the
top of the pelvis, just below your natural waistline. Let the belt
settle until it rests comfortably on your pelvic platform. Once the
pack is properly positioned, ask that it be loaded with at least
twenty pounds. Next, in front of a mirror, adjust the shoulder
straps. Tighten them so that the strap attachment point on the
frame falls level with your shoulder line. If the shoulder strap is

higher than your shoulders the pack is too large, and will keep you off balance by pulling you backward. The upper pack should ride close enough to your shoulders to keep the upper body in balance, but not so close that you're actually carrying weight on your shoulders.

With the external frame pack, once the shoulder-strap-to-hip-belt ratio is resolved, that is all you can do. With the internal frame pack it is just the beginning. The next step is to bend the frame so that it follows your back line. The most critical area for fit is the lower back. The pack should fit closely in the lumbar region so that the pack sits on top of the back of your pelvis; otherwise it will drag you down. The frame should follow the line of your middle back, then curve away from your upper back so that you can move your shoulders, then curve back in at your neck and finally back out so your head doesn't bump against the pack.

While not designed specifically for women, among external frame packs the Kelty "Tour" Pack and "The Backpacker" from Wilderness Experience are scaled to fit a smaller frame. Camp Trails addresses the small-frame backpacker with its "Compact I" and "Compact II" backpacks. The S-contoured frame of these packs may be adjusted as much as 4.5 inches to accommodate the shorter-torsoed woman.

Manufacturers that specialize in quality internal frame packs include Caribou Mountaineering, Hine/Snowbridge, Lowe Alpine Systems and Madden Mountaineering. In 1979, Hine/Snowbridge took a commendable stand by employing a woman pack designer. Lois Kirkpatrick, an experienced backpacker and climber, combined features she felt were important to women into the top-loading pack, the Apogee, and the hatch-front-loading pack, the Perigee. Because women wear packs higher at the waist than men, she shortened the distance between waist and shoulders, and adjusted shoulder straps so that they fit snugly. Fashioned from 11-ounce heavy cordura, the pack bags are scaled to 2,250 cubic inches because Lois believes women carry less than men. The frame is downsized from other Hine/Snowbridge packs to accommodate the smaller-framed person.

Lowe Alpine Systems' Kinninnic I pack was initially conceived to serve the shorter-framed Japanese market. But, because Greg Lowe's wife, who regularly packs with him, also wanted a pack that fit and worked for her, women's needs were considered. The Kinninnic I, which is designed for the short, lightweight person, features inch-thick soft foam padding on hip and shoulder straps for extra comfort. To avoid constriction of the breasts, the chest strap is adjustable. Lowe's Liberty Pack, with a full-volume pack bag that allows you to carry enough to travel long distance, offers a frame and harness system adapted to the 5'1" to 5'5" person.

The Gypsy Pack from Caribou Mountaineering also has generated positive response from women in the field, largely because of its shorter distance between shoulders and waist, and its quality workmanship.

That manufacturers are beginning to consider women's needs is evident in the fact that an increasing number are contemplating designing packs exclusively for women. Much of this is mere shoptalk, however, and may take years to realize. What equipment manufacturers need as impetus is more input from female backpackers.

SLEEPING BAGS

The sleeping bag is an ingenious two- to three-pound device which offers as much, and sometimes more, warmth as your one- to five-hundred-pound bed and blankets at home. It manages this feat in two ways. The bag traps heat radiated from your body, while the insulated filler between the bag's external and internal lining creates a dead-air space which insulates and protects you from the environment.

Sleeping bags are filled either with waterfowl down or synthetic fill. Down is the cottony undercover of the goose or duck. Each minute piece of down contains thousands of feathery filaments which entwine to effectively deaden the movement of air. Down is the lightest, most thermally efficient of all insulators.

The highest quality down comes from birds raised in cold climates and allowed to mature. But today geese and ducks are cultivated not for down, but for food. Because the younger bird offers more tender flesh, few birds reach maturity. As a result, the quality of down has deteriorated. Where a generation ago down which lofted 700 to 800 cubic inches per ounce was readily available,

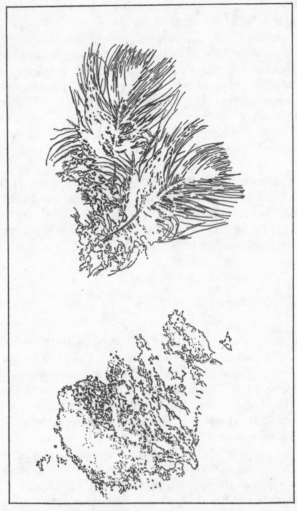

Fig. 11. Close-up of waterfowl down (above) and synthetic fi-
ber fill (below).

today high-quality down seldom lofts more than 600 cubic inches
per ounce.

Down quality is difficult for even experts to determine. When
selecting a bag, therefore, you must examine workmanship and the

manufacturer's promotional material. When manufacturers make an issue of the lofting power of down, it means that they take pride in the quality of the product. Bag construction is a second clue. Few manufacturers will demand quality sewing and detailing when the bag is filled with inferior down or chicken feathers.

To stabilize down, bags are constructed in one of three ways: quilted (the least expensive, least thermally efficient), with box

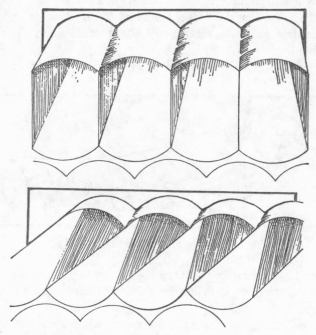

Fig. 12. Diagram of box baffles (above) and slant-walled baffles (below).

baffles, or with slant-walled baffles. Bags with slant-walled baffles are both the lightest in weight and the most thermally efficient. They also are the most expensive.

With the dwindling supply, deteriorating quality and increased price of down, manufacturers in recent years have begun using synthetic insulators. For lightness and warmth, the most popular synthetics are Celanese Fortrel PolarGuard and DuPont Polyester

Fiberfill II. Besides being less expensive than down, these insulators do not absorb water as down does, which means they work well in wet climates. Besides, they retain 80 per cent of their loft when wet—as compared with zero for down—and they dry three times faster than down. They are, unfortunately, heavier (1.4 pounds of synthetic equals the thermal efficiency of one pound of down), and because they lack compressibility, they are 30 to 45 per cent bulkier than down. When shopping for a synthetic fill bag, be aware that the "edge-stabilized" construction, as opposed to the quilt or double-offset baffle construction, offers the most durable loft.

Sleeping bags are designed in either a mummy or a rectangular

Fig. 13. Modified mummy sleeping bag.

shape. The mummy bag is more popular among backpackers because it is warmer, is lighter in weight and stuffs into a smaller sack.

Three features to consider in purchasing a bag are zipper, hood and size. Fifty per cent of your body heat can escape through your head when you are sleeping. A bag with a hood will be warmer than one without, unless, of course, you wear a wool cap to bed. Better-grade zippers have two-way sliders which allow you to open them from either end. Zippers give rise to drafts, so the shorter the zipper the warmer the bag. A sleeping bag with a full zipper, on the other hand, allows you to unzip the bottom for ventilation. Also, because it can be opened out flat, it can serve as a blanket or comforter on your bed at home. Certain mummy and rectangular bags feature complementary zippers, which means two bags can be zipped together for more warmth—and companionship.

Most sleeping bags are available now in small, medium and large sizes. You should choose the size with care, for the larger the bag the larger the space to be warmed. The best way to determine proper size is to spread it out and crawl into it.

A common mistake made by many when purchasing a bag is failing to realistically appraise their needs. As a result, they purchase a bag that is too heavy, too hot or too expensive for actual use conditions. To avoid this, carefully consider, *before* selecting a bag, in what seasons and climates you plan to backpack. If you buy a bag that is appropriate for spring, summer and fall, you can winterize it by purchasing and inserting a quilted down liner. This gives most bags a four-season temperature range.

A sleeping bag should be handled with care. Your primary objective should be to keep it clean inside and out. A flannel liner, which you can make yourself or buy at some outdoor shops, protects the inside. A large-size tarp, or bivouac bag, will shield it from snags, dust and dirt. To keep the bag smelling fresh when in use it should be opened and aired daily if possible.

ON CLEANING THE SLEEPING BAG

Despite the most conscientious efforts, sleeping bags do get dirty. After thirty or more nights of use without a flannel liner to protect it, enough natural oils, grime and odor accumulate to necessitate cleaning. Opinion is divided on cleaning. Because many down bags have been ruined by machine washing, manufacturers uniformly recommend dry cleaning. Unfortunately, dry cleaning strips down of its natural oils, which deprives it of resiliency, which eliminates loft. It is important if you choose to dry-clean that you be selective in cleaners. Most use perchloroethylene (or "perk") as a cleaning fluid; this is particularly devastating to down. In some areas establishments exist which specialize in cleaning down equipment. Check your phone book or equipment supplier for names and addresses. Or search for an establishment which uses the mild Stoddard cleaning fluid.

The alternative method of cleaning—the one many equipment

users prefer—is washing. The best, though the most time-consuming method, is hand-washing. To do a thorough job you need a bathtub, mild soap flakes, a washing-machine spinner, easy access to a laundromat—and lots of dimes. (If you cannot locate special soap for down, use pure soap, *not* detergent.) First, place the bag in the bathtub in lukewarm soapy water. Depending on how dirty it is, allow it to soak from two to twenty-four hours. Periodically, gently press soapy water through the shell into the filler. At no time should you wring or twist the bag. When you're sure it is clean, rinse at least twice in tepid water to remove all soap. Taste the water to be sure. Any trace of soap will cause the down to mat, which creates a permanent cold spot. To keep baffles from bursting, do not pick the bag up by either end. Instead, fold it over, press the water out, then *carefully* pick the bag up and place it in your washing machine. Distribute the load evenly and set the machine at Spin-Dry. Run it through twice.

Smaller home dryers create hot spots which scorch the bag. Locate a dryer in a laundromat with a low heat setting. Place the bag in the dryer with clean canvas tennis shoes (first remove the laces). The pounding action of the shoes will help redistribute the down. Check the machine every ten minutes to make sure that low heat is sustained. If not, run the dryer with the door ajar. Drying will take approximately two hours. Then, at home, the bag should be hung in the sun for half an hour to remove any trace of moisture.

The final, though most chancy, method of home cleaning is machine-washing. This method is used with apparent success by equipment salesperson and veteran outdoor woman Allison Clough. She allows her bags to soak three hours in the machine in pure soap flakes, washes them, then runs them through another cycle without soap. She runs the machine on Rinse until the water tastes clean, then puts it on Spin until the water is totally extracted. She tumbles bags dry on the air cycle of her home dryer.

Sleeping bags should be stored flat or over a sturdy hanger in the closet so that they will retain loft. They should never be stored in the stuff sack.

SLEEPING PADS

Because most outdoor surfaces are both hard and cold, and because all fillers compress under the weight of your body, in addition to a bag you need a lightweight insulated mattress. An air mattress, the traditional favorite of car campers, is neither lightweight nor insulated. Besides, at the end of a long day, it requires lung power to blow up. Also, because the air is free to circulate, air mattresses do not protect you from ground temperature. Above all, they have the predictable habit of springing leaks.

Foam pads such as Ensolite, Thermobar and Volarfoam are more lightweight, dependable insulators. Because they are closed-cell, the air is trapped, which prevents ground temperature from reaching your body. A ⅜-inch pad provides adequate insulation for every condition but snow. A 2-inch pad will insulate you from ground convection up to −10 degrees Fahrenheit. Comfort is another matter. I achieve a semblance of it by also carrying a 1½-inch-thick foam pad covered in a waterproof fabric. These two travel rolled together on top of my pack so bulk is not significantly increased, though nighttime comfort is.

The latest addition to the outdoor mattress department is "ThermaRest," a foam pad and air mattress combined in a single unit. This mattress self-inflates—you merely open a valve—and is reputed to be every woman's answer to outdoor comfort. While it is expensive—$30 and climbing—because of the comfort and compactness it offers most users consider it money well spent.

STOVES

In this age of increased backcountry use and dwindling wood supplies, backpackers seldom have the luxury—or choice—of cooking by fire. Instead, the responsible backpacker always carries a stove. However, for many, that is where the headaches begin.

I, for one, have never found a stove that works reliably and well. Either I can't get it lit, or just as it lights it runs out of fuel —or I overprime it, fuel spills and suddenly the stove isn't the only thing that is lit. Either it's too cold, too hot, too windy or too high for the stove to work—or it simply is in an uncooperative mood. It has been some source of comfort (though certainly no solution) to discover that I am not alone. Men and women both harbor private grievances. One woman nicknamed her stove "my little Molotov cocktail." This does not alter the fact, however, that if you hope to eat hot food while backpacking you must have a stove.

Your first consideration with stoves is which fuel you prefer to use. Popular fuels include white gas, kerosene, bottled propane and butane. Butane, which is stored in cartridges, leads the pack for cleanliness and ease of operation. However, it is unreliable in cold temperatures. Propane works better than butane at high altitude and in cold climates, but because it is stored in heavy containers it is of marginal use to backpackers. The presealed containers in which propane and butane are stored also make it impossible to determine how much fuel remains.

White gas is currently easily obtainable in the United States, less so in Europe. It is less susceptible to cold than propane or butane. According to author Colin Fletcher, who conducted extensive tests, white gas outperforms butane cartridges roughly two to one. Its disadvantage is that it is volatile. A spark or lighted match dropped into it can ignite it.

Kerosene is the least expensive, most universally obtainable fuel. Besides the fact that it is non-volatile (you can drop a lighted match in a puddle of it and it won't flare up), it works well at high altitude and in extreme cold, and it produces more heat per pint than any other fuel. The disadvantages with kerosene are its odor (though deodorized kerosene is available), and its high degree of impurities. Also, because it is oil based, it leaves distinct stains when spilled on equipment.

Both white gas and kerosene are contained and transported in Sigg fuel bottles. These sturdy aluminum cylinders are available in pint or quart size. They are made in Taiwan and in Switzerland. Because some Taiwan-made bottles have been known to crack with use, it is best to purchase Swiss-made containers.

Most white gas and kerosene stoves must be primed before they will start. Priming builds pressure inside the fuel tank and forces gas into the burner. A few drops of priming fluid are placed in a small bowl at the base of the burner, then lit. This flame gradually heats the tank and generator, which causes fuel in the tank to expand. As the priming flame dies the stove is turned on and the fuel vapor in the tank is ignited by the flame. Once you get the knack of priming you can light your stove quickly under any conditions, in any weather. To master it, though, takes plenty of practice at home.

There are approximately thirty different backpacking stoves on the market today. Factors to consider when selecting one are simplicity, stability and safety. Can you operate it? Is it safe? Can the stove stably support the weight of a pot filled with food?

Butane cartridge stoves, such as the Bleuet S200-S, are the cleanest and easiest to operate. Once the cartridge is attached to the stove unit, you merely turn the knob and light. While my first rented Bleuets never did work, I finally learned to test them at home *before* packing them. While the cartridge stove is a suitable stove to start with, it is not without flaws. Cartridge stoves respond sluggishly if at all when cold. The 8½-inch-high Bleuet provides an unstable cooking surface. Finally, there is the problem of empty fuel cartridges, which you must pack out.

White gas and kerosene stoves rank today as the most efficient backpacking stoves. The Svea 123 is particularly popular because it is compact (5″×3¾″ diameter), lightweight (1 pound, 1½ ounces), will run an hour on four ounces of fuel and will boil a quart of water in less than six minutes at sea level. Common complaints center on its lack of stability and its ineffective windscreen which prevents it from operating efficiently in wind.

The Optimus 8R, which uses white gas, is another favorite. National Outdoor Leadership School instructor Vini Norris uses this model. She thinks it is less susceptible to breakdown from dirt specks or macaroni clogs, and considers it easier to fix than other stoves. The Optimus 8R weighs 1.95 pounds, holds one-third of a pint of fuel, and boils a quart of water in 7½ minutes at sea level. Because it is broad-based and low, it does not require shoring up—even in snow—and will support even heavy-gauge aluminum pressure cookers stably. Unfortunately it wins mixed reviews regarding its ability to perform well in winter, and it is noisy.

Both the Optimus 8R and the Svea 123 are self-pressurizing. Because cold weather depressurizes them, a mini-pump is now

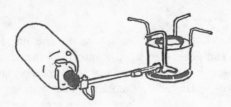

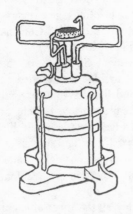

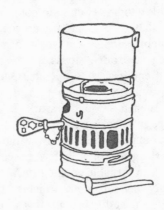

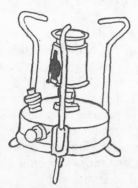

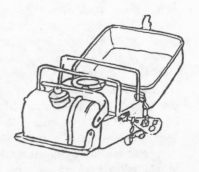

Fig. 14. Clockwise from top: Mountain Safety Research Model G; Svea 123; Optimus 8R; Optimus 00; Bleuet S200-S.

available which allows you to repressurize the tank. Theoretically this means both the 123 and 8R may be used during winter. Users caution that the pump must be handled with care, however; if you overpump, as it is easy to do, you wind up with a potential mini-bomb.

Coleman, the originator of outdoor stoves, recently introduced Peak I, a compact backpacking stove with a large burner and an integral windscreen and pot support. It weighs 1 pound, 10 ounces, holds 10 ounces of fuel (Coleman or white gas), and boils a quart of water in slightly more than three minutes. It also is reputed to have the best controlled simmer of any stove on the market. This stove has a built-in pump, which means it requires no priming except in extreme cold.

Mountain Safety Research has developed two backpacking stoves—the MSR Model G and Model G/K—which one equipment buff characterizes as the "technocrat's delight." The fuel tank, a standard Sigg aluminum bottle, is connected to the low, stable burner unit by a long, narrow fuel line. These are disassembled for compact storage. A sheet aluminum windscreen, which is included, makes this stove effective in cold and windy conditions. Using the windscreen and an MSR blackened pot (developed by MSR to assist in heat transfer), the stove will heat a quart of water in 3½ minutes. The greatest selling point is that these stoves operate on a variety of fuels. The Model G will burn white gas, Coleman fuel, leaded and unleaded automobile gas and aviation fuel. The Model G/K will burn all of these plus kerosene, diesel fuel and stove oil. With these stoves you need never fear a fuel shortage. MSR stoves are a little complicated for the beginner to operate and are the most expensive on the market. Still, the manufacturer maintains that one MSR stove can heat as much water as three Svea's or 8R's, which is one way of saying it's economical in the long run.

One favorite of long-distance and group backpackers is the Optimus 00. This stable-based kerosene stove, which features a one-pint fuel tank, weighs 1½ pounds and can boil one quart of water in three to five minutes at sea level. Although it is four ounces lighter than the Optimus 8R, it outperforms it in the water-boiling department by at least 2½ minutes. For its reliability, its ability to perform well at high altitude and extreme cold, and its ability to cook more food with less fuel, it ranks as the Sierra Club's stove of choice.

SHELTER

True to the "if a little is good, a lot is better" formula, there are at present more than a hundred different designs for outdoor shelters for backpackers. Basically these can be divided into the fol-

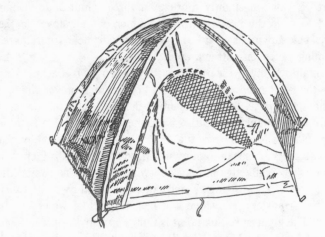

Fig. 15. Dome tent.

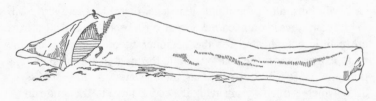

Fig. 16. Bivvy bag.

lowing categories: single-sheet shelters such as tarps; tube tents; A-frame, hoop or dome tents; and large-capacity tents. Finally, there is the bivvy bag—a 1-pound-9-ounce Gore-Tex sack with hood—which shelters your sleeping bag and yourself from wind, snow, driving rain or mosquitoes.

To avoid being overwhelmed by such a selection, you should begin the shopping process by composing a checklist. On it record how many people you usually travel with, how much or little weight you wish to carry, and how much you want to spend. Environmental factors should be considered too, principally the seasons and weather conditions in which you backpack, and insects.

Tarps are lightweight, inexpensive sources of shelter which work best in areas with trees, mild temperatures, little rain and even fewer bugs. The beauty of the tarp, besides price, is the more you experiment with tying it, the more versatile a tool it becomes. On an eight-day trip in Washington's rainy North Cascades, with the tarp as my only shelter, I stayed cozy and dry.

The tube tent is a triangular open-ended plastic tube which

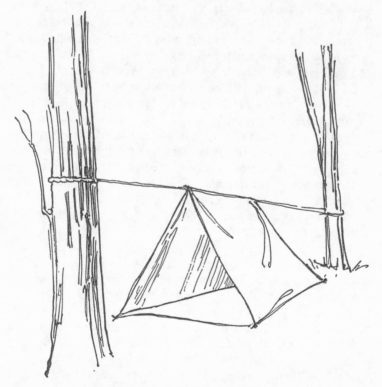

Fig. 17. Tube tent.

offers the protection of a floor. While the tube tent provides shelter from the wet ground in rainstorms, I prefer the tarp in light rains or windy conditions, because its flapping can be controlled.

With traditional tents, primary considerations are whether it will withstand the wind and stay dry in rain or snow, whether the ventilation system is effective, and whether it is easy to erect.

The A-frame, the original backpacking tent, takes its name from its shape. It achieves this shape either from exterior self-supporting poles, or from an interior I-pole plus exterior ground stakes and guy lines affixed to rocks, bushes or trees. Traditional though the A-frame may be, it has shortcomings. Interior space is cramped, and walls lack sufficient tautness to shuck wind, rain and snow. To compensate, more than a decade ago equipment designers began creating alternatives. The hoop tent came first. This tent, which resembles a mini-Quonset hut, takes its shape from flexible fiberglass poles which, when inserted in pole holders at the front and back, curve to form a hoop. This unique design increases interior space and firms tent walls, which helps deflect wind and spill rain and snow. In addition, it is easy to erect.

In 1972, Jansport introduced the dome tent. Adapted from Buckminster Fuller's geodesic dome, this tent excels in efficient space utilization. External hollow fiberglass poles which arc over the tent maintain such taut walls that heavy rains and snowstorms may pass unnoticed. The dome tent became the first stake-free tent. Although these tents can be erected quickly they are subject to the tumbleweed effect; unless weighted down, they simply head off in their own direction when the wind blows. These tents are considered the current state of the art, and so are the most expensive tents in the marketplace.

Besides familiarizing yourself with shape, it is important to know whether a tent is single- or double-walled. Most single-walled tents are made from waterproof nylon. While this may prevent rain from entering, it does not permit condensation from breath and perspiration to escape. Unless one is backpacking at low elevations or in dry climates, the resulting accumulation of moisture converts these tents into veritable steam baths. Because of this, double-walled tents are usually preferred.

Most double-walled tents follow the same design: the floor and the first 6 to 11 inches of the walls are composed of polyurethane or waterproof nylon taffeta. Upper walls are constructed with a lightweight taffeta or ripstop nylon which is porous, and which permits moisture-laden air to escape. The second wall is a separate waterproof rainfly which, when in position, protects the tent from rain and snow. The end result is an inner tent which stays dry.

When you have spent enough time with equipment catalogs to decide which tent suits you, the actual shopping process begins. In the store ask that a tent be set up, or, better yet, set it up yourself. This allows you to gauge exactly how easy or difficult it is to erect. Crawl into it, lie down, sit up; see if it feels comfortable. Check the ventilation system. Because people have suffocated in poorly ventilated tents, excellent ventilation is essential. Ideally a tent should have at least two windows near the eaves to permit cross-ventilation. To eliminate insects, doors and windows should be netted. Netting at the entrance should zip all around. Compare different models for net mesh size. There is no such thing as too-tight mesh in mosquito or no-see-um season.

Check tent construction, fabric and workmanship. The seams tell all. On a quality tent all seams are bound or flat felled. Raw edges mean slack workmanship. Check also for small stitches and double stitching at all stress lines. Finally, be sure pole holders are reinforced.

Because you may spend considerable time in the tent, its color should please you. In a cold climate a blue tent may make you feel colder. Red or orange may warm you, but also be an irritant to the nerves. Yellow is good for visibility. If you want to remain inconspicuous, green, rust or brown is best.

A tent will shelter you for years if you care for it. When you purchase one, seal all seams with a sealant such as K-Kote or Pliobond-20. Practice pitching it at home before taking it to wilderness. On the trail keep it clean inside and out. A tent kit with whisk broom and sponge, or even a damp bandanna, will help with daily housekeeping. On layover days turn it inside out and shake it. To protect its floor, never wear boots inside. In winter always brush snow off clothes and boots before entering.

Be careful where you pitch it. Pinecones and rocks will puncture the fabric and shorten the tent's life. Dead trees are unstable in wind and attract lightning: never pitch it under or near one.

Cooking in the tent is not advised. Besides the threat of fire, there is the imminent possibility of carbon monoxide poisoning. If bad weather forces you inside, place the stove near the door and open all windows.

With tent prices ranging between $100 and $400 and soaring, always rent or borrow before you buy. By field-testing different styles you can determine which works best for you before investing in this most costly piece of equipment.

᚜ᚳᚳᚳᚳᚳᚳᚳᚳᚳᚳᚳᚳᚳᚳᚳᚳᚳᚳᚳᚳ

PUTTING EQUIPMENT IN ITS PLACE

*"The experience in wilderness is not what you take
into it, but what you take out of it . . ."*

ALLISON CLOUGH

Diane Strachan has a word for it: gametanglia. To her it means accumulating more equipment than we need. It means focusing on the "buy products" of man rather than opening ourselves to nature.

Gametanglia didn't become an epidemic until wilderness became an "in" place to be. Once outdoor equipment manufacturers saw that there was profit to be made, they began concocting assorted Ultimate Answers for staying safe, warm and dry. Millions of advertising dollars were subsequently spent to convey essentially one message: unless you buy the latest model outdoor whatchamacallit *you may not survive the elements*. When one is new to wilderness, and uncertain of what it holds, such messages touch a vital nerve. We respond, knee-jerk style, by buying more than we need—without ever understanding what we need or why.

There is in this trend at least one serious flaw. As Diane says, "More accidents and deaths are occurring because people are buying expensive equipment, becoming dependent on these tools; then when they don't have them, or the equipment doesn't work, they don't know what to do."

Important lessons can be learned about equipment by just once doing without. One rainy night in wilderness with nothing but tarp, metal cup, matches and knife teaches you how resourceful you can be. It forces you to rely on self instead of equipment—which is how it should be. From it you learn which equipment is necessary and why. You learn how little you need.

Granted, certain equipment is essential: pack, sleeping bag and pad, stove and boots. But you needn't, as ads imply, buy the best, the latest, the most expensive. You can manage well with less. I've been doing it for years. With the exception of boots, every piece of equipment I own was another backpacker's discard. The fifteen-year-old sleeping bag is more chicken feathers than down, but it works well in all conditions but snow. The pack is expedition size and built for a man. We've grown accustomed to each other's shape. The parka was designed for downhill skiing. Being from an earlier generation, it is higher quality down than what is available today. Yet it came for free.

The crucial message lost in this latter-day craze to manufacture, advertise and buy too much equipment is that the finest tools you take into wilderness are your brain, your powers of observation, your common sense. They serve you best when primed with some awareness of nature's way.

The more you know of wilderness, the saying goes, the lighter you travel. On his wilderness escapades, John Muir, father of the Sierra Club, survived happily—if not always comfortably—with wool trousers, shirt, wool coat, matches and, for sustenance, a pocketful of oatmeal and raisins. Muir spent energy acquiring knowledge instead of equipment. As a result, wilderness became a less intimidating place to be.

If we follow suit, perhaps the urge to overequip, to "arm" ourselves against nature, will disappear. That is when a meaningful interchange with wilderness will begin.

CHAPTER 4

Clothes

For centuries, fashion, like tradition, has imposed its tyranny on women. Until 1920, for example, a woman's virtue was measured by her hemline and how tightly she buttoned her blouse—but honor wasn't the only thing attached to women's skirts. To hold them firm against the wind, women dutifully sewed pounds of bar lead into the hemlines of their gowns. To assist in negotiating mountains, mud puddles and everything in between, skirt elevators were affixed. These helped raise the skirt above ankle level without the wearer stooping down.

Given the costume of the day, any woman who ventured outdoors faced not one physical challenge, but two. Perhaps this was a point of early-day pride, for nowhere does history record a man successfully climbing a mountain or crossing the plains in a floor-length skirt, eight yards around, with his upper body encased in scratchy canvas and a full complement of stays!

Throughout pioneer and Victorian days fashion remained a stern dictator where outdoor women were concerned. To deviate even slightly, for whatever excuse, was to invite social censure. When, in 1895, Fay Fuller became the first woman on record to climb 14,410-foot Mount Rainier, she was branded "scandalous" for the costume she wore: full bloomers, an ankle-length skirt, boys' hiking boots and, for warmth, a wool blanket tied snugly about her waist.

Women won the right to wear trousers a few years after they won the vote. But the tyranny of fashion didn't end there: it merely assumed a more subtle form. As they had for years, men designed outdoor clothes—but only with men in mind. Shirts, parkas, pants and boots featured a fit that was decidedly male.

Women were left either to fashion their own outdoor wardrobes, or to compromise in style, practicality, comfort and fit.

Clothing manufacturers ignored anatomical differences for two reasons. Being male, and quite comfortable in clothes they designed, they couldn't imagine why women would need clothes of their own. Beyond this, they knew that any concession they made to the female figure would cost them plenty. So they simply didn't make it.

With increasing pressure on manufacturers to acknowledge women's needs, finally, in the early Seventies, a few divulged that the extra-small (XS) and extra-extra-small (XXS) sizes really were designed to fit women. And they are—if women don't care how they fit. Take the parka, for example. Because it is a scaled-down model of the XL and XXL parka, which is cut to fit men, sleeves are designed long, and shoulders, chest, waist and hips are designed straight. If you are the rare woman who also is designed straight the XS and XXS may fit perfectly. Otherwise, you are forced to do without functional fit.

The second concession manufacturers recently made was to shift clothing lines to unisex. One line fits both sexes—sort of. Even manufacturers see the folly in this. As William Ferry, vice president of Woolrich, writes, "The torso differences between male and female make it, in our opinion, virtually impossible to offer a meaningful, functional garment by simply offering the gal a man's extra-small, or attempting to offer a unisex line. Functional clothing, when put to its intended use, has very severe demands placed on it, and it must perform. For these reasons, we do not feel that unisex is a valid concept for the outdoor woman."

One other disturbing trend has surfaced in women's outdoor apparel. Supposedly to cater to women, certain manufacturers are emphasizing fashion over function. They make products pretty rather than making them work. A perfect example of this is the short-waisted parka. Because a certain percentage of body heat escapes through the lower back, short parkas offer significantly less thermal efficiency than long-line parkas. Another classic example is flowered longjohns. Some experienced outdoor women contend that longjohns fashioned for men are constructed better, last longer and, most important, are warmer than ladies' longjohns.

(Indeed, flowered longjohns actually have *less* wool in them!) The obvious solution here is for women to buy men's longjohns, except that because they are not shaped like women they are neither thermally efficient nor comfortable.

It took a few enlightened manufacturers to implement the only plausible solution—to employ women to design outdoor clothing for women. First to set the precedent was Trailwise. In 1974, this manufacturer introduced the Ladies' Logan jacket. It was a wise move. In that first year 30 per cent of Trailwise sales were to women. Today, Trailwise offers parkas, vests and a new line of hiking shorts designed by women exclusively for women. These products are offered in colors for women only: copper, blue, ruby and zircon. The shorts, in corduroy and twill, have a full leg for movement, an ample crotch and waistband, and, to ensure long life, have a reinforced bottom.

"The critical thing is that a woman get something that is going to fit," says Richard Munson, of Trailwise. "Don't settle for a sized down men's," he advises. "It will not serve you as well as a product designed for women." In a scaled-down men's parka, Munson explains, a woman's body heat is dissipated by warming extra space that would not be there if the parka was designed for a woman's frame.

Backpacker Sarah Rahaim (whose original outdoor wardrobe came from the boys' department of a local store) solved the problem of fit by designing, manufacturing and marketing QP Pants. Slacks, bermudas and shorts in this line are cut to a woman's figure, have ample leg room, large pockets, and are fashioned from sturdy khaki or denim. The "Velcro Vent"—an inner pants-leg seam lined with Velcro—spares you the effort of removing pack and pants when nature calls. It requires careful redoing, however, or the Velcro will scratch and irritate inner thighs.

With introduction of its new line, "For Women Only," Caribou Mountaineering also joined this mini-league of manufacturers who acknowledge outdoor women. Caribou's line of jackets, knickers and vests are scaled to flatter the female figure: shoulders are narrower, hips are broader and waistlines are emphasized. Filled with Thinsulate, which is designed to provide nearly two times the insulation for a given thickness than down, fiberfill or wool, these clothes feature excellent workmanship and appear to be as functional as any men's garments.

Other manufacturers which feature separate women's lines include Alpine Products, Coming Attractions, Filson, Sierra Designs and Woolrich. When establishing or expanding your outdoor wardrobe, keep these names in mind.

When shopping, seek out clothes that have been *designed* (as opposed to sized) specifically for women. The distinction is subtle but important. The sized article is merely a scaled-down model of something designed for broad-shouldered, flat-chested, slim-hipped, large-boned men. Products designed for women, on the other hand, accommodate physiological differences—short torsos, breasts, slim waists, full hips, narrower shoulders and lighter frames.

Check workmanship. Stitches should be small (12 to 15 stitches per inch is ideal) and even. Interior seams should be finished, not fraying. If the outer fabric of a parka or jacket is synthetic, ask the salesperson if it has been hot-cut. This process, in which fabric edges are melted together, contributes to product longevity. For durability, fabric should be tightly woven. Apparel that feels comfortable will function more efficiently than that which doesn't. Because its primary function is to shelter, warm and sustain you in unpredictable, potentially life-threatening elements, color and appearance (and flowers!) in the outdoor wardrobe should be secondary concerns.

As recommended when buying equipment, if your local outlet does not carry a woman's clothing line, request that they do. Such requests encourage manufacturers to recognize women's presence outdoors. With available products, be specific about what you do or do not like. When such information filters back to manufacturers, positive changes can occur.

THE OUTDOOR WARDROBE—FROM THE INSIDE OUT

To conform with the pack's acute shortage of closet space, your backpacking wardrobe must lack bulk and weight. At the same time, it must be versatile and capable of keeping you alive, dry and warm. If vanity is a concern, it should add to your appearance rather than detract. The best way to achieve these exacting ends with clothing is to layer.

While fashion magazines treat the layered look as a mere fad, for outdoor women it is far more than that. Layers shelter the body and warm it, or help keep it cool and dry. The optimum outdoor wardrobe features one to five layers. The number fluctuates depending on the season, climate and altitude in which you hike.

Layer One

Layer one is a euphemism for longjohns. This next-to-skin layer helps preserve your 98.6-degree microclimate by keeping the skin dry, by preventing direct contact with heat or cold, and by adding warmth.

Today longjohns are fashioned from cotton, synthetics and wool or wool blends. While cotton, for its softness, is a traditional choice, it is not a wise one. Cotton absorbs perspiration like a sponge. Once wet it wicks body heat from you—exactly what the primary layer is *not* supposed to do. Synthetics, such as nylon Lycra and polypropylene, are the latest addition to the longjohn line. They wear well, wash well, and are comfortable. When crafted from porous fabric they allow moisture to disperse. Many people, though, do not like the feel of synthetics next to their skin.

The warmest, most durable longjohns are made from wool and wool blends. Unlike cotton, wool continues to warm the body even after it is wet from perspiration or precipitation. Because of this, wool stands as an all-time favorite for cold climates. Wool blended with nylon holds its shape longer than longjohns made entirely of wool. The warmest, most expensive wool is Angora. Rabbit fur, from which Angora is fashioned, is smooth and rounded so it also is less scratchy to the skin. Angora can absorb up to 60 per cent of its weight in moisture, compared to 40 per cent for sheep's wool. A less expensive, equally effective alternative is a used cashmere sweater, available at Goodwill or second-hand shops for as little as two dollars.

The traditional weak spot in longjohns is the crotch. Abrasion from outer pants tends to create holes. In more expensive longjohns all seams are overcast; thus, they are recommended as a better buy.

Fig. 18. Longjohns.

Layer Two

Layer two, consisting of pants, shorts and shirts, protects your skin from abrasion and from the debilitating effects of wind and sun. For durability, blue jeans and other heavy cotton pants are popular and widely used. They have serious flaws, however. They get wet easily, dry slowly, and when wet they wick body heat. In a test conducted by the U. S. Army, a man wearing wet blue jeans suffered potentially fatal hypothermia hours before a man in the same environment who wore nothing. But that was only a test. In wilderness hikers have suffered fatal consequences from wearing blue jeans. Eugene Fear, of Survival Education Association, tells of his first Search & Rescue mission, in which the victim, Edith Anderson, became lost a mile from the trail during a light rain. It took the S&R team only eight hours to find her, but they arrived too late. Her death from hypothermia was caused, Fear believes, by the fact that she was wearing wet blue jeans.

If you are traveling in a dry climate with few river crossings, or if you pack extra wool pants or longjohns, blue jeans are acceptable. Otherwise, in conditions where you expect to get wet, nylon knit or wool is preferable.

With wool hiking pants the tighter the weave the more durable they will be. Filson produces excellent outdoor wool pants for women. Less expensive alternatives are used navy sailor's pants, or heavy wool slacks from Salvation Army or Goodwill. Another favorite for winter hiking pants is wool knickers. Outdoor writer Lynn Ferrin names her favorite outdoor pants as British women's paratrooper pants, which she found in an army surplus store.

To determine the overall quality of pants, check the crotch. If everything comes together neatly, if seams are properly serged or overcast, if there are no loose threads, they probably will wear better and longer.

Proper fit is essential. Pants and shorts should be loose-waisted, should feel comfortable and should permit absolute freedom of movement. They should never feel tight in the crotch or rub the fatty tissue of your inner thighs. If you are dissatisfied with women's pants, try men's instead. Because they are designed short in the crotch, you should test the fit by going into a deep squat. If there is any sense of chafing, select a larger pair.

Backpacking tops range from scoop-neck cotton T-shirts to heavy wool shirt-jackets. Light cotton tops are excellent for hot, dry climates. Heavy cotton "chamois" shirts, so popular now, are less practical than lightweight wool shirts, which continue to warm even when wet.

Porous, lightweight synthetic tops and shirts work well in a wet environment, or when you're exercising hard, because perspiration simply passes through. Heavy synthetics, such as Fiberpile, which is smooth on one side, furry on the other, absorb less moisture and dry more quickly than wool. A nylon Fiberpile shirt is stronger and maintains a better appearance longer than Fiberpile fashioned from polyester.

Certain wool products offer more style than practicality—in particular, heavy wool shirt-jackets, which are bulky, fit loosely and provide inefficient insulation. Instead, select something light for each layer. When choosing a shirt or top, make sure that you can bend your arms easily and stretch them over your head without the shirttails pulling out.

Layer Three

The insulation layer, layer three, traps heat radiated from your body. Heavy wool sweaters and down- or fiber-filled parkas, jackets and vests perform this task most efficiently.

Prime goose down, the feathery undercover of the goose, holds the record today as the world's warmest, lightest-weight, most durable insulator. Because of the spiraling demand and dwindling supply, it also is the most expensive. A down jacket can be 40 per cent more expensive than one containing synthetic fill such as PolarGuard, Fiberfill-Two, Holofil or Thinsulate. Besides being less expensive, synthetic fills retain up to 60 per cent of their insulating capacity when wet. They weigh more than down, however, and compress only slightly in packing, and only with some difficulty.

A vital consideration when purchasing layer three is the season and climate in which you backpack. If you are hiking in a dry climate, down is an excellent choice, but if you are traveling in an

Fig. 19. Fiber-fill vest.

area with heavy precipitation, a synthetic fill might be the better option.

Choose an insulating garment that permits total freedom of movement even when you are wearing a full complement of layers. Sleeves should extend the full length of your arm to your wrist when your arms are stretched in front of you. To keep hands warm, pockets should be large enough to accommodate hands and wrists. Because 25 per cent of body heat escapes through the lower back and hips, length is an important consideration. A

Fig. 20. Down parka.

jacket that extends over the hips will be warmer than one that stops at your waist. If a short-waisted jacket is selected for appearance or freedom of motion, compensate for heat loss by choosing warm pants.

Layer Four

Layer four protects you and your clothes from the elements. When selecting a shell, your main considerations are wind and

Fig. 21. The cagoule, or "walking tent."

rain. The shell that shelters you from one may not shelter you
from the other. Selecting a shell may get downright confusing, for
they vary in fabric, price and design from $3 plastic ponchos
which snap at the side, to $45 coated nylon cagoules (known as

"walking tents"), to $95 Gore-Tex wonders, which, enthusiasts claim, do everything when it rains but hand you the towel.

Wind-resistant shells include lightweight nylon, and jackets created from tightly woven cotton known as 60/40 or 65/35, or from Ventile cotton. This latter fabric swells up when wet, which

Fig. 22. Wind-resistant shell.

renders it water *resistant,* but not waterproof. Such shells are suitable mainly in areas where little or no rain is expected.

Waterproof products are fashioned from plastic, coated nylon and Gore-Tex. Coated nylon is indeed waterproof, but because this fabric does not breathe, when you exercise hard perspiration condenses inside. Also, after repeated wear, the coating rubs off at abrasion points. Gore-Tex breathes better than any waterproof fabric now available; however, those who have tested it claim that despite its exorbitant price, it does not work when it is dirty, and it tends to delaminate.

Standard weak spots in shells are zippers and seams. Unless zippers are soaked in silicone before being sewn in, they leak. Because of this, a zipperless pullover acts as a more effective rain shell. To ensure that seams are watertight, they should be carefully sealed from the outside. Seam sealers now available include K-Kote, Seam Stuff (for Gore-Tex), and Pliobond-20. This latter product is reputed to last longer than others, except in cold climates, where it becomes brittle and assumes the appearance, in one woman's words, of "squashed bugs."

Layer Five

Your extremities—your hands, feet and head—require considerable protection if you are to remain comfortable. In cold weather you lose up to 75 per cent of your body heat from your head alone. Avoid this by wearing a tightly woven wool watch cap or skullcap. An overexposure to sunshine at any altitude can scorch your face, neck, scalp and eyes. A brimmed hat or cotton sun visor successfully fends off the rays, while sunglasses will shield the eyes from harmful rays.

Hands need protection primarily in high altitude and when it is cold. In extreme cold the layer system for hands is advocated. First comes a 40 per cent Angora liner glove which is fingerless, and which extends up the wrists so that blood flowing into the hand is warmed. The next layer is a tightly woven wool mitten, which is covered by a water- or windproof mitt. Hands also need protection when at high altitude. High intensity ultraviolet rays produced second-degree burns on my hands on one hundred-mile jaunt. To prevent further burns, I covered my hands by day with cotton socks. Light cotton gloves are more effective, however, and should be used when traveling higher than 8,000 feet. They also serve as an excellent protection against bugs.

Socks function both to warm the feet, to wick perspiration, and to protect feet from blisters by preventing rubbing against the boot. Backpacking socks come in cotton, synthetic, silk or wool. Although it is lightweight, silk is both expensive and nondurable. Synthetic socks work best as a liner for wool. Once cotton socks get wet they stay wet, which contributes to blisters and heat loss. The most functional, durable sock is a tightly woven wool or wool blend. Another excellent choice is Wick-Dry polypropylene socks which keep feet dry and eliminate the possibility of wool irritation.

While sock combinations are a personal matter emerging from miles of trial and error, many experienced outdoor women wear either two or three pairs of wool socks when on the trail, for the cushioning and protection they provide.

Assembling a comfortable, functional backpacking wardrobe is no one-stop shopping affair. It took me three years to put together the perfect combination. Nor is it a process that must be completed before the first trip. The basic backpacking wardrobe, featured in Chapter 8, will suffice for starters. While it varies with climatic conditions, my standard three-season wardrobe is this:

LAYER ONE: Wool blend longjohn bottoms; used cashmere sweater from Goodwill.

LAYER TWO: QP Pants hiking shorts. Tightly woven wool slacks, two sizes too large (used; from Goodwill). Terrycloth backless, sleeveless body suit with crotch that snaps (perfect with shorts for day hiking and without shorts for river crossings); polyester long-sleeved shirt; hand-knit wool cardigan sweater.

LAYER THREE: Long-line down parka.

LAYER FOUR: Coated nylon cagoule.

LAYER FIVE: Hand-knit wool watch cap (for night); floppy-brimmed straw hat (for day); light cotton gloves and hand-knit wool mittens; wool/nylon liner socks (two pair); heavy wool socks (two pair).

In the standard cold night, warm day climate which predominates in the Sierra where I hike, I start the day in full regalia—everything but straw hat and cagoule. Before the hike begins, longjohns, parka, wool sweater, gloves and cap are shed. After the first mile, usually the slacks are packed and the shirt is tied around my waist for easy access—which leaves me in shorts, body suit and straw hat. At day's end I substitute hiking attire for long-johns, wool slacks and as many tops as temperature and precipitation require. Between trips, these clothes are cleaned and stored in my pack, which makes get-up-and-go easy to do.

Because emphasis has been placed on function, very little has been said about appearance. Here, then, is the good news. It is possible to remain stylish and attractive while backpacking. Pookie Godvin, for example, who heads the fashion parade at National Outdoor Leadership School, does so with color, jewelry and scarves. To a lavender turtleneck she adds a contrasting patterned peasant scarf in red. The dazzling accent of turquoise earrings makes one forget her trail-weary pants and three-pound clod-hoppers.

After enduring centuries of discomfort in the name of tradition and appearance, women at last have been released from their prisons of corsets and floor-length skirts, freed from acrimonious public opinion which condemned them for even considering the risqué bloomer. Today restrictions are gone, and in the outdoor wardrobe at least, practicality has preempted tradition. Now designers seem intent on creating functional, lightweight clothing which protects us from the elements, and which permits absolute physical freedom when hiking, scrambling, climbing—or simply stooping to sniff a sweet wildflower. Never, at least where clothing is concerned, has there been a better time to be an outdoor woman than right now!

CHAPTER 5

Food

When backpacking it is possible to expend nearly twice as many calories as you do during a normal day at home. During a summer hike with pack you might burn as many as 3,000 calories. During winter this may soar to 4,500 calories. There is a perfectly non-scientific explanation for this. When a 110-pound woman adds a 50-pound pack she becomes a 160-pound person. When she then takes to the trail—to the hills, altitude, heat or cold—her metabolic rate increases to the point that she may burn a third more calories per mile than when walking—or working—without a pack on flat terrain.

To compensate for calorie depletion, nutritionists recommend that a backpacker consume between 1½ and 2 pounds of food per day—in layperson's language, one heck of a lot of food. Quantity of consumption, though, is a minor issue. The real challenge with backpacking is finding food that can survive without refrigeration, is lightweight and nutritious, and requires a minimum of effort and fuel to prepare.

Food that meets three of these four stipulations exists now: freeze-dried, compressed or dehydrated food. Freeze-dried food was invented because astronauts needed some no-fuss food to accompany them on rocket-powered treks. To accommodate them, food technologists developed The Process.

This involves taking a perfectly tasty little steak (or egg, or Brussels sprout), freezing it at 50 degrees below zero, then placing it in a chamber where pressure is reduced to 1/1000 of the atmosphere. As a result of near-vacuum conditions, water in the food passes from moisture to ice to vapor. The chamber is then flooded with inert dry gas and opened. Next, the steak is quickly whisked

into an airtight package and sealed. Because cell structure is left intact, it still *looks* like a steak. It just doesn't taste like one.

The same thing happens to compressed food, except that once The Process is complete, the food is pummeled into tiny disks, then packaged. Dehydrated food gets that way only after prolonged boiling followed by air-drying or exposure to high temperatures.

The end result of such technological tampering is lightweight food which, to render it edible, requires little more than boiling water, adding, stirring once, and, *voilà*, dinner in an aluminum pouch.

Certainly freeze-dried food serves a purpose. It is lightweight and convenient. Teddi Boston hiked the entire 2,600-mile Pacific Crest Trail on a diet of freeze-dried food and Tiger's Milk candy bars, simply because it was lightweight. Freeze-dried food is useful for people who hate to cook, or for beginners who have yet to develop a preferred menu or the skill of outdoor cooking. Finally, it is an excellent alternative on days when you overextend on the trail and have no energy left for being creative over the cookstove.

Despite these obvious assets, there is more to food, even when backpacking, than light weight and ease of preparation. There are vitamins, for example. Even though nutritionists assure us that the protein and minerals remain unaffected, large doses of water-soluble vitamins B and C are lost through The Process. For many, the satisfaction that comes from having eaten sufficiently and well is lost also. For example, a two-person meal, in freeze-dried parlance, means barely enough for one. It usually leaves you pawing through the pack for real food to fill you up. Then there's the matter of money.

Converting whole food is not cheap. Neither is the airtight packaging required to keep it from going bad. At the going rate for freeze-dried turkey tettrazini for two, you could feed four amply with a pound of tagliarini, two cans of tuna, four packages of dried soup, pudding, and still be left with change.

Dr. Marion Nestle supplies another reason for avoiding freeze-dried food and its compressed and dehydrated relatives. "Food is better for you the less you fiddle with it," she claims.

With her Ph.D. in molecular biology, Dr. Nestle has taught nutrition five years, first at Brandeis University, and now to future doctors attending University of California Medical School. Her goal with nutrition—that which she practices and teaches—is to increase nutrient density. To accomplish this, she strives to increase the number of nutrients in the calories consumed each day.

"Fat is the most calorically dense food," Dr. Nestle explains, "so you decrease your fat intake while increasing your vitamin, mineral and protein intake." Fresh fruits and vegetables, for example, are high in vitamins and minerals and low in calories. Or with flour, for the same number of calories you get more nutrients in whole wheat than white. Sugar, with zero nutrients, is considered an empty food.

As her knowledge of nutrition has increased, Dr. Nestle's own diet has significantly changed. In place of meat, which she has virtually eliminated, she consumes unprocessed whole grains, fresh fruits and vegetables. She also has reduced her fat intake. She describes herself today as a "variety of whole foods in moderation" person. Dr. Nestle defines a whole food as one that has not been tampered with.

If for nutritional and monetary reasons you decide against freeze-dried food, the task is finding foods that travel well and are simple to prepare. There are such foods available now. They are in your local supermarket and health food store. They are the canned proteins—chicken, clams, tuna, anchovies, sardines. They are the packaged carbohydrates—cereals, grains, pasta, instant rice and potatoes and instant puddings. They are fresh onions, garlic, carrots, even oranges in the supermarket. (These are relatively

heavy, but on shorter trips they travel well.) They are nuts, dried fruit, whole wheat crackers and cheese in your health food store. Backpacking cookbooks listed in Recommended Reading assist by providing easy, appetizing recipes which utilize such foods.

Practically speaking, backpacking food is similar to what you eat at home when you're short of fresh produce and are relying on standbys from the cupboard. Breakfast consists usually of hot or cold cereal, dried fruit and a beverage. Lunch may take the form of hard bread or crackers, cheese, meat or peanut butter, fruit, nuts and a goody. If fresh trout hasn't found its way magically into your pack during the day, dinner usually entails soup, some variation of stew—including protein (fish, meat or cheese), vegetables, carbohydrates (rice or potatoes), perhaps sauce to tie them together—dessert and beverage. It's all right there on the supermarket or health food store shelves. It just takes a little knowledge and a lot of planning.

There's the catch: planning. Depending on the length of the trip, before shopping you might spend hours planning meals, specifying exactly how much and what you will eat every meal, every day—right down to the last banana chip.

Be aware when planning the menu that different foods produce different effects within the body. Carbohydrates—cereals, grains, fruits, candy, puddings—are easily digested and so provide quick energy to lift spirits and dragging feet. Unfortunately, such energy is short-lived. Longer-term benefits are derived from proteins and fats. Proteins—meat, cheese, milk, eggs—require time and effort to digest. These vital body builders nourish with warmth and energy. Fats—available in oil, margarine, butter, nuts and cheese—are the slowest to digest, and therefore warm the body longer than any other type of food.

Your backpacking menu should be designed to compensate for the demands that exercise and the elements place on the body. Basically your caloric intake on the trail should be divided accordingly: 50 per cent of your total calories should be carbohydrates; proteins should represent 25 to 30 per cent; fats should equal 20 to 25 per cent of total calories. When you are unusually active you will need more carbohydrates. When you are cold, fats will stoke the body furnace the longest. Proteins will warm and sustain you through long periods of inactivity, but may, because of the energy required to digest them, slow you down on the trail. Because they are difficult to digest, spread your intake of proteins and fats throughout the day.

Another vital consideration in food planning is how much food to buy and bring. Given such variables as appetite size, and such unpredictables as the effect of weather and exercise on the appetite, this remains an inexact science at best. There are a few tips, however, that might help. Begin with the general guideline, 1½ to 2 pounds of food per person per day. Count the number of breakfasts, lunches and dinners you plan to prepare on the trail. For breakfast, if relying on cereals, figure a suitable portion for one person (say a half cup), then multiply by the number of people and breakfasts you expect to serve. For lunch, estimate the number of crackers or pieces of bread you plan to consume. Again, multiply by the number of people and lunches to be served. Do the same with cheese and salami. To determine the proper amount of bulk foods, such as dried fruit and nuts, figure the ways in which they will be used—in cereal, stewed, as trail food, in puddings. From this figure how many dried apricots or handfuls of nuts will be consumed per day. Then multiply by the number of days you will be on the trail. Follow a similar procedure with every type of food that accompanies you.

The shopping process is nearly as time-consuming as the planning process. Prior to a 180-mile hike for four the food coordinator (me) gave the better part of four days to planning and shopping—including stops at 12 different stores. This can (and should!) be avoided by encouraging others to share responsibility for food.

Once shopping is complete, repackaging begins. With the exception of canned goods, cracker boxes, and cooking instructions (which should be cut from packages and saved), every ounce of bulky commercial packaging should be discarded. Components for one meal are gathered together—including, for a typical dinner, soup, main course and dessert. In separate plastic bags dry ingredients for that meal are measured, mixed and stored, along with cooking instructions. Seasonings may be added at this point, or may be packed separately and added when cooking begins. Once components for an entire meal are assembled, they are packed in one large, strong plastic bag. This same packaging process should be followed for each dinner. Breakfast and lunch foods usually can be left in bulk—unless you prefer adding powdered milk to cereal before leaving home to spare the bother on the trail.

Once meals are so organized, food should be distributed equally by weight among trip members. An easy way to separate food from the rest of the pack contents is to store it in colored stuff sacks—dinners in one colored sack, lunches in another, breakfasts in yet another. In *Simple Foods for the Pack,* Vikki Kinmont and Claudia Axcell recommend a fourth stuff sack for condiments such as soy sauce, seasoning, sugar, tea bags, coffee.

Yes, it requires more time, effort and thought, but women who have switched from freeze-dried meals to supermarket and health foods measure the rewards in ability to perform, and in a sense of health and well-being. This is not to imply that women of this school are purists. Many rely on dehydrated vegetables for texture and variation. Some reconstitute tomato flakes to create a totally convincing spaghetti sauce from scratch. Many pack one or two freeze-dried dinners as emergency rations. It's just that they don't rely on these as primary sustenance.

There is a growing school of women today who take an even more concerned approach to nutrition on the trail. These are women committed to the New Age principle that the more loving energy you put into food, the more wholesome benefits you derive from it. They are women like Colorado Outward Bound instructor Leslie Emerson. "There has been an ethic created while you're in the mountains. 'Don't take time for food, just get the instant fast stuff.' But that's not my rhythm. I'd rather take the time. With a little forethought you can make and carry what you need," Leslie says.

The degree of forethought varies with the individual. Months in advance, some women will begin drying their own fruits and vegetables, or, from organic vegetables, concoct their own hearty soup bases which they then dry and powder. Other women will pack just the basics and, come mealtime, let inspiration be their guide. They will bake their own yeast breads (using a reflector oven) or whip up a pizza or toss together a peanut curry on the trip. To sprouts (they've sprouted during the hike) they will add a few wild onions, sesame seeds, lemon juice and oil. It will make you wonder what you ever saw in lettuce. These, usually, are outdoor experts, women who have confidence and practice with trail cooking as well as dedication to natural foods.

Because I have yet to master skills for natural foods cookery outdoors, my typical dietary day goes as follows. The day begins with the first glint of light. Nightwear, such as it is, is changed in the bag for trail clothes, which have spent the night in a pillowcase, serving as my pillow. Before packing, I sit quietly contemplating the dawn, sipping a cup of Deborah's Eye Opener. (Premix at home one part each Tang, milk powder and brewer's yeast. On the trail add water, stir until lumps dissolve, sip. Yeast takes getting used to. Do it before you leave home.) Brooks Range guide Deborah Vogt created the recipe and attests that clients who drink it seem happier and peppier. For me, given the protein, vitamin and sugar surge, all things become possible at that early hour —including lifting a pack and actually walking with it.

An hour or two later, once the sun is fully up, I stop at a lovely spot and start breakfast. Breakfast is a crucial meal for a backpacker. It raises blood sugar and provides the energy required to walk distances under the weight of a pack. My trail breakfast seldom varies: stewed dried fruit from the night before, or a handful of dried fruit to start. A Sierra cup filled with wheat germ, nuts, dried fruit, honey, powdered milk, to which I add boiling water. On cold mornings, for extra calories and warmth, I add a dollop of margarine. This one-dish hot cereal provides maximum protein, vitamins and minerals with minimum bother. A cup or two of hot Ovaltine or carob drink premixed with dried milk follows.

With the first twinge of hunger I reach for my daily ration of Gorp. Gorp is a trail acronym for Good Old Raisins and Peanuts, but actually is any combination of favorite high-energy goodies. My recipe comes from Bill Shephard, an early backpacking benefactor: one part each unsalted cashews, muscat raisins and M&Ms. (M&Ms are a favorite with backpackers because, with their sugar coating, they don't melt.) This high-energy nibble food is consumed throughout the hiking day to keep energy and spirits from sagging.

After another few hours of hiking comes lunch: one or two open-face sandwiches of Bavarian pumpernickel with cheddar or dry jack cheese, or peanut butter and honey; nuts, dried fruit or an orange, many drafts of reconstituted lemon or grape drink. If I've done something commendable to deserve it, a few squares of semisweet chocolate follow. (Hard cheese, such as dry jack, and semisweet chocolate are selected because they resist melting.)

Depending on weather, light conditions and the proximity of water, hiking ends between three and five. Once camp has been established and I have indulged in a refreshing bath, dinner preparations begin. Boil water for soup first: oxtail topped with sherry (carried in a two-ounce plastic vitamin bottle) and whatever wild greens are available. While sipping the soup, boil macaroni eight minutes. When tender, drain, add cubed cheese and salami. Stir and eat. While the macaroni is cooking, add reconstituted milk and walnuts to instant butterscotch pudding. Let it set. While eating, boil more water for tea. Before bed, toast the stars, the day, the joy of being there, with a final cup of hot Ovaltine. The calcium and warmth of this drink keep me from spending nights perched on the edge of my Ensolite pad.

My trail food favorites and daily food routine evolved over years of trial, error and countless pots of scorched food. Because outdoor cooking and menu planning does take practice, perhaps the answer in developing your own routine is to take a graduated approach. As a beginner, while developing cooking skills, always include a few freeze-dried dinners as a fail-safe. As experience increases, begin incorporating simple menus, using food from the supermarket or health food store. Once you have become an outdoor expert, start working with natural foods if that appeals to you. By then, if your sprouts fail to sprout, or your yeast bread fails to rise, you will at least have enough confidence in your outdoor cooking skills to know that you won't starve.

THE HOW AND WHY OF FOOD DROPS

You should plan to carry between 1½ and 2 pounds of food per person per day. On a 14-day trip you would pack, at most, 28 pounds of food. With additional clothing and gear, this makes for one heavy pack. While the rule is to limit pack weight to one-third of your body weight, when walking longer distances this is not always possible. If you are not up to carrying additional weight, suggest distributing it equally among other trip members. Another alternative is staging a food drop.

While there are no set guidelines on food drops, one (or more) should be considered when traveling more than a hundred miles or walking longer than two weeks. Food drops are relatively simple to accomplish. Once you determine your route, locate the addresses of rural post offices in nearby towns or villages. In a heavy carton, prepare a food box which includes sufficient food to last through the next leg of your journey. Ask that a reliable family member or friend mail this on a designated date to guarantee that it arrives before you do. Always clearly mark "Hold for arrival" on the package and specify the date so it will not be returned unclaimed.

Jeannie Smith, the only woman on record to walk both the Pacific Crest Trail and the Continental Divide, recommends that on longer journeys you make it easy on yourself by using every possible food drop.

HOW TO ANIMAL-PROOF YOUR FOOD

Ever since the first peanut butter sandwich was shared with the first hungry bear, human food has become a coveted item among animals in the wilderness. Bears, coyotes, raccoons, squirrels, chipmunks and mice are the most rambunctious foragers. By their size and ability to harm, bears are the major concern, but smaller animals are cagey and no less troublesome. On one trip, during which I failed to hang my food, one resident rodent nibbled holes and swiped food from fourteen different plastic bags in my food sack. The only way to discourage this is to animal-proof your food.

When backpacking in bear country—particularly in national parks—the challenge is outsmarting the bears. This is no easy task. In the Seventies, to foil bears, rangers in Yosemite National Park suspended massive cables between trees high above the ground. Backpackers were encouraged to drape food sacks from these. Within two months bears had cracked the system. Larger bears simply hoisted lighter-weight bears on their shoulders, which put the cables within easy reach. Traveling hand-over-hand, the "food courier" would pass among the packs, selecting and knocking to the ground those containing peanut butter, honey or bacon. Other sacks were left largely untouched. Luckily not all bears are so sophisticated, but because they are large, strong and smart, you must be diligent in efforts to protect your food and yourself.

When backpacking in areas where grizzlies dwell, food storage and food preparation should take place as far from your tent as feasible. Otherwise, one veteran outdoorsman warns, you could become food.

At night before retiring in bear country, or when leaving your pack unattended for long periods during the day, store every scented item—food, toothpaste, hand lotion, soap—in a large stuff sack or distributed equally among smaller sacks. Locate a sturdy tree limb at least ten feet off the ground. Tie a rock to one end of your ⅛-inch nylon cord and toss it over the limb at least five feet from the trunk, while holding the other end of the cord. Lower the rock to waist height. Tie the stuff sack to the other end of the cord and raise it to a few feet from the limb by pulling the length of cord with the rock on it. To hold the bag in place, the extra length of cord should be wrapped around the trunk of a tree, as high as you can reach, and tied securely. While this system discourages most rural bears, in national parks or areas where bears are accustomed to humans, a counterbalance system must be rigged. A shorter length of cord is needed for this method. The weight of the food is equally distributed between two stuff sacks and each sack is tied to one end of the rope, or a rock equal in weight to the single food sack is tied to one end of the rope. The two sacks, or the sack and its counterbalance, must be hoisted to the appropriate height, with the midpoint of the cord resting on a tree limb; a long, fallen branch is used to lift the sacks. In the morning the food can be brought down by using the same long branch to push one food sack over the limb. (Never break or cut a branch from a living tree for this purpose.)

Animal-proofing food in areas inhabited only by smaller mammals and rodents is a somewhat simpler task. Either the stuff sack can be tied to a limb five feet from the ground with the extra length of rope tied around the trunk, or the food can be stored in large pots with heavy rocks placed on the lids to discourage foraging.

THE BACKPACKING KITCHEN

No matter what style of food appeals to you, you will need certain basic tools for preparing it.

THE BASICS

Stove
Cookset with two nesting pots (1½ and 2 quarts) and pot gripper
Sierra cup
Tablespoon
Small ladle
Spatula

Pocketknife
Small can opener
Hot pad (or use your wool gloves)
Plastic bags for garbage
Dishtowel (or bandanna)
Biodegradable soap
Pot scrubber

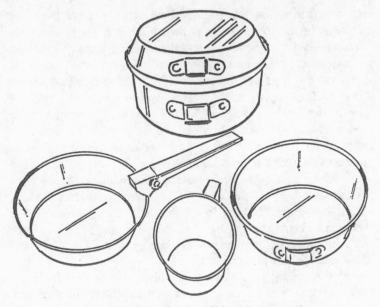

Fig. 25. Disassembled cookset.

THE LUXURIES

Bowl for eating
Insulated drinking cup
Wooden stirring spoon

The Sierra cup, a lightweight but sturdy 8-ounce aluminum cup,
works wonderfully as eating bowl, measuring cup and drinking
cup. During the day it travels hooked to the belt or belt loop,
which makes sipping from streams easy. For hot drinks, insulated
cups are tops. Once you use one outdoors you may be tempted to
add it to your list of essentials.

If you purchase pots individually instead of buying a cookset,
consider a Teflon frying pan. Backpackers who use them recommend them highly. If trout fishing is on the agenda they are considered an absolute must.

A clever pot tip comes from Vini Norris at NOLS. She uses a
4-quart heavy-gauge aluminum pressure cooker from Recreation
Equipment Incorporated. This 2-pound-13-ounce device cooks

soups, stews, vegetables, grains and even, Vini claims, fruit cobblers, in half the time—which means half the fuel. While a certain intimidation factor accompanies pressure cookers, this can be allayed by practicing with it at home before taking it along.

Many backpackers, myself included, have adopted an organic approach to dishwashing. Because soap does untold damage to our waterways, and because, when not thoroughly washed from dishes and pots, it causes diarrhea, quite a few backpackers have stopped using it. Many also have discovered that pine needles, gravel and sand work just as well as, and carry fewer germs than, pot scrubbers. Whatever your method, never wash dishes nearer than 100 feet from your water source. There is nothing less appealing than decomposing food particles in otherwise crystal waters.

If, as John Steinbeck once wrote, the line between hunger and anger is a thin one, so, too, is the line between nourishment and joy. Make your outdoor meals memorable and, in all probability, your outdoor adventures will be too.

CHAPTER 6

A Few Words About Feet

W. C. Fields once said that if he hurt his foot he could always count on sympathy, but if his feet hurt all he ever got was laughs. Feet, those innocent five-toed appendages, have been a source of humor and pain ever since humans graduated to a biped existence. While humor may elude us (particularly when sore feet belong to us), the cause of foot pain is easy to understand.

Feet serve as the body's connection to earth and are one of our more intricately designed parts. Each foot has 26 bones—26 potential little troublemakers. Due to gravity and distance from the heart, circulation in feet is sluggish at best. Foot skin, which inhabits the dark, dank world of shoes and socks, is unusually sensitive to friction of any kind.

To these entirely human conditions are added two other complications if feet belong to a woman. These are fashion and physiology. Shoe designers with little concern for foot health pick a shape, any shape, and call it style. Many women go for it every time. Foot function and shape is altered by these shoes—by the pointy toes, spike heels, stiff platform soles. The result is similar to, if less extreme than, Chinese foot-binding. Once liberated from fashion's rigid molds, the foot may undergo dramatic change. Dr. Harry Hlavac, podiatrist and author of *The Foot Book,* tells of women who, in their first year of running, have had feet flatten and expand as much as two sizes.

High heels are no help either. Because of them, calf muscles, tendons and ligaments shorten. When the heel again meets the ground, as it does in hiking boots, because flexibility and elasticity have been lost, foot placement may be altered. The foot may pronate (roll in) or supinate (roll out). When such motions are exaggerated, foot problems are practically guaranteed.

Because the anklebone leads eventually to the knee joint, some discussion of knee problems fits here too. Women have twice as many reasons for knees to go bad when backpacking than men. Besides the standard causes—improper foot placement and under-conditioning—women have a greater potential for soft-tissue injury to tendons, ligaments and muscles around the knee. Too, their broad hips accentuate the angle of the thighbones, which increases the likelihood of improper knee motion.

A few summers ago psychologist Pat Story signed up to co-lead a group of high school students on a leisurely hundred-mile backpack trip into Yosemite National Park. She arrived at the trailhead for this, her first lengthy trip, having done no conditioning. The first day she did fine. But the second day, when the trail began covering two-thousand-foot ascents and descents, her knees began to hurt. By the fourth day they had perceptibly swollen and, with the aid of a walking stick, Pat was forced to cover the required ten miles a day with knees that did not bend. Pat subsequently admitted that the mistake she made was not conditioning before the trip. Since taking up a regular program of running, she has backpacked even longer distances with virtually no problems from knees.

Foot and knee problems are easy to diagnose. Corns, calluses and bunions indicate foot problems. So do twitches or spasms in muscles, and foot fatigue. Knee problems show up in pain, stiffness or swelling under or around the knee joint. Usually people with problematical knees or feet know it. However, sometimes the backpack unexpectedly brings these problems to light. As Dr. Hlavac says, "A heavy pack puts strain on any foot imbalance problems and exaggerates any impact-shock problems in the knees."

There are ways to diminish the likelihood of sore feet and knees —before and even while backpacking. Heading the list of positive measures one can take is proper selection of boots. For women this is no small accomplishment. Outdoor Women, a national organization, surveyed members and learned that their most common problem is the lack of properly fitting boots—or the nonexistence of boots for women. In 1976, when the survey was taken, the standard solution was to buy boys' boots. Given the female's usually narrower heel, this seemed an inadequate answer at best.

Fortunately, a few boot manufacturers since have acknowledged that women's feet are shorter and, from the ball of the foot to the heel, more triangular and narrower than men's. To accommodate women's lighter frames, some also have reduced the weight of the boot. Four manufacturers have designed boots using lasts that correspond to women's feet. These include the Vasque "Gretchen II," Donner Mountain Corporation's Pivetta "Muir Trail," Fabiano's "Madre" (all sizes) or "Padre" (under size 8), and "Mountain Trail" by Danner Shoe Manufacturing Company. When selecting your hiking boot, fit and weight are the primary concerns. Not price. Not appearance. Fit and weight.

Before discussing these, however, a proper introduction of hiking boots is in order. A suitable backpacking boot is a moderate-to-lightweight, over-the-ankle, front-laced boot, with a lug sole which loosely resembles a waffle. The body of the boot should be constructed from high-quality whole grain leather. I emphasize this because costly errors have occurred in the boot buying process. Outdoor leader Arlene Ustin confesses that on her first outing —rock climbing lessons in New York—she showed up in knee-high high-heeled dress boots new that week from Bloomingdale's.

Because, as Dr. Hlavac believes, "Most shoe salesmen are concerned more with sales than with proper fitting," you must determine which boot—if any—fits well. Proper fitting begins with proper socks. One thin liner sock and one heavier sock is best. When trying boots on, first kick the heel down so it falls into the heel cup, then lace. Boots should be laced loosely across the toes, tightly across the instep, then gradually looser near the boot top. To determine if boots are a proper length, stand on a slanted surface. If toes touch boot ends, boots are too short. Next, spend ten to fifteen minutes walking around the store. It takes this long for the foot to adapt to the rigid cast and to become sensitive to any high spots. Make sure your arch is compatible with the boot arch and that your toes have freedom to wiggle. You should not feel seams or pressure around the ball of your foot. If there is pressure at the base of your big toe, the boot last is too long. Go up on your toes. If your heel slips, either the boot is improperly laced or the heel cup is too wide. A loose heel, or "heel slop" as it is known in the trade, is the leading cause of blisters in hiking boots.

Next note the weight of the boot. Standard hiking boots vary from 3 to 6¾ pounds *per boot.* In two hours of walking around my home, one on-trial pair of boots produced knee twinges, a classic symptom of overweight boots. They were quickly exchanged for lighter boots. If the option exists, always choose the lighter boot (unless you engage in marathon walks or strenuous mountaineering), for, as a rule, one pound on the foot equals three pounds on the back.

Fig. 26. Comparison of a man's boot (right) and a woman's boot (left).

Some manufacturers have succeeded more than others at reducing the weight of women's boots. For example, Donner Mountain Corporation was the first to seriously address the issue of boot weight. In 1980, they introduced the revolutionary DMC-PTF series. The "PTF 600" is a walking shoe that weighs 1 pound, 4 ounces. The "PTF 1000" is an over-the-ankle hiking boot that weighs 2 pounds, 2 ounces per pair! The secret behind weight reduction is that the body of the shoe and boot are fashioned from three-layer Gore-Tex laminate, covered by heavy-duty nylon. As a result, both models vaguely resemble running shoes. Toes and heels are protected by chrome-tanned leather, and both models feature Vibram soles, steel shanks for arch support, and toe caps and heel counters for foot protection. While there are savings in weight, there are none in cost: both models are competitively priced in the $50 range. Also, retailers have complained that they are difficult to fit, so try before you buy.

If the boot passes these tests, buy them—but only from a store that allows you to return them if, once wearing them at home, you find them uncomfortable. Boot expert Jim Owens, of The Smilie Company in San Francisco, advises, "Wear boots at home for two to three hours at night after a day in which you've done considerable walking. Feet tend to get edema after they've been used. Boots must be comfortable when your feet are swollen or you should take them back." If boots continue to feel comfortable, however, wear them as often as possible to break them in before introducing them to the trail.

Boots dampened by sweat, snow and water lose their insulating value. Once wet they rapidly draw body heat away, which can endanger you. To prevent this, boots should be waterproofed. The general rule in waterproofing leather boots is to use oil or grease on oil-tanned leathers, and wax or silicone (Sno-Seal, Leath-R-Seal) on chrome-tanned leather. If you do not know how your boots were tanned, consult the shop from which you bought them.

Socks, too, should be selected with care. Two no-nos in the sock department, in Dr. Hlavac's opinion, are the one-size-fits-all stretch sock and the tube sock. Both confine and cramp the foot, which leads to problems. To this list Jim Owens adds the cotton sock, which ruckles and, once wet, stays wet. The sock combination he recommends is a Wick-Dry interior sock and a heavy wool exterior sock. When walking farther than ten miles a day, he wears two pairs of wool socks for the cushioning they provide. By wearing two pairs of socks, friction, heat and the possibility of blisters are reduced. Be sure when doubling up socks, though, that the outers are big enough so they don't cramp or wrinkle the inners. Otherwise foot circulation will be constricted and your feet will grow cold.

Two major criteria in selecting socks are resilience and sweat absorption. Generally wool is most effective in these categories. A soaked wool sock retains 70 per cent of its insulating value. It is the only sock which will keep your feet warm when wet. With wool socks the foot moisture is wicked through wool fibers and transferred from the foot, either through the boot or out the top of the sock. The disadvantage of wool is it shrinks when washed, and because it has low abrasion resistance it wears out in toes and heels. A wool/nylon blend sock that has been shrink-treated generally will wear longer.

Always, if possible, wear clean socks. Dirty socks insulate poorly, absorb less sweat and thereby increase the chance of blisters.

Because few of our daily activities strengthen foot skin, beginning three weeks before embarking on a trip of any length, either apply rubbing alcohol twice a day to dry and toughen skin, or massage the foot with lotion. By working the skin in this way you prepare it for the increased friction it will encounter in long-distance walking.

If, while conditioning, you experience a knee twinge or two, start strengthening your knees. This is best accomplished by developing the quadricep or thigh muscles. Dr. Hlavac recommends a series of ten knee lifts without weight to start. (See description in "Conditioning.") Gradually three- to five-pound weights should be added to each leg during knee lifts. To further minimize impact to knees and feet from long-distance hikes, purchase Spenco cushioned insoles and place them in the boots.

So much for preliminaries. The moment of truth arrives when you don backpack and boots and start walking. Unfortunately, for many women, a half hour after the moment of truth arrives, so do blisters.

Blisters, considered the most common foot problem, are caused by friction which separates the layers of skin. Once separation occurs either blood or a clear serous fluid fills the space created. Blisters are pleasure robbers at best. At worst they are killers. In 1924, Calvin Coolidge, Jr., son of the thirtieth president of the United States, developed a blister on his toe while playing tennis on the White House courts. He ignored it. It became infected. He died. Some blame his and other blister-caused deaths on the lack of antibiotics. It's a moot point, for how many of us have easy access to antibiotics when we are backpacking?

To avoid the need for antibiotics, there are a few tried-and-true ways to prevent blisters. One, keep feet clean and dry. Wetness and dirt particles are a source of irritation. Two, pay attention to hot spots. The minute you sense one developing, stop; remove boots and socks. Allow your feet and socks to air dry. Once they have, apply moleskin to the irritated area. By this method you may stave off a troublemaker.

Dr. Hlavac blames blisters on too much or too little friction. For those whose feet perspire freely, he recommends foot powder. An equally effective, lightweight and inexpensive alternative is cornstarch, which can be carried in a small plastic bag.

Jim Owens avoids blisters by carefully taping predictable trouble spots on his feet—his heels and the top of his toes—with two-inch adhesive tape. To eliminate the weight and bulk of the metal spool, he advises purchasing this tape from hospital supply houses.

If, despite your best efforts, blisters develop, you have two choices: leave them alone, or lance them. Because of the chancy character of blisters, most podiatrists recommend hands off. To minimize discomfort, cut moleskin larger than the blister. Into this cut a doughnut-hole the shape of the blister, then apply. This eliminates friction. Leave the moleskin on for the remainder of the trip; to remove it is to chance opening the blister.

If you decide to lance a blister, maintain absolutely sanitary conditions. Begin by washing feet and hands with soap and water. Sterilize the needle by heating it with a match until it glows red hot. Insert the needle at the base of the blister and press gently to release fluid. Apply antiseptic and a bandage. To lessen the possibility of infection, wear only clean socks. Dr. Hlavac recommends white socks to eliminate possible irritation from dyes.

One final common problem on the trail is cold feet. This usually is a warning that you are losing too much heat elsewhere from uncovered hands, from a draft at your waist or from an exposed head. The head receives the greatest amount of blood and heat. It also loses the most heat—depending on the climate, anywhere from 50 to 75 per cent of the body's heat production. When you cover your head, heat is shunted back to the body, and finally to the feet.

This leaves but two footnotes—and both relate to pleasure. During the day, each time your path crosses a creek or stream, slip out of boots and socks and slip into the water. Your feet will thank you for miles after. At day's end, just before bed, with whatever lotion or oil you have handy, indulge in a do-it-yourself or, with your trail partner, a do-it-to-each-other foot massage. There is but one word for the experience: aaaahhhhhhhhhhhhhhh.

CHAPTER 7

On Finding a Partner

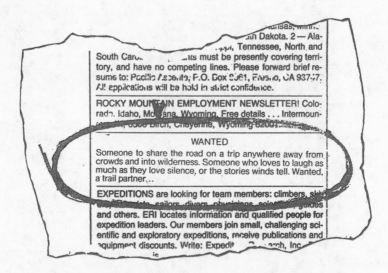

...nsas, ...
...th Dakota. 2 — Ala-
...ppi, Tennessee, North and
South Caro... ...ts must be presently covering terri-
tory, and have no competing lines. Please forward brief resume to: Pacific Ascents, P.O. Box 2061, Fresno, CA 93747.
All applications will be held in strict confidence.

ROCKY MOUNTAIN EMPLOYMENT NEWSLETTER! Colo-
rado, Idaho, Montana, Wyoming. Free details . . . Intermoun-
tain, 3500 Birch, Cheyenne, Wyoming 82001...

WANTED
Someone to share the road on a trip anywhere away from
crowds and into wilderness. Someone who loves to laugh as
much as they love silence, or the stories winds tell. Wanted,
a trail partner...

EXPEDITIONS are looking for team members: climbers, ski-
... sailors, divers, physicians, scientists, guides
and others. ERI locates information and qualified people for
expedition leaders. Our members join small, challenging scientific and exploratory expeditions, receive publications and
equipment discounts. Write: Expedit... Research, Inc.
...ie

Have you ever had an urge to write an ad to find a partner to
share a mountain, campfire or meandering trail?

Have you ever stayed home because you were the only one you
knew who loved to traipse in the wild, to feel the bulge and pressure of a home on your back?

I have—and intuition tells me I'm not alone.

Women, as a rule, are introduced to backpacking by husbands
or male friends. Should such relationships change, women find
themselves with backpack and without friend. I found myself in
just such a spot, but for a different reason. On my first trip a
woman friend and I traveled together. Beginners both, we incor-

porated every classic mistake into that trip. We arrived at the trailhead underconditioned and overpacked. We hiked too far and ate too little (actually, raccoons stole our food). Our stove wouldn't work, and by the end of two days neither would our legs. It seemed a perfect way to begin—for me at least. My friend, however, announced that she had better things to do with her time—which left me with backpack, without friend.

Since then, to rummage up partners I have: 1) clerked in a backpacking shop; 2) become an outdoor writer to interview likely candidates; 3) fallen in love; 4) volunteered to lead trips; 5) led them for pay; 6) joined group outings; 7) initiated a few of my own. I also have gone alone and picked up a partner or two on the way.

Of these, the tactic I recommend most, for beginners anyway, is group outings. There is a certain logic behind this: it is easier to find a group than it is to find a lone partner. At least eight national organizations host annual outings which combine like-minded people with wilderness adventure. With 3.5 million members, the National Wildlife Federation, for one, sponsors educational one-day, weekend or week-long outings in many states.

With 53 chapters throughout the United States and Canada, the conservation-minded Sierra Club stages both national and local outings. Local chapters in each state coordinate and sponsor day hikes, weekend backpack trips, rock climbing, bicycle tours and extended backpack trips. Many local chapters also sponsor singles groups with special activities. For the address of your local chapter, write the national headquarters of the Sierra Club, 530 Bush Street, San Francisco, California 94108, requesting membership information (though it is not necessary to be a member to attend the outings). If you are interested in longer outings, or trips outside your area, also request a copy of the national outings catalog, which is published in January.

There is a predictable character to group travel: leaders frequently are men (although, within the Sierra Club, this is changing); the majority of participants are women. One survey showed that 60 per cent of participants in group outings are women. This is understandable. As beginners, women seek the security of a group. Usually the larger the group, the safer they feel. Men, on the other hand, feel more comfortable outdoors, and tend to have male friends who also enjoy wilderness. As a result they usually initiate trips on their own.

The beauty of group travel is that one good trip invariably leads to another. Once you find people you enjoy, there usually follows an invitation to do it again. (If others don't extend it, you should!) My first group trip—a 70-mile circle of Yosemite's high camps—happened nearly a decade ago. Many people I met then are still companions on and off the trail.

Once you gain expertise you can organize a group of your own or, with a sponsored group, can volunteer as co-leader or member of the commissary crew. Due to two outdoorsy parents, Marti Leicester joined the Sierra Club at age two. By sixteen, she began participating in the commissary crew and as assistant leader on trips. In the next few years she backpacked—free—in Yosemite, the High Sierra and Hawaii. Marti, now twenty-nine, claims she has never lacked for partners. To qualify for such jobs you must be a member of the organization and have attended at least one sponsored outing before. It is a small price to pay for the chance to travel free with a ready-made group.

The alternative to group travel is scouting up mates or friends. In choosing whom to ask, remember that the quality of companionship is more important in the backcountry than the sex of your companion. "When you're out there it's like life amplified," Karen D'Antonio says. "You get down to basics because you have the material things taken away. It's just you and the person you're with. Your interactions become really important."

Because, when backpacking, risk is a reality and dependency a must, the quality of give and take between partners is essential. So is friendship. To cultivate or reinforce this bond, take a few day hikes or weekend trips together. (Guidelines for planning a weekend trip are found in Chapter 8.) Having survived these preliminaries, you move into the planning stage. The trick with planning is to do it together. If you have backpacked before, you know your average daily mileage and how many layover days you require. You know how many meals suit you and what foods taste best. Make sure you incorporate these into the plans. While certain elements may involve compromise, mileage is not one. If your partner thinks a daily twenty-mile hike is grand, and you prefer ten, either improve your condition or go in search of a different partner.

One seldom-celebrated beauty of the backcountry is that it allows men and women to push past stereotyped sex roles. With the physical exertion backpacking demands, you soon discover that almost anything he or she can do, you can do too. This does not necessarily mean that you should do more than your partner. On any trip, work and weight should be shared. If your partner is accustomed to "the little woman" handling domestic chores while he goes off to fish, educate him in new rules of the road before you hit the road.

If the rules don't stick, you might follow psychologist Pat Story's example. Before the trip it was agreed that chef chores would be shared. When her male partner missed his turn once, she said nothing. But when the pattern persisted, she balked. As one mealtime approached she became engrossed in a long novel. She read until 11 P.M., when he begrudgingly asked what she wanted for dinner. To avoid such scenes, establish chore lists before you leave. If your partner hates to cook or keep camp, figure other ways the load can be shared.

Whatever the sex of your partner, whatever the friendship is, be aware that backpacking forges a bond between you which will last for years. This alone should encourage you to be selective about your backpacking companions.

These people—your partners—play a starring role in the one thing that lingers when the trip is over: memories. If you pick, plan and communicate carefully before and during the trip, your memories—and your partner's—will be happy ones.

CHAPTER 8

How To Plan Your First Trip

Once the decision is made to take up backpacking, most beginners face the same considerations: how to do it, where and when to do it, and who to do it with. If you choose to go alone or with a small group of friends, you must determine your destination and the total distance you wish to hike. A good rule with the first trip is to make it easy. A one-night, two-day junket spanning between five and ten miles is reasonable. Given the number of unknowns in a first trip, anything more challenging than that could be inviting trouble, or a short-lived interest in backpacking.

Your route must be selected with care. It should feature clearly marked trails, flat to moderately hilly terrain, and abundant natural beauty. Altitude, enervating climbs and steep descents can discourage the uninitiated or underconditioned. Avoid them in the beginning.

The best way to pinpoint a suitable destination is to consult the experts. Ranger stations in your nearest national or state parks or forests, function in part to inform future visitors of the condition of trails and campsites. A phone call or letter requesting advice and maps is suggested. (For the address and phone number of your nearest national park, consult listings under United States Interior Department in your phone book, or write to the Information Office, National Park Service, Interior Building, Washington, DC 20240. State parks located near you are listed under the heading of Parks & Recreation in state listings in the phone book. Or consult your local library for the address of State Park headquarters.) A second approach would be to contact the local branch of the Sierra Club, or the owner, manager or backpacking expert in an outdoor equipment shop. Always identify yourself as a beginner so recommendations can be tailored accordingly.

If your trip takes you into a national park or forest, a wilderness permit may be required. Contact the National Park Service or Forest Service information offices nearest you for information regarding wilderness permits.

Wilderness permits serve to regulate wilderness use. By limiting the number of people entering an area, wilderness managers can prevent crowding, trampling of vegetation and earth, and overuse of firewood. Permits are issued free and, where authorized, serve as campfire permits. They are required prior to entry into wilderness, and are valid only during the specified dates of the trip. It is wise to secure a permit well in advance of the trip, particularly during summer and holidays. They may be obtained by writing or calling the park or forest you plan to visit. Once completed, they should be returned by mail at least fifteen days before the trip. Otherwise they may be secured at ranger stations or field offices near your point of entry. To travel without a wilderness permit in areas where one is required results in a $25 fine if you are caught.

Because navigational skills are likely to be nonexistent at this point, the trails you hike should be clearly marked, and you should carry easy-to-read maps, available at park headquarters. It is wise, on the first trip, to stick to well-traveled trails where help is as handy as the next passerby. Before setting off know exactly where you are going, and how to get there and back.

Once destination and date are set, begin collecting equipment. Essentials for a three-day trip include backpack, sleeping bag and pad, shelter—either tent or tarp, depending on temperature and precipitation—stove, fuel and cooking implements. If you are traveling with others, shelter, stove, fuel and cooking implements are community gear. The responsibility and cost of assembling them should be shared.

When gathering gear for your first trip, you should use what you have, or rent or borrow, but *do not buy* until you have backpacked at least once and find you enjoy it. Equipment can be a major investment—and a poor one unless it sees adequate use. No one knows this better than Pieter McCormack. Invited to join three women friends for a two-week Sierra trip, Pieter purchased backpack, boots, sleeping bag and parka. Two days before the trip, exhaustion from overwork forced her to cancel out. Today more than $400 of new equipment remains unused, and Pieter now acknowledges that she simply has no interest in the outdoors.

With backpacks, it is wise to rent rather than borrow. When you borrow the choice is limited, and so is your chance of achieving a comfortable fit. The most uncomfortable beginners I have known are small-statured women who borrowed a pack from a husband, son or boyfriend six feet tall or more. When you rent a pack you have the chance to choose the proper size, and an experienced salesperson usually will adjust the straps and suspension system to fit your frame.

Because of climatic variables, borrowing a sleeping bag can be tricky business too. The bag may be designed for winter in the Himalayas; you may be heading for a desert. The bag may be a bulky Dacron model designed for car camping only. Before borrowing, inquire whether the bag has down or synthetic fill, and check its bulk and temperature range. If it does not suit your needs, for your own comfort and safety, rent instead.

Whether you rent or borrow a stove, make certain before leaving home that it works, that you are capable of working it and that you have ample fuel.

Unless you are a bona fide city woman with fancy clothes only, chances are that you already own the principal components of the basic backpacking wardrobe outlined in the diagram. The three exceptions might be parka, poncho and boots. To avoid having to buy a down- or fiber-filled parka, either borrow from friends, or substitute with one heavy, tightly knit wool ski sweater which may be purchased at a secondhand shop for $5 or less.

Secondhand shops are recommended because outdoor clothes are subjected to constant abuse from dirt, soot, exertion, water and snagging by rocks, brush or trees. Besides, there is a certain economy involved. Before one trip I purchased a long-sleeved cashmere, two hand-knit wool sweaters and a pair of wool slacks for $6. The slacks, torn by a tree snag during a river crossing, were discarded at the end of the trip with no sense of loss. I still wear the sweaters.

Plastic ponchos with side snaps are available at many outdoor shops for under $3.00. In addition to protecting you from rain, these also serve as a pack cover or as a ground cloth under your sleeping bag, though manufacturers do not recommend this. (While these ponchos are intended for one-time use only, don't underestimate them. Mine has served as a perfectly respectable ground cloth for years.) Given unpredictable weather conditions in wilderness, and the imminent threat of hypothermia from rain-soaked clothes, it is imperative that you pack a poncho or some sturdy rain gear *on every trip*.

With hiking boots priced between $50 and $150, footwear for the beginning backpacker poses a dilemma. I hiked my first four hundred blister-free miles in lightweight Converse tennis shoes. I only switched to hiking boots when I began taking longer trips and carrying heavier loads. Since then, tennis shoes have been the focus of controversy. Some specialists maintain that their thin soles do not adequately cushion feet, that they are dangerous on uneven or gravelly surfaces, and that they offer no ankle protection. If, because of this, you opt for more sturdy shoes, consider crepe- or rubber-soled walking shoes, or inexpensive over-the-ankle hiking boots if you can find them. But, buy no boots or shoes unless they feel comfortable, and only backpack in them after they are broken in.

On short trips, because you are packing less weight, you have more flexibility with food. You can carry oranges, fresh vegetables or even cans, if you choose. The important issue with food planning and purchasing is that it be a joint process. That way everyone is happy with the results . . . or shares the responsibility for unappetizing food.

The No-Fuss Menu introduces you to outdoor cooking the easy way. With the exception of the first night, when you use your imagination, little more is required than boiling water for soup, cereal, beverages or instant dinners, or reconstituting powdered milk for instant pudding. If you follow these guidelines, remember that freeze-dried dinners seldom fill or satisfy. Either buy extra, or carry additional nuts, cheese or dried fruit to fill the void.

Once food has been repackaged and organized according to the guidelines in Chapter 5, assemble all items on the Essentials List on a large floor space. Now the fun begins. To lessen the chance of pack contents getting wet from rain, frost or dew, start by lining the pack's larger compartments with sturdy plastic garbage bags.

For added protection I also line the stuff sack carrying my sleeping bag.

While packs vary in design, the rule of thumb when packing is to store light, bulky items—sleeping bag, spare clothing, foam pad—at the bottom; heavy items—stove, fuel, pots, food—in the middle; and items which you use through the day or need first when you stop—an extra shirt, parka or poncho, lunch, tent—at the top. By packing this way, the weight is over your feet and center of gravity for stability. Each side pocket should be assigned a function. In my pack, one contains kitchen implements—pocketknife, can opener, pot holder, matches, fuel. (If fuel is carried in a Sigg bottle, wrap the bottle in a plastic bag. By storing it upright in an outside pocket you lessen the chances of spillage.) Another pocket holds toilet paper and all practical toiletries. One is reserved for beauty implements—comb, sunscreen, dark glasses, a tiny steel mirror, lip salve, hand cream. The fourth holds pathfinding tools—compass, pocket flashlight, spare matches, pencil for journal writing, plus a one-quart plastic water bottle. Maps, notebooks or slim paperbacks should be stored in the flat zipper- or Velcro-closed pockets featured on most packs. When packing clothes, rather than folding them neatly (which consumes space and produces lumps), stuff and scrunch them in. The wrinkles that develop will vanish once exposed to air and exertion. Items that may be stored outside the pack include rolled sleeping pads, sleeping bag (if the pack does not permit inside storage), hand towel, which I safety-pin to a flap, tent poles and stakes in an appropriate carrying sack. For accessibility, or when my main compartment is overfull, I drape my parka over the pack when I hike. This is recommended only if you have some way of securing the parka, for a lost parka in wilderness is a potential life-threatener.

Efficient packing is largely a matter of organization and consistency. Once you have determined the appropriate place for an item, always store it there. Stuff sacks, or less expensive plastic bags, aid greatly in organization. Different colored stuff sacks may be assigned for specific functions. One can carry stove and pots, another food, another first-aid items and repair kit. A fourth can hold clothes. Plastic bags, or smaller stuff sacks, help keep contents in order. Some women pack breakfast, lunch and dinner in different colored sacks, which are then contained in a larger sack.

Plastic bags are used in the wardrobe sack to separate the dirty from the clean.

When you are packing, there is no such thing as too many plastic bags. I build my supply by saving them from grocery shopping. Where possible, to reinforce them, I always double bag. In my cook sack, sooty pots are contained in plastic bags, and so is the stove. Empty plastic bags serve as carryalls for inorganic garbage, which must be carried out—freeze-dried-food containers, film wrapping, aluminum foil, etc.—and for organic scraps, such as orange peels, that do not decompose for years.

Once packing is complete, lift the pack. It will be heavier than expected. The final step in packing the pack is unpacking the pack to carefully determine which nonessential items can be left behind.

Before starting out on the trip, learn to put on and walk with a loaded pack. Ease into this gently. For starters, place your pack in an upright position on an elevated surface—chair, car fender or boulder. Slip into the shoulder straps, starting with your knees bent, so that the burden of weight is supported by your thighs instead of your back. Straighten your legs and stand up. Position the pack so that the bottom of the waistband rests on the top of the hipbones. Adjust the waistband, then the shoulder straps. Because the waistband shifts weight off the shoulders to the pelvis, your body's center of gravity and strongest anatomical point, always keep it taut when you are walking.

To cushion your body from the shock of walking with a loaded pack, concentrate on keeping your knees flexed or slightly bent. Rather than attempting to attain perfect posture, when carrying a pack heavier than twenty pounds (and whenever walking uphill) angle the torso forward about five degrees. This helps keep weight off your shoulders and on the pelvis and thighs where it belongs.

Practice walking with a loaded pack as often as possible before the trip. Either carry groceries home from the store, or load it with books—adding one or two with each new hike.

Although planned mileage may seem short, do heed tips for conditioning in Chapter 1. Many backpackers push themselves harder on short trips because time, and therefore the chance to see and enjoy, is limited.

To the novice, to those supercharged by television and the fast pace of urban life, wilderness may seem monotonous at first. What is there to look at? What, really, is there to do? To answer these questions, to cultivate your sense of the green world, before heading out read one or two books listed as general nature reading in the Appendix. Take binoculars or a hand lens along. If boredom encroaches, rout it by looking closer—at a leaf, a rock, at birds' or insects' maneuverings. You are venturing into a realm of minute and majestic miracles. To appreciate them, your mind and your eye must be trained, however cursorily, to see. If you lack time for reading before you depart, take along a specific nature guide to identify trees, flowers or whatever interests you. Learn one or two new things about nature each day. You may be amazed by the end of the trip how connected you feel to the natural universe simply because you took time to get involved.

Your first trip may not prove, in the long run, to be your best trip, but with proper preparation and planning, chances are good that it will be the start of a promising new hobby. And that is the best of all possible ways to begin.

NO-FRILLS CHECKLIST
FOR THE
TWO-DAY TRIP

EQUIPMENT
Backpack
Tent or tarp
Tent poles and pegs
Stove
Fuel
Sleeping bag
Sleeping pad
Nylon utility cord—80 to 100 feet

CLOTHING   See Basic Wardrobe for the First Trip (below).

FOOD   1½ to 2 pounds per person per day

TOILETRIES

- Toothbrush and toothpaste
- Biodegradable soap
- White toilet paper
- Comb
- Sunscreen
- Lip protectant
- Dark glasses
- Nail clippers
- Hand towel

TOOLS

- Pocketknife
- First-aid kit (including moleskin, Band-Aids, antiseptic cream, gauze, insect repellant, snakebite kit when needed, aspirin and medications for special needs)
- Plastic water bottle
- Plastic trowel (for digging fire pit and privy)
- Matches, preferably waterproof
- Match safe
- Plumber's candle
- Pocket flashlight
- Plastic bags
- Stuff sacks, large and small
- Repair kit (including needle, thread, lightweight wire, rubber bands, safety pins)

COOKING TOOLS

- Cookset, or appropriate pots
- Spoon (and fork, if desired)
- Can opener, if required
- Sierra cup or bowl
- Insulated cup
- Pot holder

BASIC WARDROBE FOR THE FIRST TRIP*

Wool watch cap
Sun visor, or brimmed hat for protection from sun

* This wardrobe is intended only for moderate terrain, mild-climate backpacking. Desert, high altitude or winter backpacking require adjustments to accommodate climatic conditions.

Fig. 28. Wardrobe basics for a three-day trip.

Dark glasses
Wool sweater or shirt
1 turtleneck (cotton or wool)
1 T-shirt (cotton or synthetic)
Parka or wool jacket
Poncho (nylon or plastic)
Wool mittens or gloves
1 pair longjohns
1 pair hiking shorts
1 pair long pants**
1 pair wool socks
2 pair lightweight wool or nylon blend liner socks
Hiking boots or shoes

NO-FUSS MENU FOR A TWO-DAY TRIP

Breakfast

Tang (served hot or cold) or a handful of dried fruit
Instant hot cereal, to which may be added nuts, dried fruit, a dollop of
    margarine and powdered milk for warmth and sustained energy
    and/or
Granola Bars
Coffee, tea or instant hot cocoa

Lunch

Hard bread, such as pumpernickel, or hard crackers (packed in their
    box)
Cheese, salami or canned sardines
    and/or
Peanut butter and honey, carried in plastic Gerry Tubes (available at
    your outdoor shop)

** In areas with low precipitation, heavy cotton or jeans. In wet, cold
areas, wool is advised.

Reconstituted milk or powdered fruit drinks

Dried fruit, nuts or trail mix (available ready-made in health food
stores, or concoct your own)

Dinner

First night:

If you are spending the first night at the trailhead, or a short
hike in from it, the first dinner can be fresh food brought from
home: steak strips marinated in soy sauce, garlic and wine in a
Ziploc bag, for example, and fresh corn. Or you may want to
prepare soup and your favorite entree at home, then freeze them in
Ziploc bags. The food will defrost on the drive to the trailhead. At
dinnertime they can be tossed in pots, heated and served. Otherwise,
choose a favorite easy recipe, such as tuna and noodles. To replace
fluid lost through exertion, start each meal with soup (the packaged,
reconstituted variety will do), and accompany the meal with water,
reconstituted milk or fruit drinks.

Second night:

Packaged soup

Freeze-dried dinners—your choice, but bring extra servings in case
you're still hungry after eating one

Instant pudding or stewed dried fruit

Coffee, tea or instant hot cocoa

Section Two
WHAT IT TAKES

Profile / ERICA FIELDER

In October, 1979, on the eve of the day she would turn thirty-two, Erica Fielder and her lightweight knapsack boarded a commuter bus, rode to a nearby mountaintop, and there disembarked. She hiked cross-country for about a mile, away from roads, stretched out her Ensolite pad, pulled sketch block and paints from her knapsack and began capturing on paper the spectacular sights she saw: sun converting sky to a luminous pink-orange; pervasive arms of fog curling around the Golden Gate; the first twinkle of night lights in the city below; nearby and distant trees which would serve as her walls for this commemorative night.

When darkness fell she responded as diurnal creatures do, by preparing for sleep. She buttoned her jacket, a piece she had crafted from two compatible wool plaids, then curled up on her pad to be entertained by the dance of stars and the intermittent song of night creatures. She slept until some inner sense announced the coming of predawn. She was there, she and her watercolors, to witness and record the miraculous details of the start of a new day.

The birthday present she gave herself was twenty-four hours in wilderness alone. It is not something most women easily do. To wander alone is to assert that you are an expert. Erica has that presence about her, yet she met her first backpack less than five years ago.

For more than twenty-six years, Erica harbored the kind of physically inept self-image that so many young women have. Her first weekend backpack trip hardly changed that, but it did re-awaken a love of outdoors planted in early childhood by her geologist father. Now she sees that trip as a turning point. In the next few years this former physically inactive textile designer apprenticed herself to a botanist and a naturalist, began leading children on nature walks, parted from her husband, participated in National Outdoor Leadership School's (NOLS) five-week training course, began leading backpack trips for women, coauthored the book *Ecology for City Kids,* and co-founded the national organization Women In the Wilderness.

"I haven't said no to experience," Erica says. "I remember when I was twelve telling my mother that I intended to have experiences, to put myself into them, to really feel them. She was very upset with that. To her experiences meant danger. To me they mean danger, but is that ever exciting!"

Erica is stretched now on the carpet in a sun patch which temporarily holds sway in her plant-filled living room. I am aware, as always on the occasions when we have met, of the stark and subtle characteristics which distinguish her. First there is her name, a shortened version of ericaceous, the genus of heath plants. Her mother loved botany, and so gave her daughter a flower name. Then there is her physical presence. She stands just over six feet. Two fine braids fashioned from her waist-length auburn hair frame her face, a face which appears perpetually flushed, either by sun or some inner well of exuberance. Such exuberance manifests itself frequently: she has just interrupted our conversation to introduce a jumping spider, a tiny creature who spins webs and snatches unwary insects on a nearby window ledge. For Erica it is the resident clown, the beloved house pet. We study its antics for a time, then continue our talk. The subject is skills building.

"I am forever grateful," she says, "for the chance NOLS gave me to do things over and over until I knew them so thoroughly I could do them in my sleep—map reading, use of map and compass, food preparation, locating and setting up a camp. When I do these things, even today, I get that same thrill I had during that course that I really know what I'm doing, and I'm proud of myself.

"I learned too," she says, "that I am a physically strong person. That sense of 'I can't do this, I hate sports, I'm too awkward, I can't run fast'—that's still there a bit. But on top of that is this solid feeling that I can carry my gear, I can handle myself, I can survive." The big test at NOLS was a four-day survival experience: a thirty-mile hike with a heavy pack, no food and a group of three she was assigned to lead. "I knew in such a deep, deep place that I could do it, that even though I was lying by the trail seemingly incapable of moving from hunger and weakness, that I could get up and go on a few more days. Knowing that, I never fear getting lost or having a bear eat my food. With that training I raised my sense of myself and my outdoor knowledge hundreds of per cent."

Erica subsequently made most of her own gear—sleeping bag, tarp, rain gear and clothes—then set about developing a backpacking style of her own. Today she either travels with a soft pack alone—containing matches, rain gear, food, compass, knife, Ensolite pad, plus clothes she is wearing—or she totes what she calls the "urban special"—a heavy pack filled with all the things she thinks she'll miss. Once she reaches a desirable location she establishes base camp, leaves the pack and continues on with her soft pack. "My style changes with this pack. I feel an incredible sense of freedom, a true feeling of lightness and adventure that I don't experience with my pack."

Her goal is to fit closely with nature, to gain some deeper understanding of it. Rather than walking well-trod paths, she follows animal trails. Rather than extending the day with fire or flashlight, she rises with the sun and retires when it does. For books she takes nature guides to identify birds, wildflowers, mushrooms and insects—and perhaps one intellectual work she normally wouldn't read at home. "Only when weather conditions force me to remain under my tarp will I sit and read. I don't want a book that will grab me and keep me spellbound. I want nature to do that," she says.

Her one admitted indulgence while backpacking is food. She spends hours preparing it—baking herb or cheese bread, making curries, whipping up a pizza or cinnamon rolls. For fresh vegetables she sprouts seeds. For a treat she concocts a hot vanilla milkshake. A gourmet vegetarian, Erica believes that the vegetarian diet lends itself to backpacking. "A lot of foods I eat in the mountains I have incorporated into my everyday life," she explains, "so it's easy for me to do a trip. I simply go to the cupboard and take out the stuff. It makes it inexpensive too. I never buy freeze-dried food."

Through NOLS Erica gained vital perspective: "It is difficult for women to feel comfortable and safe within the city because we're constantly surrounded by warnings, cautions, by newspaper headlines which terrify us. There's a constant sense of frenzy and tension. The natural environment, on the other hand, can be like a womb. It is the point of our origin. To return there is to have access to a place where we can learn that calmness, that love of being in solitude—a sense of freedom, of safety. Every time I go out I add to my sense of comfort. With that reinforcement I become more effective in my everyday work."

She wanted to share the feeling with other women, but she had other incentives too. "I noticed that a lot of women were frustrated in the way they were being taught to backpack. Men held the knowledge about backpacking. What they held was, 'You've got to get to the top of the mountain by sunset, you've got to walk this fast, you've got to eat freeze-dried food'—even though the stuff tastes terrible.

"From men, women were being taught another form of dependency. They were taught to cook, but weren't taught how to light a fire. They were taught to carry backpacks, but weren't given the information they needed to set up a camp, tie their knots, to hang their food in a tree.

"I saw a real need for women to teach women, for women to learn a nonaggressive, nonconquering attitude toward backpacking, toward themselves and the wilderness. Women didn't have aggression in them and they didn't want to learn it. They wanted to learn the flowers they were passing. They wanted to know they could sit and write a poem, or sleep comfortably in the sun for a while, that they could wander or dream without having to achieve any monumental feat."

Insights gained from leading nearly 150 women backpacking supplied the seed for Women In the Wilderness. At Erica's invitation, a core group of outdoor women gathered in San Francisco in 1975 to establish what became a national organization with nearly a thousand members. Until its demise in 1980, WW sponsored outings and strove through its quarterly publication to provide role models, encouragement, philosophy and advice to women who love the outdoors.

There was about the organization a spiritualism and an animism which was pure Erica. "I was the airy fairy one of the bunch," she offers with a contagious giggle. From living at the garden community of Findhorn in Scotland and from intensive nature study, Erica has experienced the spiritual side of nature. It has shaped her beliefs. She believes, for example, that water is the physical manifestation of the spirit of the earth. It flows through everything; it takes on different forms to permeate us. When in wilderness she celebrates this by drinking from every stream, whether she is thirsty or not. Before tasting she will stage a small ritual, holding her cup, sometimes merely thanking the water. "I've experienced that when I'm in ritual places animals are not afraid of me," she says. She recently performed a ritual before a stream which crossed a beach in northern California. When she was finished she discovered a sea lion directly behind her, attempting to see what she was doing. As he turned to leave, Erica instinctively put up her hands, in what she realized later was a gesture of peace and submission. The animal stopped, and for long moments the two examined each other without fear. Then he quietly returned to the ocean. "Whenever I've done a water ceremony I've always received some gift in exchange. The gift here was the knowledge of how to communicate with animals."

That women approach wilderness with a different awareness than men is, for Erica, a given. But they also face different challenges. Many females are taught fear at a young age. Erica is no exception, yet on her first backpack trip she was warned that the only thing women need fear in wilderness is men. "It's men," she says, "who steal from other campers. It's men who rape. It's men who are the aggressors. It's men who drive dune buggies over the delicate desert. It's that attitude in juxtaposition with wilderness that seems so frightful. Because of it I'm concerned that women will become fearful of going out by themselves."

She encourages women to remember, whether they are traveling alone or together, that they are still property in some men's eyes, that they are there to be conquered. "Women need to be cautious, to camp completely out of sight, to just blend in. It's safer for you and your gear. Know a trail is going to have people on it. If you feel threatened, give out a sense of assertiveness as you walk. Put out an aura that lets people know you can take care of yourself." This is not to imply that Erica is anti-male. On the contrary, she separates herself from men only when she needs to develop a certain strength or skill.

To backpack with a man, Erica believes, is to share an experience as potentially powerful as marriage. She labels the process "bonding." "Things that create this bond," she explains, "are the sense of being a unit with another person—each carrying his or her own weight and sharing so they're supporting one another being out there. There's a dependency on one another for survival. There's also freedom; there's the great outdoors in which two people can go separate ways, so there's freedom of interaction when they're together. Then, finally, there is the sharing of the real experiences that wilderness offers."

Whether traveling with a man, with another woman or alone, Erica's advice is the same: "Go! Just go! If you have any desire, follow it. Follow your tiniest voice that says, 'Maybe I want to try this.' Being in wilderness one drops away urban trappings. There is a process of simplification which takes place, a learning to be entertained by oneself without dependency on outside things. This creates an individual who is more of a self-support system. As this develops a woman cannot stay very connected to old systems, systems which encourage dependency. She can return to the city with a feeling of self-confidence and unity.

"We're talking about strong medicine. We're talking about life-changing experience. The decision to pick up that pack and do something with it is the process which starts the initial change."

It needn't, on the other hand, be that heavy. Backpacking can be an activity women simply enjoy—or contend with, as the case may be. As Erica readily admits, "Sometimes I wonder why I'm working so hard just to get out there with the dirt and bugs for the chance to eat burned food over a campfire."

Fortunately for Erica—as for most devotees of the sport—the compelling reasons to backpack simply outrank burned food and bugs.

CHAPTER 9

The Origin of Hesitations

In 500 B.C., the Greek historian and essayist Xenophon wrote of women: "The gods created the woman for the indoor functions, the man for all others. The gods put woman inside because she has less endurance for cold, heat and war. For woman, it is honest to remain indoors and dishonest to gad about. For the man it is shameful to remain shut up at home and not to occupy himself with affairs outside."

Xenophon helped foster a precedent which twenty-four centuries of civilized society doggedly upheld. That it was alive and well as recently as the 1890s was evidenced by this quip, which appeared in *Punch:*

> *"A lady an explorer? A traveller*
> *in skirts?*
> *The notion's just a trifle too*
> *seraphic:*
> *Let them stay and mind the babies,*
> *or hem our ragged shirts;*
> *But they mustn't, can't and*
> *shan't be geographic!"*

The only problem with Xenophon's classic quote is that biologically, sociologically and psychologically it is full of holes. As sports medicine specialist Dr. Evalyn Gendel says, "It has been medically proven, and is biologically true, that women have more stamina and endurance than men in exposure to heat, cold and such long-distance pursuits as marathon running. This is due in part to the female's subcutaneous fat, which provides insulation as well as energy in long-distance travel and high-altitude climbing."

Historically, one need look no further back than covered wagon days to gain evidence of this. In repeated instances, during three- to five-thousand-mile treks, all the men died and only the women survived. Dee Brown, who authored *The Gentle Tamers,* believes that pioneer women did so well because they had more optimism than men in the face of hardship, more flexibility and more physical and psychological endurance at the farthest reaches of suffering.

Because Xenophon failed to identify his "gods," we must presume he spoke for himself. Certainly his intent of keeping women home was plain to see. But that's not the only inhibiting effect such doctrine had. Because men spent more time there, wilderness became known as an exclusively male domain. Any woman who ventured there by choice invited as much social censure as a man who preferred to stay home and tat. This heritage is with us even today. Planted deep in most women's psyches is the insidious question, by going outdoors will I lose my femininity, will I become like a man? As any former tomboy knows, absolutely not.

There is a time in young girls' lives given to freedom of motion, to dirty fingernails and dirty hair, to boys' Levis and beanshooting and climbing trees. It is a time which comes, for most of us, just before menses, just before the body affirms it is female and will be a mature woman soon. It is a time when dollhouses and frilly dresses are replaced with a vigorous involvement with outdoors.

Jungian psychoanalyst Jean Shinoda Bolen was a tomboy once. She knows the inherent value of being a tomboy in making women healthy and whole. "Being a tomboy is not a matter of being masculine," she says. "Rather the girl is by her nature more of a physically active sort.

"One nice part about the tomboy period," Dr. Bolen claims, "is that for a while the girl is unself-conscious about who she's supposed to be. She's just out being herself. She has the chance to be daring, to take risks. She enters games with boys and experiences a give-and-take with them as equals. She gains a sense of being an all-right person. In contrast, the little girl who remains a walking Barbie doll, who always is self-conscious about who she's supposed to be, is very handicapped." Contrary to society's dubious opinion of tomboys, Dr. Bolen believes that "Most women who have gone on to be somebody in the world have experienced some kind of active tomboy phase." If outdoors contributes so much at that early age, if our femaleness not only endures but thrives, certainly it will at a later age.

Other hesitations which have traditionally encouraged women to remain indoors include discomfort, dirt and bugs. Physical discomfort only became an issue once humans discovered there was another way. That most likely happened when we learned to control fire or to construct primitive roofs and walls. Still, comfort remained a luxury until technology and push buttons were born. Now overstuffed easy chairs and an indoor climate of 68 degrees are considered the natural state.

Since comfort became the norm we have evolved into a society of softies which grows increasingly reluctant about exploring an environment where hard, cold and wet is the rule. The logic on which such hesitation rests goes like this: "Why substitute my pre-warmed Sealy Posturepedic for some barren, unsheltered spot on the ground?" Actually it is a valid point—if comfort is the only consideration.

A woman's next hesitation centers around dirt. America sustains a double standard where dirt is concerned: in young years boys are expected to be dirty, girls are expected to stay clean. This rule doesn't end at simple grime. Until recently a statute in Kansas declared it "improper for a young girl to sweat." Such statutes—and there are many still on the books—shape the education and belief systems today. "I'm not against men," Dr. Gendel says, "but they are the ones who wrote those statutes, and even today some men actually believe them!"

Still, men aren't the only ones to blame. As a girl grows up mother and modern media inculcate her with what Outward Bound instructor Marlene Simonson labels "the perfume ethic." A suitable motto for this might be, "A dainty lady is not a dirty lady; a dainty lady always smells nice." What is involved here is far more than scent. An earnest devotee of the ethic, be she teacher or pupil, sees a broken fingernail or mussed hair as a personal affront. The perfume ethic is in us all to a varying degree. It assumes its most advanced and repressive form, however, when it stops us from exploring outdoors.

The final hesitation focuses on bugs. The sad part is that, for most women, bugs didn't always have a bad name. When first introduced in childhood days we saw them as creeping, crawling or fuzzy curiosities. Bugs didn't always benefit from this (I remember eating one once to see how it would taste), but we did, for they provided yet another living link to explore.

Before long, the lessons began. Usually they took the emphatic form: "Don't touch!" Some lessons were more subtle—like TV ads for Raid. Some were downright indirect. I remember watching my mother be afraid of mosquito hawks, those long-legged rattly creatures that haunt the night. For the attention and teasing it earned from my father, "frightened" became an attractive thing to be. At first my fear was mere mimic. Before long it became my own.

So it is with most children. Gradually natural curiosity gives way to fear. By the time a young woman matures, bugs aren't something to live with (or eat), they are something to flee from or kill. The happy addendum to this narrative is that the condition is reversible. Curiosity resumes once a woman gains appreciation for even one bug's unique form and function in nature's complex web.

With hesitations we have a choice: allow them to limit us, or see them for what they are—the offspring of erroneous dictum or social conditioning. Hesitations are intended merely to give one pause. Where wilderness and women are concerned, they should never be allowed to do more than that.

CHAPTER 10

Variations on the Theme "I Can"

In order to achieve anything positive in life a person must first believe she can. This deceptively simple concept often determines how high one reaches in life, and the success one knows.

These are provocative thoughts, but how do they relate to a backpack—or, more pointedly, to you? Answers to this began forming one day as I was attempting to climb a 200-foot-high rock face. Actually, I was stuck. I couldn't see how I could maneuver a four-foot move when my legs barely stretched three. Rather than undertaking creative problem solving as I hung there, I began reviewing my can'ts (I can't move; I can't stop my legs from shaking; I can't be the strong person I'd hoped—and so forth). Finally, out of desperation—or an inundation of can'ts—I asked the woman holding my belay rope to pull me up. She had more faith in my abilities than I; she refused. Because I had no alternative I did finish the climb. After that I began examining the power of can't versus can.

We are taught as young girls that there are many things we can't do. First there are the physical lessons. We are told we cannot throw a rock, baseball or Frisbee as far as our brothers, we cannot run as fast, we cannot lift the weight that they can. From these and similar dicta we learn all that our bodies cannot do.

There are sociological can'ts imposed too. When we begin to risk and adventure we are told we mustn't. It isn't safe. Further, we are taught that Mom needs us, that it isn't right to wander when there are people to satisfy right here at home. In the words of one woman, we become "elegant pleasers"; we learn to place others' needs ahead of our own.

After ten to forty years of such conditioning someone proposes a friendly little backpack trip. For many women two responses occur. One, "I can't possibly leave Fred" (or the kids, or the dog, or the parents). Two, "I *can't* carry a backpack!" (or walk ten miles, or sleep without a bed).

How do you know what you can or cannot do if you have never tried?

Given the traditional upbringing, most women are bound by more can'ts than men. Fortunately there are exceptions to the rule. One is Leslie Emerson, now twenty-eight, and an instructor for ten years at Colorado Outward Bound.

As an infant Leslie was bundled up and taken into wilderness, there to spend months at a time. She learned to walk in fields of pinecones and boulders. When in the city she found the smoothness of sidewalks strange. She was raised at the heels of her mountain-climbing father. At age six she began to climb. She would place her feet where her father did, and would follow wherever he led. Of those times Leslie says, "I can remember as a small child yelling out, 'I can't do this!' and my father would say, 'We're going to wipe that word out of our vocabulary. Can't doesn't have a place here.'" No distinctions were made between what she and her brother could do. Her father's expectation was simply this: "Always take a step forward. That gets you in a new place and some new kind of learning." As a result, Leslie admits she is a person who is not inclined to say "can't."

By eighteen, when she joined Outward Bound, Leslie was the next best thing to an impossible role model. She stood six feet tall, blond and beautiful. Her outdoor skills were unmatched by many people twice her age. If she lacked anything it was insight into the pervasive power of can't. When she taught her first course to teen-age girls her lessons began.

"What I learned is that women lack the self-concept that says they can do most anything they put their minds or hearts to," Leslie says. "It took years watching women of all ages fumbling through to realize they're just not imbued with that. Instead, there is hesitancy and self-doubt.

"The first reflex all women have coming through the program is to say, 'I can't.' Once they've said that you have the sense of high brick walls being erected between them and what is possible."

Sometimes wilderness offers perfectly valid reasons to say can't —at least they seem valid at the time. While a student at Outward Bound, Marlene Simonson resorted to can't when she decided she was entirely too young to die. Marlene remembers those long moments before her first rappel (that feat of descending a rock face while supported only by climbing rope). While instructors set the rope, Marlene plumbed her list of can'ts. The reason she finally gave for why she couldn't rappel was that she had just undergone shoulder surgery two months before. "Not one word of it was true," she admits now, laughing. But she wasn't laughing then, particularly when, in the next moment, she found herself executing her first shaky rappel.

Marlene subsequently became an Outward Bound instructor. In 1976, in her thirties, she began focusing energies on teaching women thirty and over exactly how much they can do. "We don't even say 'you can' or 'you can't,'" she says. "We just assume participants will, so the support they receive from us is always positive." Such support is beneficial—as long as it lasts. After graduating, one woman wrote that on returning home she suddenly became aware of the number of influences in her life that were saying, "You can't."

She is not alone. For most of us can't assumes one of two forms. There are external can'ts which arise in dialogue with family or friends, and there are internal can'ts, ones we perpetuate on our own. Either way they are a barless prison; they impose unnecessary limits.

Now that we have examined the constrictive nature of can't, one seemingly contradictory point must be introduced—namely, not all can'ts are bad. "In wilderness that's especially true," Leslie says, "because things can change from one moment to the next in terms of weather patterns, temperature and conditions of terrain. Maybe can't is appropriate for this time and place. It's a situational ethic."

There is another instance in wilderness when can't does apply. His two legs can span six feet, yours can cover only three. You honestly cannot achieve what he does in the way that he does. You can, however, create a style of your own. "I'm willing to say there are male/female differences, but I wouldn't want those to get carried to extremes," Leslie says. "I'd rather we as individuals take stock of our styles, rhythms and capacities. Try not to set up an external standard of what is possible based on what someone else can or cannot do."

As I learned on the rock face, can't is a choice one makes. It is saying no to the opportunity to expand capabilities, to probe broader realms of self. Next time a can't threatens to overwhelm, substitute "I can!" for it. By making a habit of this you might be amazed at all you are able to do.

CHAPTER 11

On Developing Skills

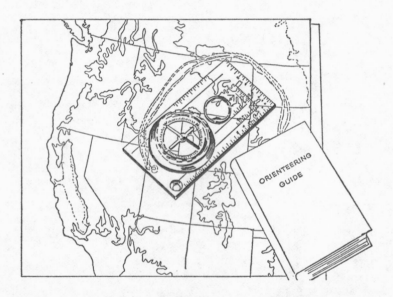

Backpacking is a deceptively simple sport in which just about anything can go wrong—and frequently does. You pick up your pack incorrectly and your back goes out. You cross a mossy log bridging a turbulent stream. Your foot slips, you slip. Now you're no longer walking, you're swimming. So is your pack. You reach camp just as it starts to rain. Your stove forgets how to work and, because they are wet, so do your matches. By sleep time the wind is up and your tarp is down. When you raise it again it flaps like pterodactyl wings next to your ear. Next morning as you pick up your pack again one clevis pin pops from the frame. A shoulder strap sighs to the ground like a dog's tail too weary to wag. For these reasons, before you grow earnest about the sport, it is essential that you acquire certain skills.

Skills building for many women smacks of Boy Scouts and Eagle badges and Always Being Prepared. Actually it's less regimented than that. Usually the desire for skills increases in direct proportion to your love of and urge to be outdoors. Skills considered vital for staying comfortable and alive include fire building, knot tying, map and compass reading, shelter building, river crossing and first aid. Beyond this, you should be able to interpret messages the body sends and, under any climatic condition, should know how to stay warm and dry or, in the desert, cool and wet.

There are a few traditional ways to develop skills: institutional learning; learning by doing; learning by teaching, by putting yourself in a situation where you are expected to know. Today the number of institutions teaching outdoor skills is legion. These include YWCA, local recreation departments, night schools or universities, and professional outdoor schools such as National Outdoor Leadership School and Outward Bound. Primary considerations are time, money and the degree of motivation you have. The Y and public universities offer night courses for small fees, or none. Frequently these include a weekend expedition which permits practice in the field. Professional outdoor schools, on the other hand, cram everything you need to know, and then some, into eight-day to three-month courses which range in price from three hundred dollars to two thousand dollars.

After several years of do-it-myself skills building I decided to let the pros give me a hand. As I learned only *after* participating, the trick to outdoor schools is taking their recommendations for physical conditioning and multiplying by two. If the school advises 10 push-ups a day for one month before your course, do 20. If it suggests daily two-mile runs, shoot for four instead. The worst thing you can do is show up unprepared—which is precisely what Clorinda Hite did.

Clorinda is an appealing, spindly waif whose 5'8" frame is dominated mainly by legs and eyes. A native of Kentucky and a nurse by trade, she signed up for Colorado Outward Bound because she thought it might be fun. She had never worn a pack, never harbored any burning desire to lug forty pounds. Once her pack was loaded, patrol mates had to help put it on. Her body responded in a perfectly understandable way: "My legs began to bow," she says. "I wasn't sure I'd be able to walk."

The first thing she learned about backpacking is that everything worth seeing is at the top of some hill. "We never walked down to a destination," she says, "just up." At first she tried being brave, but quickly discovered it took more effort than it was worth. As she walked she would stumble and mumble, and when all else failed she would cry. "I cried up one whole trail," she recalls, "until I realized it was interfering with my breathing."

Everything about the trip was miserable and hard. Besides the physical exertion, Clorinda was put off by the food. "It was bulgur," she recalls, "bulgur in every way, shape and form. But the thing that bothered me most was eating and drinking out of one little cup."

As she was leaning against a rock one day breathing what she hoped would be her last, her instructor reassured her as best she could: "Don't worry, Clorinda," she said, "backpacking isn't for everyone." By the second week Clorinda began making promises to herself: "I promise I'll never do anything this hard again." She kept the promise the first three months she was home. Then new awareness dawned: "I realized that in spite of everything I probably had enjoyed it." By Christmas she requested a backpack as a gift so she could take up the sport on her own.

Outdoor schools offer far more than the chance to bear up under the weight of a pack. At Northwest Outward Bound, one of the regional outcroppings of this national school, my patrol mates and I were initiated into the adventure in the traditional way. We began by hauling ourselves hand-over-hand across a river on a rope suspended between two trees, by leap-frogging over a six-foot-high "electric" wire, by learning technical knot tying to hold us secure in future climbs, by perfecting what looked like awkward gibbon acts on an eight-phase rope course which took me six tries and three hours to complete. After loading fifty-pound packs, after a chummy get-acquainted campfire and a midnight dinner of mainly soup, then and only then did the day's hike begin. Following a two-mile sprint highlighted by the perilous log crossing of a thunderous stream, day one finally ended at 2 A.M. the next morning. Day two commenced three hours later at 5.

Featured skills in the eight-day span included rock climbing, map and compass reading, knot tying, first aid and snow skills such as glissading and ice ax arrests. We learned to rappel down rock faces and ice cornices, then claw and scuttle our way back up. We learned to survive compatibly as a group. We learned exactly how physical we could be on little food and even less sleep. We learned to remain mobile and rational despite omnipresent fear. We gained inner certainty that under most conditions we possessed the capacity to survive.

It became apparent from this that there are two parts to acquiring skills—learning the technical side, and learning that you have the physical and emotional stamina to perform when the need arises. It is in this latter realm, in pushing you to experience your vast physical and emotional potential, that outdoor schools particularly shine.

There are two disadvantages to skills building the professional way. One is expense. While the investment is worth it, for many women it is beyond their means. Many schools address this by offering full or partial scholarships. The second disadvantage is that, despite all you are taught, your retentive capacity is somewhat squelched by fear. The solution is to practice new skills in a non-stress situation once you return home.

Leslie Emerson is a firm believer in this. "Make sure you break that institutional umbilical cord and go try things on your own," she says. "Going out there and walking a lot of miles and making a lot of mistakes on your own time is the only way to truly integrate what you have learned."

Learning by doing is essential, whether prefaced by institutional training or not. It is, in fact, the primary way we learn. You're never sure you can build a successful fire or erect a stable tarp until you've done it successfully on your own. The catch to this method of learning is that it seldom happens when traveling with a man, for most of us harbor a traditional, if subtle, tendency to lean. If you wish to bolster skills, travel either with another woman with a mutual desire to learn, or with people of either gender who possess fewer skills than you.

In keeping with the Japanese proverb "To teach is to learn," the third way of building skills is to place yourself in the position of educating others. The key here is to start small. Girl Scouts, for example, is a grand way to begin—not as a Scout, per se, but as leader of a new or small troop. For women eighteen and over, the Scouts offer monthly leadership training sessions which teach Scout traditions, policies, games, crafts and outdoor skills. Four times a year the Scouts offer special training in outdoor cooking and specific skills for backpacking leadership.

Once you have a fundamental grasp of skills you can hire on as co-leader for a trip. After my first year in backpacking I applied as one of three leaders on a ten-day high school snowshoe trip. I'd never seen a snowshoe, let alone worn one, but by virtue of having to know I learned more about snowshoeing and winter camping than many backpackers ever know. Because women leaders are a desired but rare commodity, opportunities to teach often abound. For starters, contact your school district, recreation department or local Girl Scouts.

Backpacking is like college. The longer you're involved the more you realize there is to learn. Once you master such basics as silencing tarps (alias pterodactyl wings) you move to a more delicate state of the art—predicting weather from cirrus puffs, or setting direction from the face of your watch and the slant of the sun. Given nature's intricacies, there is no end to what you can know.

Skills add comfort and safety to wilderness trips, and they add something more. Any woman who ventures freely in a world without push buttons or walls automatically gains a self-reliance which accompanies her not only when traveling with backpack—but wherever she goes.

A PRIMER ON FIRE-BUILDING

Fire in wilderness is a friend, a foe, and for many of us an unknown force. We carry matches to start one, but lack the knowledge to construct one, or to appreciate its short- and long-range effects. Eugene Fear of Survival Education Association claims that only 20 per cent of wilderness travelers possess the skill to build a successful campfire in dry conditions. The guidelines that follow serve only as a starting point, for fire-building as a skill requires practice, while fire as a phenomenon in wilderness deserves considerable thought.

❦

During certain seasons, and in certain wilderness areas, fires are off limits. Because of this, check with appropriate personnel—managers or backcountry rangers—before departing, to determine fire regulations. Secure a fire permit if one is required.

If you decide on a fire, once you have established camp, scout the area for an existing fire ring. This is a circle of fire-blackened rocks constructed by previous campers to contain a fire. If a ring exists, use it. Otherwise, look for a clearing away from tree trunks or overhanging limbs, and some distance from boulders, so they will not be blackened. The best spot is a dry stream bed, for when water flows again all traces of fire will be washed away.

Next, begin gathering downed wood, pinecones and small sticks. If the ground is dry, pine needles and dry leaves can be gathered as fire starters. If the wood supply is already depleted, *do not snap limbs from living shrubs or trees.* Instead put off building a fire. If downed wood is available, gather it and store it in graduated sizes: small twigs, slightly larger sticks, pinecones and small limbs. Only gather as much as you intend to use—and always use less then you intend; otherwise you disturb the ecological integrity of the site.

When the wood supply is at hand, if no fire ring exists, and if the top soil is soft or pliable, dig a small fire pit. This need be no larger than one foot square and six to eight inches deep. First subdivide the designated area into sections by marking the dirt with a stick. Then, using a plastic trowel if you carry one, begin digging, cutting and carefully removing soil in sections. You will note the soil consistency changing the deeper you dig. If you are unable to remove the soil in sections, be aware of these different strata so they can be replaced in order. If you find that you have to chop through roots, scout out another area to dig your pit, instead of damaging or killing a shrub or tree.

At the bottom of the pit place any paper you have salvaged—

gum wrappers, a page from a notebook, or pine needles and leaves. On top of this place the smallest twigs. Over this foundation, using pencil-sized sticks, build a small tepee-like structure. This permits air to circulate, which is essential for a successful fire. Once the tepee is completed, using a candle or matches which have been stored in a plastic bag or waterproof container, light the paper. If the starting flames seem hesitant, gently blow at the base to encourage the flames to catch. Once the fire is well started, carefully add larger wood, one piece at a time, making sure that its weight does not collapse the tepee and snuff the fire. When adding wood remember the axiom, "Indian builds small fire, huddles close, stays warm. White man builds big fire, keeps warm gathering wood." Once the fire is established, sit back and enjoy.

Before retiring, douse ashes and any remaining embers with abundant water. If roots pass through the pit, be particularly certain that they are cold and wet, for fire can be transmitted through root systems. In the morning before breaking camp, begin replacing soil in the order in which it was dug. When the pit is filled, tamp soil gently with your feet, and sprinkle with additional top soil to remove any trace of fire. Finally, scatter any of the gathered wood that you have not used, so the visual integrity of the site is preserved. If you restore the area with sufficient skill, those who follow will never know that a successful fire was built on this site.

In wilderness today fire is a mixed blessing. Ecologists laud its ability to clear underbrush and promote tree growth. As a result, an increasing number of controlled fires are being set in national forests and parks. However, although fire rejuvenates, it also destroys. One sees increasing evidence of this along backcountry trails.

With fire, wilderness users tend to place their needs over nature's. They seek light, warmth, cheeriness; they light a fire. Nature suffers the consequences. A tree which may have taken two hundred years to germinate, grow, die, fall and commence its dissolution to dust, is consumed by a campfire in minutes. An ecological process is halted, the wilderness is diminished.

But nature is not the only one slighted. By huddling in a tenuous ring of firelight we separate ourselves from night wonders, from stars, animals and quixotic imaginings. We destroy night vision, and a powerful bond to night. We think fire shields us from fear and elusive mysteries of night. It does not. It separates us temporarily, that is all. We think it warms us, but mittens and a wool cap do the same—and they leave no scars.

In the morning we pack and leave. But traces of our visit remain, in charred earth and boulders blackened for eternity, in earth scraped bare of tree droppings. Fire rings and scorched grass in some alpine meadows take 10,000 years to disappear. Is that the mark you wish to leave behind?

If you must build a fire, do so carefully. But, remember, campfires deplete and destroy. Like the wise Indian, always keep yours small.

SHORT STEPS TO SKILLS

More than a decade ago Gene Fear founded Survival Education Association because he believes most of us have lost the knowledge and ability to stay alive even eight hours in wilderness when separated from our equipment. The point is well taken. Because of it, and because of the unpredictable character of wilderness, you should start out prepared. The following tips will assist in sharpening skills.

Map and Compass Reading

• Read *Be Expert With Map & Compass* by Bjorn Kjellstrom.

• Enroll in a course in orienteering through your community college or YWCA, or request that such a course be taught by your local backpacking shop.

• Once you have secured the appropriate topographic map from a backpacking shop or by writing the nearest office of the U. S. Geological Survey, head for a nearby wilderness area. Begin by sitting stationary. Position the map properly, then compare actual geography with the map's contour lines. You will begin to recognize configurations on the map. Take a short hike while holding the map before you. With practice you will begin to see similarities between geography and what you see on the map. Certain trail maps may contain discrepancies due to changes in trail, vegetation and terrain. For your own protection when backpacking, always carry at least two different maps depicting the area in which you are hiking, if possible.

Shelter-Building

• Using a tarp or a large plastic sheet, nylon cord and available sticks and rocks, practice erecting it in your backyard as if to protect yourself from wind, sun, or rain. If your tarp lacks grommet holes, roll small pinecones or rocks into each corner as stabilizers; tie these in place with a nylon cord. Tie the other end to trees or to rocks or sticks which are subsequently pounded into the ground. Before raising your shelter, determine if it is to block wind, rain or sun. The way you place the tarp, and the design you select, determines how much protection you gain from the elements.

If you will be traveling with a tent, practice raising it before you leave home.

First Aid

• Take a course in mountaineering medicine through your local Red Cross. If this is not offered, take advanced first aid.

• Read *Mountaineering First Aid* by Dick Mitchell. This is available at outdoor shops, or by sending $3.95 to Seattle Mountaineers, 719 Pike Street, Seattle, WA 98101.

• Write for free first-aid pamphlets, "By Nature's Rules," available from Safeco Insurance Company, Safeco Plaza, Seattle, WA 98185.

Knot-Tying

• Purchase and practice on Early Winters Knot-Tying Card. Send $2 to Early Winters, Inc., 110 Prefontaine Place South, Seattle, WA 98104.

• Excellent knot-tying instruction can be had through the Boy Scout Handbook. Contact your local Boy Scout Council, or send $3 to Boy Scouts of America, P.O. Box BSA, North Brunswick, NJ 08902. According to former Boy Scouts, the older the handbook the better. If your local council cannot supply you with a vintage copy, check out used-book stores or your mate's or brother's bookshelves.

• If you have time to master only one knot, make it a figure 8. This serves you well in most instances.

River Crossings

Each year backpackers lose their lives while making unsafe river crossings. When crossing a river always take time to locate the safest possible area to ford. This may be where the river narrows, where the current slows, or where downed trees can brace you. During crossings the pack can be deadly. Once they have lost their footing, many people drown because they are weighted down or pinned under logs by the pack. If possible, throw the pack across. If not, and if you are making a solo ford, locate a long branch or stick to help balance you. *Always* release the buckle on your hip belt before crossing.

If you have packed tennis shoes, wear them during river crossings. Otherwise wear your boots as a protection against sharp, slippery rocks. Remember, wet boots are a far better alternative than losing your footing . . . and possibly your life.

When the current is swift or the water deep, if you are traveling with two or more, tie a belay line between two trees on opposite shores. The first person, who carries the line across, should not tie into it, but should merely hold onto it. The alternative is to lock elbows and enter the water at a slight angle to the flow of the water. Each person should take small steps and should move only when the others are stationary and secure in their footing.

Snow Camping

• Because of the demands freezing temperatures place on the body, never backpack in snow unless you are accompanied by experts, or unless you have completed a course in winter camping. If neither option is available, teach yourself snow camping the practical way. In snow country, camp a short distance from your car, then practice digging snow caves, setting up shelter, cooking and sleeping.

• For further information read *Snow Camping*, by Nordic World Editors. This is available for $2.95 from World Publications, P.O. Box 366, Mountain View, CA 94040.

For additional information on skills, contact your local Girl Scouts requesting free brochures on outdoor survival and skills.

CHAPTER 12

The Essential Skill—
Staying Alive

At least 90 per cent of those who wander in wilderness do so unprepared in body and mind. Most of us suffer a common malady: civilization. With instant access to warmth, shelter and water, we have lost our sense of the body—and the ways the elements affect it. We have relinquished the sound judgment of the pioneers. We have given up outdoor skills. So complete has our transition to the indoors been that many of us have even lost the ability to stay alive for the few hours it takes a Search & Rescue team to locate us.

"If people want to live a little longer in wilderness, or in any emergency situation," Gene Fear says, "they must learn to manage their bodies better." But, first, we must understand how the body functions.

Imagine, for a moment, that your body is an ambulatory egg. Your skin is the shell. Your heart, lungs, stomach and brain comprise the yolk. Muscles, tissues, arteries and capillaries, which insulate these vital organs, are the white. To preserve health and life, the yolk of the egg must sustain a relatively constant temperature—in our case, 98.6 degrees Fahrenheit. Outdoors, because of exposure to the elements and physical exertion, this is not always easy to do.

Unlike the egg, the human body has the ability both to generate and disperse heat. It produces heat in one of three ways. The first is through basal metabolism—the act of eating and digesting. When one eats a single candy bar, body temperature temporarily rises at least five degrees. The second is involuntary heat production, which occurs with shivering. For a short time shivering will increase the body's heat production as much as eightfold. The third is voluntary heat production, which results from exercise. At rest, the body produces about fifty calories of heat per hour. Carrying a heavy pack up the trail can increase this ten times. Anything that weakens the body—loss of sleep, inadequate food intake, fatigue, dehydration, lack of acclimation, fear—reduces the body's capacity to produce heat.

There are five ways in which body heat is dispersed. First is *radiation*. Like a home radiator, the body is continually giving off heat to its surrounding environment. This generates a thin layer of warm air which surrounds our body, and which is considered our micro-environment. If this heat is captured and held close by clothing the body stays warm. If not, it can chill. *Convection,* the motion of air currents over and around the body, carries radiated heat away and replaces it with colder air. Even a moderate breeze can disperse body heat faster than it can be produced. *Conduction* occurs when the body comes in contact with cold surfaces—a cold boulder, for example, or cool water. Anytime the body touches any surface colder than 98.6 degrees, it loses heat. *Evaporation* is the fourth way the body loses heat. Whether you are exerting yourself or not, the body is always emitting an invisible shield of perspiration. As this evaporates the body is cooled. Finally, the simple act of breathing, or *respiration,* disperses heat. Each breath you take enters cold and leaves warm.

Outdoors the body is exposed to numerous elements, each of which may produce physiological changes. These include heat, cold, wet, wind and altitude.

HEAT

The sun holds undisputed title as nature's primary heater. Sun warmth dominates deserts and canyons, and also generates intense heat in unexpected places—on glaciers, in mountain moraines, on mountain tops. As the body absorbs sun warmth and generates additional heat through exercise, it begins working to increase the flow of heat away from the body. To maintain a comfortable temperature in the "yolk," blood vessels dilate, or open up. Increased blood flow radiates excess heat out through the extremities, then through the skin. Sweating begins. If this does not effectively cool the body, it responds in headaches, dehydration, heat exhaustion, and—the potential killer—heat stroke. A flushed face, excessive thirst, fatigue and irritability are warning signals that the body has dangerously overheated. Immediate steps should be taken to cool the body. Once you have sheltered yourself from the sun, remove clothes to help dissipate heat through convection, radiation and evaporation. To cool by conduction, immerse yourself in cool water, or lie on cool boulders. Drink liquids to replenish fluid loss, and to reactivate the body's cooling system.

COLD

In a cold climate, the process is exactly the opposite. To stay warm, the body must produce heat at least as fast as it is lost to the environment. When this is not possible, body temperature begins to drop. To preserve its core temperature, the body begins withdrawing heat—first from the skin, then from tissue and muscles in the extremities. At first one may notice cold feet. Next the skin begins to feel numb, and the fingers lose some flexibility. If the individual does not respond to these cues by donning a wool cap or warm, dry clothes, or by ingesting food or warm liquids, the tissues contract and serve as insulation to prevent further heat loss. When the core temperature starts to plummet, muscles begin an involuntary contraction; you begin to shiver. Persistent or violent shivering signals that the body is on the verge of hypothermia.

Hypothermia is the rapid, progressive mental and physical collapse which accompanies the chilling of the body's inner core. It is caused by exposure to cold, and is aggravated by wetness, wind and exhaustion. It is the number one killer of wilderness travelers.

This insidious killer is easy to avoid—if you are attentive to body signals. When the feet begin to feel cold, don a wool cap. In cold climates, between 50 and 75 per cent of body heat is lost through the head. When the head is covered, heat and energy are shunted back to other parts of the body. If you are wearing wet or even slightly damp clothes, change them for warm, dry clothes. If shivering continues, make camp immediately. Once shelter is set up, remove any wet clothes and crawl into a sleeping bag protected from the ground by an insulated pad. Because your body has lost the ability to generate heat at this point, warm water bottles, fire-warmed rocks, or the body heat from another person in the bag will compensate. Drink warm liquids.

Hypothermia is branded "the killer of the unprepared." It strikes when you least expect it. Most deaths from hypothermia occur not in sub-zero weather, but in mild temperatures—between 30 and 50 degrees.

WET

The cold that kills most rapidly is cold water: cold water running down neck and legs, cold water held against the body by sopping clothes, cold water flushing body heat from the surface of clothes. When a body is exposed to water, either through precipitation, perspiration or immersion, it loses heat 240 times faster than a body that remains dry.

Protect your clothes from the elements. In snow or rain always wear waterproof rain gear. In cold weather avoid overheating through exertion. The perspiration which results dampens your clothes. When clothes are wet they lose 90 per cent of their insulating value. Beyond this, wet clothing causes an accelerated loss of body heat because the evaporation process draws out much heat from the body. At the first sign of rain or wet snow put on your rain gear. When you stop walking, add more clothes to stay warm, or replace wet clothes with dry ones. In wet climates always carry wool. Wool can absorb 17 per cent of its weight in moisture before it feels wet, cotton 7 per cent, polyester only 1 per cent!

If you cannot stay dry and warm under existing weather conditions, abandon the day's goal and make camp out of the wind and rain. Otherwise you court exhaustion and hypothermia.

WIND

Wind robs the body of heat by convection. When it blows it disperses the thin layer of warm air surrounding the body and replaces it with cold. While this helps cool you when the body is overly warm, it poses a serious threat when it is cold and your clothes are wet. Wind drives cold air under and through clothing, and it refrigerates wet clothes.

Wind alters not just body temperature, but existing air temperatures. A 2 mph wind can drop the effective temperature as much as 20 degrees! When wind picks up to 20 mph, a 30-degree temperature drops to 3 degrees. The phenomenon is known as the wind-chill factor. When the wind blows, be prepared to compensate for heat loss with warm, dry clothes!

ALTITUDE

The lack of air pressure and resulting lack of oxygen at high altitude imposes yet another stress on the body. Inadequate oxygen in the blood, compounded by exertion and dehydration, may bring on altitude sickness. This manifests itself in many forms, including headaches, nausea, dizziness, weakness, labored breathing. In extreme cases, high-altitude pulmonary edema, or cerebral edema—both potential killers—may develop.

Altitude sickness seldom occurs below 8,000 feet, though a sense of lassitude may occur when backpacking at 4,000 feet or above. Those who suffer from altitude most are those who ascend rapidly, and who engage in vigorous exercise at high altitude.

To avoid this malady, acclimation is a must. Full acclimation takes up to six weeks, but a three- to four-day stay usually prevents symptoms. On a weekend or three-day trip, arrive a day early and sleep as high as you can so the body becomes accustomed to lower air pressure. On the first day do not push the body too hard, and take every opportunity to rest. If altitude sickness develops, aspirin for headaches, Dramamine for nausea, and caffeine for reducing lassitude will help. If symptoms persist, descend 1,000 to 2,000 feet and remain at that altitude until the body acclimates.

DEHYDRATION

Because of dry air at high altitudes, fluid loss through lungs and by sweating is greatly increased. One day of heavy exertion at high altitude without adequate fluid replacement can produce a loss of three pounds of fluid weight. When fluid is not replaced, dehydration occurs. Its symptoms include weakness and lethargy. To ward off dehydration when backpacking at 10,000 feet or above, force yourself to drink at least one gallon of water or fluid per day. At lower altitudes you should increase your fluid intake two quarts over what you normally consume each day.

In wilderness your body will either work for you or against you. By growing sensitive to its processes and needs, and to the intricate effect the elements have on your body, safety and pleasure in wilderness will be enhanced—and life and health will be preserved.

IF YOU ARE LOST

According to Search & Rescue experts, women are least likely to get lost in wilderness, and most likely to survive if they are lost. Women have the advantage, experts believe, because they have been raised to be cautious and, if they are mothers, have learned to think ahead.

Fine in theory, but women still get lost in wilderness. You can increase the chance of a safe return by following these procedures.

Before Leaving Home

• Never start out without first supplying a responsible family member or friend with a brief itinerary describing where you are going and when you will return. Allow a half-day or one-day margin on your return date. Promise to call this person as soon as you exit from the wilderness. Ask that they immediately notify rangers or appropriate official personnel if they do not hear from you. A search will begin. (You will be expected to bear the expense of this.)

• Educate yourself. Leading survival expert Gene Fear has condensed twenty years of education, training and experience in search and rescue procedures into his book, *Wilderness Emergency*. It should be considered required reading. For a copy send $5 to Survival Education Association, 9035 Golden Given Road, Tacoma, WA 98445.

• Create your own survival kit. This should include a one-pint can with the top cut out and a lid of sturdy plastic taped in place, a 7-bushel leaf bag with a hole cut in the sealed end for face or head, a large garbage bag, a plumber's candle, a box of strike-anywhere matches, 6 to 12 sugar cubes, tea bags and bouillon cubes and a roll of adhesive tape—all stored in the plastic bag. The tape is for repairing clothes or plastic bags, or as emergency bandages. The can will serve to collect and heat water in, and as something to drink from. If you lack shelter the plastic bags will sustain body warmth by trapping radiated heat. Never leave your pack, even for a short day hike, unless you take along a stuff sack or a day pack containing a survival kit, extra food and clothes.

On the Trail

If you do not see landmarks that seem familiar, if you feel disoriented, you probably are lost. Sit down immediately. If you cannot correct the error by mentally retracing your steps to discover where the mistake was made, follow the advice of Lois McCoy, a leader in the Search & Rescue movement: hug a tree! According to Lois, this benefits you in two ways. While hugging a tree your feet are not moving; you are not getting yourself any more lost. Two, it gives time to calm yourself and think. People who continue moving often waste vital energy walking in circles, or walking downhill into ravines where they are less visible. It is better to stay put.

If your pack, containing shelter, food, dry clothes and maps, is with you, you are not lost, merely disoriented. Stay calm and stay put until, by studying maps, you have discovered your directional error. Retrace steps only by day. Do not move if night is approaching.

If you are without your pack, primary energy should go to conserving body heat. If you have a tarp, set it up as shelter. If you do not, locate or construct some natural shelter. Put dry insulation beneath you—limbs covered by leaves, for example—to reduce heat loss by convection. Collect wood. Ten armloads will be sufficient to warm you through the night. Set a fire and prepare to light it.

If you are wearing wet clothes, remove them and dry them—with sunshine or fire warmth—if you can. Replace them with dry clothes if you have them. If you do not, wrap yourself in one or two large plastic bags to preserve body warmth.

If you have easy access to water, collect it and heat some over the fire. If you have tea bags or bouillon cubes, add one and drink the fluid. This will both calm and warm you. Sit quietly and mentally retrace your steps. If you have maps, consult them now to determine where you are and how best to return to the trail. If you lack maps, short scouting hikes *taken only by day* may help locate the main trail, but leave your temporary site only if you are certain of its location and how to return to it. To ensure this, every hundred yards turn and study the path you have just covered. Familiarize yourself with vegetation, ground slope, geologic formations. You will note as you do that the path looks entirely different when viewed from the opposite direction. To guarantee a safe return, mark arrows in the soil, or tie thread or fabric strips to trees to mark your trail. If you cannot locate the main trail, return to your campsite and stay put. Spend time gathering wood, and keeping warm, dry and calm. Know that panic is your principal enemy. Get angry, get active observing your surroundings, do anything to keep your mind occupied, but do not permit panic to take hold.

To assist Search & Rescue teams in finding you, keep a fire going. Feed it occasionally with wet leaves. The smoke will be visible at some distance. If you have a whistle, intermittently blow three long signals to indicate distress. Make yourself as visible as possible by staying in a clearing, and by spreading out any colored items which contrast with your natural surroundings.

If you abide by these rules, the chance of correcting your directional error, or of being found alive and safe by others, is excellent.

CHAPTER 13

Parting Thoughts

For centuries the tradition of men leaving, of women being left, proceeded merrily along. Then, a few years ago, the lightweight backpack was born. It was just the ticket women needed to go outdoors. We did so timorously at first, traveling mostly with men, but gradually the number of us wanting to be outdoors exceeded the number of men willing to take us there. So, we began back-packing in groups, with other women, or by ourselves. As a result, one time-honored tradition has taken a subtle turn. Now some women are doing the leaving, while men are being left behind.

It would be one thing if women managed this new role with ease, but it simply isn't so. From examining women's sentiments on the subject it becomes clear that we may have come a long way in some departments, but when it comes to leaving men, we've got a long way to go.

One primary hurdle is social training. From birth pre-women's lib females were schooled that it was their role to nurture and sup-port. Mostly that meant being there to cook a meal, iron a shirt or soothe a weary brow. Now, suddenly, women are finding value in placing their needs and desires over their men's. Only they're not sure how he will respond.

"The hard thing about leaving is you don't know what you'll be coming home to," says Dr. Deborah Dain. A skilled outdoor woman, for three years she has sustained a positive relationship with Jim. Usually she shapes her schedule to fit his, but when some irresistible trip comes up, she goes. She went one summer to Alaska to backpack and explore. The next year she joined a high-altitude physiology study on Mount Logan in the Yukon. "I have these underlying fears," she says. "Maybe I'm being too independent. Maybe he will not put up with this."

The concerns women grapple with are two: Is he capable of caring for himself? Will he, in our absence, find someone new?

Men, meanwhile, experience discomfort of their own. "Whenever Maureen announces she's taking off without me my stomach just starts to churn," Willi Fuller claims. Willi has been leading family and friends backpacking and mountain climbing for years. More than many men, he understands the urge to go. But understanding doesn't ease the pain of being left.

The reason is simple: most men have a balanced life and physical comfort as their goals. When their mate heads for the hills with a backpack, balance instantly goes out of whack, while they are left to provide comfort on their own. Few men face such disruption passively. Instead, as women have for years, many initiate a campaign of "the pulls."

Pulls are designed to activate guilt feelings, to encourage partners to stay home. They take many forms. One is disbelief: "You're really not going to *leave* me (and/or the kids), are you?" Another is enticement. Here he thoughtfully recounts all you'll be missing while you're away—social gatherings, sporting events, him. When women hold firm, not a few men have stooped to the most seductive pull of all: the alternative plan. In this he posts a reward for your staying—usually some romantic trip *à deux*.

There are, to be sure, men who abstain from the pulls. They recognize benefits in a woman growing on her own. Yet even they have difficulty coping. "Jim always has been supportive of me going," Deborah says, "but when it comes to me leaving he gets uncommunicative and difficult to deal with." Sometimes such reaction is as hard to handle as a concerted campaign of the pulls.

The problem with leaving is this: when someone you love is encouraging you to stay, it makes it twice as hard to go—which is why some women never do. There are ways to resist the impulse not to go. Scientific problem solving is one. In this you list all the reasons why it is important for you to leave. Elaborate on the good it will do. Remind yourself that it is something you want to do. In another column, list the (one hopes few) reasons why you think you should stay. If positive outnumbers negative, you've supplied an objective rationale for going.

If that system fails there are friends, those stalwart pioneers who have successfully left before. By contacting them you probably will hear what has been said often before: separations contribute to the relationship if you're not gone too long. Sally Stapp Campbell and her husband, Dan, both lead outdoor trips. Sally leaves Dan many times a season, sometimes for two weeks or more. "It used to be real hard for me to go," she admits, "but we both need space to do things by ourselves." Deborah agrees: "My trips have affected our relationship in a positive way. If I do things I want to I'm keeping myself happy. If I hang around to fulfill his needs I start getting antsy about things." These thoughts are shared by many.

A trip away can be, usually is, a good thing to do. The first step —announcing and activating the plan—is the hard part, but there are ways to ease even that. If you feel shaky about leaving, figure out why. If you worry about how your mate will care for himself, together work out a livable plan. If you feel anxious about how and with whom he'll be spending time, tell him. Sharing stressful emotion sometimes is like releasing pressure from a balloon.

Apprehensions grow stronger as the day to leave draws near. Men experience tension, while women sometimes give in to tears. "I always cry the night before I leave," one woman says, but such emotion is not limited to women. Willi Fuller talks of tightness in the chest, the result, he thinks, of holding feelings in. The best way to handle parting is to pack the day before you leave. This frees the evening for you to spend alone, nurturing and indulging each other's needs.

So much for husbands or sweethearts, but what about kids? Sometimes the maternal link is stronger than that which binds woman and mate.

When a mother contemplates leaving, her mind fills with vivid imaginings. "Child Abandoned by Backpacking Mother," headlines scream. "The accident wouldn't have happened," the story starts, "if the mother had stayed home . . ." To these are added a timeless attachment and concern. Can the children stand being on their own? Will they eat? Who will bandage their knees?

Such fears are put to rest by thorough preparation, by making sure that meals and bruised knees and goodnight kisses are handled caringly by somebody else. Still, it is not easy to go.

One woman who speaks of the divisive pull of personal interest and love of child is Pat Kielsmeier. A decade ago in Colorado, Pat, who was married then to an Outward Bound instructor, began orienting herself to outdoors. Three years after her daughter, Laurie, was born, Pat enrolled in Outward Bound. During her first time apart, she discovered the value in maintaining individual identity. Pat is working full-time with Outward Bound now; she started leading courses four years ago, when Laurie was five. During summers teaching responsibilities separate her from her child two weeks at a time.

"I think it's a myth that as kids get older it's easier to leave them," Pat says. "That's just not true. No matter how old kids are we're always going to feel tension in leaving them. That's part of being a mother. But, we have got to go ahead and do this or our kids will be thirty-eight and we'll still feel this way."

Pat, who leaves Laurie with her parents or with friends while she's away, has gently schooled her in the need for time away. "My being away doesn't mean I don't love you or don't want to be with you," she tells her. "It's just that you don't need me all the time, and I don't want to need you all the time."

There's the catch. Need. Sometimes a woman's need to be needed stops her from leaving her kids. With Mom gone children might discover that they can get along better than they thought they could. Kathy Evans—wife, backpacker and mother of three—admits, "In leaving your family, even temporarily, you are relinquishing your familiar role and the idea that you really are indispensable. If you go, your family will see it can be done without you. A lot of women won't give up that power."

But, to both mother and child there is long-term value in temporary partings. A woman who acknowledges and indulges independent desires, who does things by and for herself, sets an example of health and strength which her child is likely to follow. As Pat knows, "My doing this will allow Laurie to have minimum guilt feelings for leaving me to go exploring or adventuring on her own."

The first parting is hardest, and so, on any trip, is the first day away. The missing begins moments after you leave, but something wonderful happens, too. Once you get away you realize that your anxieties don't matter. You regain the exhilarating sense of being complete within yourself. Suddenly all those worries about what your mate, family or friends are doing are replaced by the hope that, in the time apart—like yourself—they'll be having a good time.

Section Three
WHAT IT'S LIKE

Profile / DEBORAH VOGT

Many people consider Alaska the last true wilderness. Much of its vast ruggedness resists subjugation. Whole mountain ranges and valleys have never known the plod of human feet. Animals living there—moose, caribou, wolves, wolverines and bears—pass entire lifetimes without encountering a single human being.

Outside urban centers wilderness grabs hold. Few neatly fashioned roads or trails penetrate. To reach its core you fly. Once the tiny bush plane departs you face rare isolation. It might be a thousand miles to the nearest grocery store, hot shower, or source of help.

It is a land cast in head-high brambles, turbulent streams, in miles of marshy tundra. In summer hiking tundra is like crossing soppy, spongy bed springs. A sense of solid earth is gone. There is strain, and omnipresent sucking sounds as boots meet icy rivulets from which tundra vegetation grows. To walk five miles in these conditions is equal to walking ten in any other place.

There are basic rules for backpacking there: "Guard your equipment from damage" and "Never surprise a bear." Failure to comply with either carries a threat of being maimed or killed. To avoid chance encounters, bear bells are affixed to the pack, or the hiker learns to sing, recite poetry or conduct lengthy monologues.

It is wilderness at its most exacting, inspiring best. It is a good place to explore once wilderness skills are mastered. It is, all agree, no place to begin.

It was hardly an auspicious start. On day one in Alaska, her love, Bob (the reason she was there), announced he'd found someone new. On day three her former love, two other men, and she set off on a six-week backpack trip to explore Alaska's remote Brooks Range.

It would be comforting to think Deborah Vogt was "experienced" on this trip. She was not. Her total time with a backpack included one weekend in the Sierra the year before, featuring ten-mile daily hikes she thought would kill her. Understandably fear joined her on this trip. She was concerned maybe she couldn't do it, maybe she couldn't keep up. Luckily, one man was in worse shape than she, which positioned her in the middle—alone, but at least not last.

Each morning started the same way. Bob and his hiking partner, Robin, broke camp and left. Deborah—in a determined effort to keep up—followed. Ken brought up the rear. Entire days would pass without her once spotting the others. Guideposts were footsteps—when she could find them—and common sense. Sometimes the trail crossed fast-paced streams. She learned to ford them alone. Once it led to the base of an 8-foot cliff. She maneuvered that too—alone. "If Bob and I had still been romantic," Deborah says, "I would have just grabbed his hand every time I needed help. It would have been a totally different experience. The fact that I had to confront it on my own was at first very intimidating—terrifying almost. Then, as weeks went on, I began getting immense fits of pride in my ability to cope. By the end of three weeks I was convinced that if the plane didn't pick us up it was no big deal, I'd just walk back."

Three weeks out, two days in Fairbanks to resupply, another three weeks out. What Deborah saw and achieved in those six weeks changed her life. "I look back on that trip as an almost religious experience," she says. "It was so profound. For the first time I really felt all parts of my life were under my control—that I was acting completely rather than reacting or being passive."

Deborah had achieved things I'd only dreamed: annual lengthy stays in wilderness, building a log cabin by hand, living simply without modern conveniences of any kind. She was happy to share the experience, I eager to learn from it. On the strength of that we became friends.

Although our Bay Area homes stood twelve miles apart, this day we were exploring watershed regions of the mountain which formed our respective backyards. Cossack, the Alaskan malamute, was along. Four feet in height, his head measured level with Deborah's waist. Although he was wolflike in appearance, his massive tail was generally in a wag, his face in a lolling-tongued grin. He was leaping now at the prospect of a walk and freedom from his leash.

Our goal was a distant lake—an eight-mile walk-run. We traveled light; no water, no food, just clothes and blithe spirits engendered by a spring day. In tailored clothes—which she usually wears —Deborah is a sensual woman without the frills. Today she was pure tomboy: shorts, a halter fashioned from kerchiefs, New Balance running shoes, Ragg socks. Still, the prettiness was there, in prominent flushed cheekbones, in slightly slanted eyes. Hers is a face which by configuration alone could be Alaskan, but the coloring is wrong: silky short hair the color of old gold, blue-green eyes which sparkle like waters traced by a pale moon.

We ran awhile, then walked and talked. Always with Deborah talk turns to Alaska. She probes current legislation, conservation issues, people. She as readily expounds on the life of a bush hermit as shares a vignette about being with the Governor when word of his reelection came. Today the subject was her own life and experience there.

She returned the second summer to assist Bob Waldrup (or, simply, Waldrup, as Deborah refers to him now) in leading backpack expeditions through the Brooks Range. Initially she coordinated food, but gradually, with experience, began advising and guiding. From all she experienced and gained there, by the end of that second summer her decision was firm: Alaska would be her new home. From glittery, fast-paced, all-the-amenities San Francisco, she moved to a rustic one-room cabin five miles outside Fairbanks. It had no running water and was heated only by a wood-burning stove. By chopping wood, by carrying two five-gallon water containers at a time, by traveling mainly on skis, Deborah maintained her physical conditioning. To save money she turned the electricity off. "I wanted to see how little I could get by on," she explained. She worked only to pay minimal rent, and to afford food for herself and her dogs. With a team of four malamutes, Cossack among them, dog sledding became her favorite sport.

Winter jobs varied from night waitressing (so she could dogsled by day), to executive secretary, to manuscript typist. One winter she served as sole proprietor of lodge, airfield and gas station in Bettles, a community of fifty-four people, and the jumping-off spot for northern Alaska. Her day off each week was spent dogsledding or transporting food and mail by bush plane to remote home-steaders and hermits. Always with these jobs her agreement with employers was, "The end of May, the end of me." Early each June Deborah was back doing what she loved most—exploring and guiding Brooks Range expeditions.

At first, Deborah and Bob led trips sponsored by other organi-zations. After two years they formed a company of their own. In what they did they were unique, for they alone possessed the knowledge to conduct tours in this demanding terrain. As Deb-orah says, "We were two of the ten most experienced people in the Brooks Range."

Such experience hardly tempered clients' dismay when they learned that their leader was a woman. "I always think it ruins the expeditionary sense for some of these men," Deborah says. "They think, 'Here I am going off on a Brooks Range expedition, and if a girl can do it it can't be that hard.'"

Actually it was—and is—that hard. With all essential equipment, packs easily weigh up to 70 pounds. Deborah, herself, may carry a 75-pound pack—well over half her 130-pound body weight. Flat though the terrain may be, walking tundra is never easy. Several clients describe it as the toughest hiking they have done. Because of her condition and experience, Deborah manages it with relative ease. "Some clients on these trips have completely changed their generalities about women," Deborah comments. "A lot of men have never met a woman that could or would do the things we do. It surprises them that we not only do it, but actually enjoy it."

For the first few years clients were mainly men. That is changing now. "It hasn't gotten any easier," Deborah assures. "It's just that today a lot more women consider themselves capable of carrying a heavy pack and of doing hard trips." According to Deborah, women backpack differently than men. "They have less spring and more stamina," she says. "Men hike faster than women and use up more energy. Women will plod along at a less spectacular, more sustained pace. It may take them an hour longer to reach camp, but when the time comes to climb down the bluff to get water, to make dinner or do camp chores, women are the ones to do it. Men often have a tendency to put up the tent, crawl in and just collapse."

We paused in our walk long enough to identify birds, plants and animal tracks. Deborah's opinion usually prevailed. No, it's not a mountain lion's track, it's a large dog. No, it's not an alder, it's a rare species of oak. At one point in the trail, where earlier I had met a pack of feral dogs, we searched briefly for a den. By crashing through dense underbrush Cossack alerted skittish inhabitants of our approach. "He never runs this free in Alaska," Deborah said. "Usually he stays within ten feet of me." In Alaska Cossack makes an ideal wilderness companion. Bears mistake him for an overgrown wolf, an enemy worthy of respect, and keep their distance. Still, even here he is protective of his mistress. As if on cue he bounded back to check in. Deborah landed a mighty wallop on his side, and he again took off. We followed him down the wooded trail at a trot.

To lead expeditions in Alaska seemed challenge enough, but Deborah also wanted to experience wilderness alone. Early one fall, a bush pilot ferried her to a remote lake. Cossack, a mere puppy then, accompanied her. With camp established she watched the sun settle low as it does at night in this part of the northern hemisphere, then she retired to her tent. What happened next may have been a dream, but to Deborah it seemed real. She awoke to see darkness in the shape of a bear at the foot of her bag. Terror immobilized her. As the form approached she sensed it was death. Gradually its shadow encompassed her lower body. When it reached her head she knew she would be dead. She was calm then, recognizing, she says, that "death is not so bad." She had had a good life. Her one regret was that Cossack must die so young.

Death did not overcome her that night, but the experience purged her of the fear of death and the fear of being alone.

Wilderness Alaska had become her fascination, the source of her livelihood. In 1974, the opportunity arose to also make it her home. In what became the final chapter in federal homesteading, the Bureau of Land Management made available certain parcels of land in the western Brooks Range. Waldrup joined her in realizing the dream. In spring he skied in, surveyed the area and staked fifty acres. In fall, Deborah and a carpenter followed his lead to the land, using a map and what directions Waldrup could provide. Finding it wasn't easy, for the complex, brushy valley was inhabited by beavers who had, during summer, altered the course of many streams. Because the carpenter was a stranger she described the experience as a "three-week long blind date"—a successful one at that. They raised the first structure, a bear-proof cache braced twenty feet in the air on three lopped trees. Equipment, clothes and food were stored there. The next fall, Deborah, Waldrup and three others felled and peeled forty trees, the basis of the cabin. Their main source of power was muscle, their tools only those they could carry on their backs from an airstrip twelve miles away. The next spring, another carpenter set the cabin's foundation, frame and walls. Once roof and walls were raised and chinked with sod that fall, and a wood stove and mosquito netting for windows were carried in, the cabin became habitable. Now it serves as unofficial headquarters, a place where guides and clients go at the end of trips to celebrate the unique life-style there.

The homestead, to Deborah, is not exactly wilderness. There is, after all, the airstrip where one can take a shower or get a cold beer. That only operates part-time during summer, though. Otherwise the nearest neighbor is a forty-mile hike. The homestead provides Deborah with a sense of permanence. She longs one day to spend twelve months at the site to usher in and experience the seasons.

What time she has spent there, and in other wilderness places, has both calmed and sensitized her. "It's a physical relief to be in a quiet place," she says. "My body doesn't have to defend against noise anymore. There are tensions within that I was not even aware of that finally let go." During the day she may hear two, maybe three sounds. That is all. She has extended her hearing faculties to pick these up. "I can hear a beaver playing in the water a hundred yards away," she claims. "I can detect when water changes direction as the result of wind."

As her connections with wilderness were deepening, so too was her involvement with Alaska in general. In spare time she began volunteering with Alaska Legal Services. That plus a nine-month assignment as court liaison officer with Fairbanks Native Association rekindled an interest in law. The timing was perfect. With her growing commitment to Alaska and her awareness of its increasing need for legislative protection against exploitive oil interests, Deborah longed for a more influential voice. "I wanted to have more say about the use of Alaska's lands," she recalls. "I had vague ideas that a law degree would allow me to have a louder voice."

She applied to Hastings Law School in San Francisco and was accepted. After one year, based on her performance, the Dean encouraged her to apply to the University of California's prestigious Boalt Law School. There she completed the last two years and earned her degree.

In the span of eight years, from a nine-to-five urbanite, she had become a one-of-a-kind Brooks Range guide, Alaska's last female homesteader, and now a lawyer and professional woman. As we picked our way back home, Deborah explored what she considers the cause of this dramatic change—her first backpack trip in the Brooks Range. "Fundamentally a trip like that just shakes your foundations so severely that your whole perspective is altered." She acquired emotional and physical self-reliance. She learned to take active control of her life. "In a sense," Deborah says, "I've never gone back to the way I was before that trip."

Following graduation, she returned to Alaska. For once, summer months were spent not in the Brooks Range, but in Juneau, her new permanent home. She passed bar exams there. In August she visited the homestead briefly. There wasn't time to linger, though, for in September she started her new job.

Deborah Vogt currently serves as Assistant District Attorney in charge of natural resources for the state of Alaska. Where preservation of the wilderness she loves is concerned, Deborah has only just begun.

CHAPTER 14

The Quality of Our Teachers

The world's most inspiring classroom has never known a blackboard, a ceiling or fluorescent lights. Chairs, as we know them, are nonexistent, and so are desks. No standard texts are required there —in fact, most books are considered cumbersome and out of place. This classroom operates on a twenty-four-hour schedule. Students do not arrive or depart with the gong of some bell. They come and go at will. The classroom of which we speak is wilderness; the student is anyone who wanders there by choice.

At any age, at any stage in your wilderness experience, there is much to know. To travel safely you must master outdoor skills. To appreciate the intricate workings of the system your senses must be attuned, refined. To develop a sense of unity, to understand fine and finite happenings there, you must acquire knowledge to decipher what you see.

The process takes time, and it takes teachers—lots of them. But who are nature's teachers? Loosely defined, they are anyone you walk with who knows more than you. They may be professional outdoor persons, naturalists, family members or friends. Frequently they are men. Why? Boys are raised to believe that outdoors is their domain. They play there, learn there, fight there, grow there. From these experiences emerge a storehouse of memories, real and imagined. They supply the base of knowledge and confidence most men have outdoors. Girls are just the opposite. Unless they dally overlong in the tomboy stage, they grow up to see outdoors as alien land. For women to grow comfortable, some transference of knowledge is required. This process usually is launched by the person who invites them outdoors.

There are as many styles of outdoor teachers as there are styles of men. The quality of instruction hinges mainly on the man's character, incentive and degree of sensitivity. Good teachers make the learning process safe and exciting. Bad teachers heighten the insecurity a novice feels. Then there are the non-teachers, those individuals who ignore teaching responsibilities altogether.

Annie Ketchin was introduced to wilderness by such a man. The urge to be outdoors had been in Annie always, but in her wealthy Southern family the opportunity had not. This pixieish woman with almond-shaped eyes arrived in Colorado at age twenty. Here her outdoor education began. By twenty-one, she was making first ascents of mountains in Peru. The transformation sprung more from Annie's desire than from instruction, for the man she traveled with lacked any ability to teach. Ski "lessons," for example, consisted of ushering Annie to the top of the highest slope, then leaving. Rock-climbing "lessons" took basically the same form. "He was the type who had very little grasp of what anybody else was going through," she says. "I was placed in one predicament after another and just had to get myself out. That is a way of learning. It also is a way of becoming overdosed very quickly so your learning is not very useful to you."

It's that old sink-or-swim method of teaching. But there's a catch to it. Just because a woman doesn't drown doesn't mean she's learned to swim. Annie herself learned so fast that before long she joined Outward Bound as an instructor—but midway through her career she lost contact with what she knew. "I realized suddenly that I was doing everything by the seat of my pants," she says. "That took the wind out of my sails, and shattered my self-confidence." The experience was similar to the young child who begins examining the processes involved in taking a step, and suddenly loses the ability to walk. She felt crippled in her ability to teach. She admits she was not a good instructor at the time. "The concept of learning by the seat of your pants and overextending a little bit has a lot of validity," Annie says today. "But it also can backfire—which is one reason, I think, why so many women don't go back."

A teacher can by his technique instill a sense of awe about outdoors, or can encourage a student to retire permanently indoors. My array of teachers included one of each. One was a graduate of the "If they don't speak the language, scream it and maybe they'll get the message" school. Everytime he wanted to teach me something he raised his voice to a low-pitched shout. The trouble was that the louder he shouted, the more I resisted the lessons he had to share. The other teacher was a skilled and sensitive naturalist. From him I discovered the miracle in a single leaf, the inspiration of a star. Because of him I am active outdoors.

By his own awareness and sense of self a man determines, unconsciously perhaps, how much a woman learns. Some men believe women should remain dependent, and so they dispense information or emotional support sparingly. Others (and one hopes that their number is growing) value competent women, and so infuse them with as much knowledge as they can. Outdoor leader and professional river runner Bob Licht is like this. He consistently encourages students and friends to stretch past constrictions of ignorance and fear.

One beneficiary of Bob's teaching is Laurie McCann. On her second official outing, Laurie was invited to co-lead with Bob a backpack trip the two-hundred-mile length of California's John Muir Trail. "It was like an intensive assertiveness training course for me," Laurie recalls. "I learned I was really strong, that I could do things I never thought I could before. The trip offered really concrete validations of my physical and mental strengths." When she was confronted by fear, by the sense that the task involved too much risk, Bob encouraged her anyway. Laurie questioned the wisdom of pushing herself, but afterward was always glad she had.

Once she had perfected her backpacking skills, Laurie started river touring. Now she runs rivers in kayaks and instructs other women in doing the same. Much credit for who and where she is today, she feels, goes to Bob. "He has been like a guru in terms of what I learned from him about myself and what I can do. When talking about women in wilderness I always keep the perspective that he's the one who really made it possible. He was my teacher for five years. I always want to acknowledge him in what I learned."

Leslie Emerson had an equally positive learning experience. Her teacher was an able mountaineer, a university professor by trade. He also happened to be her father. "He never articulated much," Leslie says, "so I spent a lot of time watching as I moved with him through the terrain. I'm thankful, in hindsight, that he didn't instruct in a formal way. By watching him interact with the environment it made me open my senses. It made me curious why he did what he did when he did. It was a puzzle to put together—which kept me open and watchful. It gave me an autonomous feeling. Even at age six I felt myself a sensing human being in that environment rather than just existing in a lock-step bond with my father." As a result of such instruction, Leslie began teaching outdoor skills herself when she was eighteen. With Leslie and Laurie the maxim is the same: good teachers create good students who eventually become good teachers themselves.

This is not to imply that women are taught solely by men. Some women recognize inherent disadvantages in the system—she gives up her strength, he does more than he should—and seek out women teachers instead. Some purposely enroll in all-women patrols in outdoor schools to practice skills or to develop strengths they feel they cannot in the company of a man.

Women usually teach differently than men. There is, for one, a lack of paternalism, and little enticement for the student to lean. Vini Norris of NOLS says, "Being women, we recognize the games our women students are playing and simply don't join in." Women teachers are a source of inspiration. With Stephanie Atwood, my Outward Bound instructor, I experienced a mixture of pride in her strength and a sense of possibility—a feeling that "If she can do it, so can I."

As with men, there are drawbacks to being taught by women. While the goal-oriented male will push the student until the mountain is climbed or the skill learned, the woman instructor, who is generally more responsive to human needs, may back off if sensing tiredness or immobilizing fear in her students. Women teachers also take fewer risks. When confronted by a potentially threatening task, they are more inclined than men to relinquish the goal and choose safety. While there is certain merit in following a conservative path, there also is less chance for the student to extend beyond self-imposed limits or fears. Still, Pat Kielsmeier, of Outward Bound, highly recommends women teachers. "There's less competition between women," she says, "less trying to measure up, and more chance to take responsibility at the outset. She recommends that women seek out other, more experienced backpacking women to travel with and learn from.

There is another side to the education process, and that is the
role the learner plays. Every student has responsibility for the
shape her education takes and how much information is absorbed.
This responsibility is heightened with wilderness skills, for there
are times in wilderness when one's life depends on how much one
knows. Active participation in the learning process is, therefore,
mandatory. Still, in fairness, being a learner is not all fun and
games. Developing physical agility and wilderness knowledge
seems at times a gambol in awkwardness, a wallow in exasper-
ation or fear. Always there is the genuine wish that no one will
notice how silly you look or how stupid you feel.

The main problem with learning is that somewhere in the col-
lective subconscious it is written that learners are lesser people,
that what they don't know is a reflection of how inadequate they
are. As far as Outward Bound instructor Beth Barker is concerned, "That's ridiculous! A learner is not necessarily lower in
any kind of hierarchy than a teacher." Being a teacher, Beth assures, is "just plain old time in the woods. If students had spent as
much time there as I have, they would have the same skills I have.
There's nothing magical about my ability or understanding of the
place."

The most important skill a person brings to wilderness, Beth
believes, is the ability to see oneself as a learner. "In fact," she
says, "we are all learners. You can be very competent and still be
a learner, and you can be very inexperienced and be a learner.
What is involved is being attentive to what is happening." What is
involved, too, is being eager—sincerely believing that you can do
it, it's just a matter of time.

Those who have taught wilderness skills to women see a pattern
in the way they learn. Because much of the information is technical, women take longer than men to absorb the salient points. But
once they grasp the knowledge and accept it as their own they
quickly develop a grace of technique which few men have. One
other observation is made: women have a harder time moving out
of the instruction phase. They hesitate to own what they know, to
accept that they can manage in wilderness on their own. It is a
trait born of centuries of dependence on men. The first step in
overcoming this tendency is simply being aware of it.

A proper introduction to wilderness is no slapdash affair. It can easily occupy a lifetime if you let it. There are lessons in wilderness that will never be found in traditional universities, or between the covers of some book. If at first you don't sense and appreciate this—instead of cancelling your enrollment in the classroom of outdoors—either brush up your learning technique, or round up a more inspiring and inspired teacher instead.

CHAPTER 15

Pacing

Remember Thoreau's classic line about the guy who insists on marching to a different drummer? Well, each time we take up a backpack we do exactly that. There dwells within us all a specific rhythm, a particular speed at which we most comfortably travel. It is known as our natural pace. It is determined in large part by our height, sex, age, physical condition and mood.

In some ways one's pace is nearly as personalized as one's fingerprint. Yet, unlike the fingerprint, pace has the capacity to change—and does so periodically. Usually the younger and more determined the woman, the faster the pace. At the outset of her outdoor career Emmy Stonington felt compelled to do everything men did as fast as they did. After nearly a decade of sustaining a three- to four-mile-an-hour pace under a fully loaded pack, she began taking her own measure. "As I get older," says Emmy, who just turned thirty-two, "I'm feeling less need to make trips a driving push. Now I know enough about what I want that if I don't want to do something I won't. Now I go to be together with friends rather than to compete with them."

The more experienced the woman, the more flexible the pace. Outdoor leader Nancy Skinner, now forty-eight, is the proud possessor of three different paces. There is her two-mile-an-hour pace, used when leading others. There is her natural three- to four-mile-an-hour pace, which she slips into when walking long distances. Then there is her cavalry charge, which she takes to when alone and burning off excess energy or angst. By sustaining this pace Nancy admits she can achieve a state of altered consciousness: leaves begin to pulsate, the trail ahead lengthens or shortens, reality assumes a different feeling.

Pace differs from fingerprints in one other way, and that is its classic ability to cause trouble. Stick two or more people together who walk at different speeds and, if you're not careful, you have the makings of war. After four years of instructing at NOLS, Vini Norris learned to anticipate at least one big blowup over pacing per course. Reality seldom fell short of expectation.

At the root of problems caused by pacing is xenophobia—fear of difference. A conservative estimate is that 95 per cent of us are plagued by it. We like others to be, think, act (and walk) as much like us as possible. When they do not there is friction. We may forgive our friends for having different fingerprints, but can we forgive them for leaving us behind or slowing us down? Can we forgive them for reminding us that our physical condition or age leave something to be desired? Can we forgive them for standing in the way of what we hoped to achieve while backpacking?

Pacing is related to yet another fear—the fear of being abandoned. Most newcomers, according to Nancy, arrive at the trailhead united by a single thought: "I won't be able to keep up, they'll leave me and I'll die!" It is in us all to varying degrees, which is why so many of us engage in that tricky little game called Keeping Up. For the safety in numbers, for the love of others' company, we find ourselves double-timing like a bunch of Marine recruits, or slogging along like dispirited Volga boatmen.

Keeping Up is played most frequently by women who backpack with men, for with pace men have a decided physiological edge. While the average female is composed of 23 per cent muscle, the average male consists of 40 per cent muscle. Conversely, women have more fat than men—25 per cent compared to 15 per cent. Because fat weighs less than muscle, a woman will weigh less than a man of the same height, and will have less power to propel her body.

While leg strength is comparable between men and women, leg length may vary dramatically. Therein lies an important difference, for the longer the leg the longer the stride. A six-foot man may easily manage a three-foot stride, while a shorter woman may average only half that. Automatic problems arise when this couple walks a mile together. Covering the distance in three-foot lengths, he will take approximately 1,760 steps while, with a stride half his, she will take 3,520 steps. But that's not all. Given his extra power, if he doesn't slow down and she wants to keep up she must take faster, and therefore smaller, steps. To his 1,760, she might take as many as 5,000 steps. This leaves her at the end of the mile gasping, puffing and pleading for a break. He, meanwhile, may be humming strains from "Why Can't a Woman Be More Like a Man?"

He can outpace her on flatlands and he can outpace her while climbing hills, for men also have a greater ability to process oxygen than women. Oxygen is transported by hemoglobin, which is found in red blood cells. For men the average hematocrit (percentage of red cells in a volume of blood) is 40 or above, while most women function on a level between 30 and 35. Exercise physiologist Dr. Joan Ullyot considers this a significant handicap. "Since the hemoglobin in red cells transports oxygen to the tissues, it follows that most women won't be able to carry as much oxygen as men," she says. "Add to this lower hemoglobin the fact that many women are chronically iron deficient because they don't replace monthly blood loss, and you get a limit on oxygen-carrying capacity which can seriously reduce performance." To compensate for this, Dr. Ullyot recommends taking a daily iron supplement.

Pacing differences are hardly limited to members of the opposite sex, as I discovered last fall in joining two friends on a five-day trek. She stood six feet in her socks, while his thighs measured exactly twice mine. I instantly assumed my place in line—last—where I remained for the duration of the trip. She, meanwhile, took an easy lead and maintained it. Besides periodic apologies for holding them back, mostly I entertained my lonely self on the trail by rehearsing adaptations of Shaw: "Why can't that woman be (short) like me?"

One other element affecting pace is motivation. People backpack for different reasons. Some go for exercise, or to achieve specific physical goals. They tend to walk fast. Others go for social reasons—to be with friends, to be away from problems. They are more inclined to saunter. When backpacking with others, then, we have a choice; either master skills at Keeping Up, or grow sensitive to our own distinctive rhythm and walk to that.

Beyond mental and physical factors, pace is also determined by terrain, ground cover and how much you carry. When hiking a level dirt trail with a lightweight day pack, the conditioned woman can manage four miles an hour. Add a thirty-pound pack, a two-thousand-foot ascent or descent, the challenge of altitude, and a ground cover of snow or talus, and the pace may slow to one mile an hour. Veteran outdoorsman Tom Winnett sets a standard pace with pack on level terrain at two miles per hour. But when hiking hills he adds an hour for every thousand-foot ascent or descent. Using this formula, a six-mile hike that climbs two thousand feet will require five hours on the trail.

Still, there are exceptions to that rule. At first many women aren't certain they can bear up under a pack, let alone walk with one. Such uncertainty, combined with beginners' characteristic lack of conditioning, slows them down. They may cover no more than one mile an hour. Once they become experienced and conditioned the pace may increase to 2½ to 3 miles an hour. Women who travel faster than that under a hefty pack are either very young, very determined, or very experienced.

I have, at one point, been all of those things and, as a result, have witnessed significant variations in my pace. During my first one-day backpack trip I covered 13 miles in nine torturous hours —less than 1½ miles per hour. Three years of conditioning later, I returned to the same area to hike 21 miles in six hours, better than 3 miles an hour. Last year, out of necessity, I covered 4 miles an hour in hills with a twenty-five-pound pack. I had learned by then how to ration my breath and extend my steps. On steep ascents I marched in rhythm to my huffing—two steps to every one breath. I quickly became drenched from exertion. On flat areas I stretched legs as far as they would reach, and commenced bounding rather than walking. I played mental games, picturing my legs as springs, and my body weightless as wind-wafted eiderdown. There was exhilaration in that pace, but the quieter pleasures of packing were lost. Not once during the sprint did I stop to analyze animal tracks, to admire light patterns or rock formations, or even to identify the random bird which heralded my passing.

The single best way to discover and improve one's pace is to practice. It may seem a slip in logic to advise people who spend their lives walking to practice walking—but it is not. We cannot discover our natural rhythm until we step beyond start-and-stop walking, until we methodically begin covering unbroken distance.

For most it takes four or five days on the trail, long enough to sluff city awkwardness, to adapt to uneven surfaces and continual motion. One day the feet begin taking a firmer plant, the body moves easily and well. Sometime after that, when thinking on other things, you suddenly become aware that you are in synchrony, that you are walking in step to some soundless music. It is like a spiritual experience in some ways; there is a sense of connecting to levels deep within yourself. You have come home. You have found your pace.

Once you recognize it, ever afterward you will sense when you slip into that perfectly tooled groove. The longer you remain in it the less time it will take in subsequent trips to rediscover and resume it.

Discovering your pace may be a solitary process, for only by walking alone can you heed the rhythm of your heart, can you walk in steps measured to the length of your leg. In *Zen and the Art of Motorcycle Maintenance,* Robert Pirsig writes of finding one's pace: "Mountains should be climbed with as little effort as possible and without desire. The reality of your nature should determine the speed. If you become restless, speed up. If you become winded, slow down. You climb a mountain in an equilibrium between restlessness and exhaustion."

For years Lynn Ferrin has walked to her own pace. She has done it on short walks, she has done it on month-long treks in the Himalayas and the Andes. Although she travels with groups, during the day she purposely keeps to herself. For her the rewards are abundant. "My most precious memories of trekking in far countries are of moments and experiences while I was alone on the trail," she says. "I remember once crossing a pass in the Khumbu region of Nepal and finding myself socked in by clouds. An old Nepalese Sherpa woman appeared in front of me. She laughed and began looking me over, feeling my jacket and jeans and hat, fondling cloth and textures new to her. I responded by fondling her amber necklace and her beribboned braids, both of us giggling and stroking each other. After a while we hugged and went our separate ways. I will never forget that jolly, wrinkled old face, the two of us absolutely alone in the mist in some faraway mountains, communicating with each other in a very affectionate way."

One requirement for walking alone is some familiarity with

wilderness. This is best achieved, Lynn believes, by growing adept at reading topographic maps. Before the day's hike begins, with the map spread before you, get some idea of how many feet you will ascend or descend, how many streams you will cross, how dense the vegetation will be. If the path seems easy to follow, allow yourself to walk alone. For some sense of security arrange checkpoints where you and your partners will meet. You might designate points on the map, or you can walk by the clock (for example, the leader walks an hour, then waits for followers to catch up before continuing on). The only times when walking alone is inappropriate is when terrain or weather are unpredictable. Then, for everyone's safety, it is best to stay together.

If women harbor one overriding concern about pace it is that theirs is not fast enough. Long before we ever set foot on the trail we start worrying about speed. If speed is good in automobiles, assembly lines and fast-food chains, the thought goes, it must be good in wilderness. It is, but only for those who choose to remain hooked to compulsions which regiment urban life. It is not for those who go to get away, to be calmed and stilled by the songs and sights of wilderness.

There is an answer to pressures imposed by ourselves or others regarding speed. It is a motto Nancy Skinner shares with senior citizens who join her Stately Backpacking courses. "The slower you go," she tells them, "the more you see." Nancy has discovered the real secret to pacing. It is not how fast or how far you travel that matters, it is how much pleasure you gain in the process. Remember that the next time you feel the urge to march to a drummer different than your own.

CHAPTER 16

The Pleasure of Her Company

"That trip wouldn't have had half the impact on me if men had been along," said Susie Stewart after returning from a ten-day backpacking trip with twelve other women. Susie, a wife, mother, designer and frequent participant in art fairs, was accustomed to traveling only with her family. To go without them—to spend time in the company of women only—was, for her, a revolutionary thing to do. She did it. She liked it. This year she's planning on doing it again.

Women backpacking with women is a novel idea. Until recently it was something that happened only in smallish groups of friends. Then, in the early Seventies, it graduated to a national trend when women leaders in Outward Bound recognized a growing value in being together outdoors. The first all-women's course, offered by Southwest Outward Bound in 1974, was attended by women from throughout the United States. In 1975, Colorado Outward Bound introduced two women's courses in their annual curriculum. National Outdoor Leadership School quickly followed suit. Since then organizations such as Outdoor Women have formed expressly for bringing women together outdoors.

The timing couldn't be better. For more than a decade now, women have challenged the old rules. They have, in effect, kicked the pins out from the patriarchal system. They have pushed back the all-too-confining walls of a woman's place. They insist that they want to do more, earn more, be respected and appreciated more. These perfectly legitimate movements toward social and personal change can flounder badly if women themselves do not become more self-reliant, more aware of physical and mental strengths, more confident, more appreciative of self. According to those who have tried it, one good way to accomplish this is to backpack with other women.

Interesting things happen when women backpack together. The bond of common experience, which women share, merges into immediate rapport. There is unspoken understanding and emotional support. It is what feminists speak of when they refer to sisterhood. It offers particular value when backpacking. To be encouraged when trying something new is to increase the likelihood of growth and success. "I haven't seen anywhere near the personal growth happening for women in co-ed groups as when they travel with women only," says Outward Bound instructor Marlene Simonson.

When women backpack together they experience their physicalness more. They learn to do and achieve on their own without the help of old what's-his-name. When men are absent Pat Kielsmeier notices an equalization. "There's not a chance of you carrying a twenty-pound pack and someone else carrying an eighty-pound pack. You wouldn't do that to your woman friend," Pat says, "unless she was *really* big." These experiences open women to an awareness of strength. Laurie McCann, who leads annual all-women backpack trips, says, "After all these women's trips the feedback we get is strength. In most participants there is a new sense of independence, a 'Wow, I can really do it!' attitude."

It is exactly what Outward Bound leaders had in mind when they conceived all-women's courses. "Options open to women are, in fact, increasing," wrote Pat Kielsmeier in her proposal to Outward Bound. "To take advantage of this, women must learn to make large life choices. This requires self-confidence. But there is a lack of self-confidence and a lack of experience among many women, especially older women." Today Outward Bound offers all-women courses only to women age thirty and over. The magic age thirty was picked, Marlene says, because women that age and older have been subjected to certain conditioning and limitations that younger women have not.

Still, there is significance in wilderness for women of all ages. Realizing that society offers teenagers no official rite of passage into adulthood, Unitarian minister Ann Heller created a program called Walkabout. It was a unique idea. Ninety-eight young women were divided into seven groups of fourteen to spend one

month in wilderness on a Walk of Consensus. They alone decided
where they would go, how far they would walk each day, what
they would eat, where they would camp. Adult leaders intervened
only in physical emergencies.

With wilderness as their backdrop and facilitator, the young
women began communicating and sharing in a way many had not
before. There was, Mrs. Heller says, "a sense of permission for
women to be together. It was okay to hug each other, it was okay
to care about each other, to hold one another if they cried or if
they were happy. So many young women said this just couldn't
have happened in the rest of their lives."

The month passed strenuously, joyously, and on a night before
Walkabout concluded a special ceremony was held, a communion
of sorts with each other and with nature. "We were in a high
mountain meadow," Mrs. Heller recalls. "The night sky was peb-
bly with stars and always there was the distant voice of moving
water. The only light was firelight reflected on the faces of girls
and women with flowers in their hair."

They sat in a circle. Leaders walked to the center of the circle
with each young woman and back again, singing a song. By their
words and gestures they thanked the young woman for being who
she was. Later one participant, an adolescent, wrote of her experience, "All I know is that I have to come back. It was something
about the spirit there. I don't know yet exactly what I want out of
life, but somehow up there I was closer to it."

"All we did," Mrs. Heller adds, "was say to her, 'Look, little
sister, you are beautiful. You are good.'"

Besides personal validation, there are other advantages to traveling with women only. In subtle and significant ways women approach wilderness differently than men. On our own we usually
walk slower and see more. When we are open to mystical thought
we find extended meaning in natural objects. Redwood trees and
old oaks, for some women, have souls. Such spiritual musing is
seldom expressed or explored in the presence of men. Outward
Bound chief instructor Emmy Stonington has led all-women patrols, and has joined women friends in desert backpacking and
winter ski touring. "With women there have been mystical experiences or amazing conversations which I simply have not experienced on co-ed trips," she says. (Men take issue with this point,

maintaining that they too experience heightened sensitivity to nature when traveling without women. Perhaps separation inspires this. Perhaps the energy spared from upholding images or sex roles goes instead to refining senses or deepening thought and awareness.)

There is the chance to be "laid back," as Emmy characterizes it, when traveling with women only. This results, she believes, from the pace, level of skills and lowered expectations which women take into wilderness. "When I am with women I don't put as much pressure on myself that I should be achieving on a demanding level as I do when I'm with men. With women it is far easier to assert my particular needs. That has been important to experience."

There is yet one final advantage, the chance to acquire or refine skills. It is a process that seldom happens when men are around, for by tradition women are encouraged to let George do it instead of learning to do it themselves. Many married women have admitted that the reason they enrolled in all-women's courses was to see exactly how much they knew, or how many skills they could acquire on their own.

Just because backpacking with women is a good thing to do does not mean that it is an easy thing to achieve. According to Emmy, "Women in general give a higher priority to men and to activities with their mate than to doing things with their close friends. This tendency is so prevalent, you have to work around it." A few years ago four experienced outdoor women decided to stage an all-women wilderness trip. Emmy gleefully accepted the role of coordinator. A year in advance she contacted twenty women by letter, inviting them and allowing them to name where they wanted to go. Only six even bothered to reply. A date and site were subsequently selected. One year later, when the actual trip occurred, not one of the four originators—or the other sixteen she had invited—accompanied Emmy on the trip. "Evidently it has to be some huge commitment where money is raised or they have a goal like climbing Mount Everest before women take a trip seriously. Men friends and couples are much less prone to back out of trip commitments."

Even if trips do survive the pre-trip stage, they don't always proceed as planned. Because Diane Filippi always played helper to her experienced male partners, she felt she was experiencing backpacking secondhand. To amend this, she organized and planned an all-women's trip for four. She invited one more experienced woman as her backup in case, by her lack of knowledge, she landed the group in trouble. Before they reached the trailhead, the backup, Robin, had assumed control. She told the group how far they could walk each day, and designated where they would camp. She refused to carry community gear, insisting that with Diane's stronger boots the responsibility should be hers. She told them what they could eat and when. "It was like being in the military," Diane recalls. What was planned as a five-day trip ended in three—but not without further hassles.

Following that trip Diane revised her thinking. "It is not the people you travel with who keep you from the experience," she believes, "it is how you position yourself." It is your own active involvement which determines how much you grow and gain from a trip. Diane subsequently backpacked with two other women with a similar level of skills—and loved it. To increase her sense of peace and harmony in wilderness, she then enrolled in a course in fly fishing. By her own decisive actions she advanced past her self-proclaimed role as "guest" in wilderness, and is now a vital participant. Still, lessons from her misadventure serve as a positive springboard for us all.

When backpacking with women, select as traveling companions women you know and trust. (Diane's contact with Robin was limited to infrequent social luncheons or dinners.) If the friendship is not strong, take a few day hikes together to determine how well you interact when separated from familiar surroundings and friends. Actually, the same rule applies to men.

When in wilderness be prepared for a certain personality change. In traditional roles women are trained to be accommodating. Under most circumstances they relate to people amiably and well. In wilderness traditional behavior may falter in the face of unfamiliarity and fear. Some women confront these dual challenges by growing aggressive, others by withdrawing into themselves. It may happen to you. Understand it and try to remain flexible.

When you are a beginner, select partners more experienced than you. However, once you are experienced, choose women with a similar level of skills. In this way the responsibility for planning, the community gear and the chores will be equally shared. Highly conditioned, motivated women should seek partners on the same level. To do otherwise is to inflict frustration on an entire group. Diantha Bowie, a teacher who spends entire summers outdoors, admits, "I always have a sense of anger with women friends. I want to go fifteen miles, they want to go five. To meet someone as determined, I almost have to go with a man."

Much as I hate to impart paranoia in wilderness, if you are traveling in a group of four or fewer some system of defense should be devised or carried. Select inconspicuous campsites; walk assertively; if you sense impending trouble from men who pass, mention your male companions who are following. (See *On Self-Protection* in Chapter 21.)

While on-trail problems resemble those experienced when traveling with men, most women who have adventured with other women feel that the experience is worth the effort.

If traditional sex roles hinder you outdoors, if they limit self-development or the chance to discover your own strengths and skills, seek out the pleasure of *her* company, and see how much you gain in return.

CHAPTER 17

Beauty and the Backpack

There are a dozen international corporations that have made millions by convincing women that beauty comes from a bottle. There is nothing wrong with the concept except that it misses one major point entirely. Beauty is a composite of every thought, every activity, and every thing a woman puts into—as opposed to onto—her body. It is vigor. It is the sparkle of clear eyes. It is a supple body made so by regular exercise. This type of beauty is not something that diminishes with time (as those of the bottled-beauty school believe); it is something that is enhanced by it.

This definition of beauty is shared by every woman I know who backpacks. It is, in fact, one reason why they backpack.

The very act of walking long distances firms muscles and trims the figure. Extended exercise stimulates circulation and encourages rapid elimination of cell wastes through the skin. There are mental benefits too. Scientists claim that exercise inspires a sense of well-being. The hormone epinephrine—a chemical linked with happiness—doubles in the body after just ten minutes of sustained aerobic exercise such as jogging. While the hiking, climbing, huffing and puffing involved in backpacking may seem less exertive, it does mellow and lift the mood of anyone who engages in it.

But, while there is beauty gained from backpacking, if you are not careful, there is also beauty lost. Your skin, hair, nails, even eyes, can take an absolute beating from unaccustomed exposure to sun, wind and cold. There is a way to avoid this, and that is to follow a few basic guidelines—before, during and after your trip. For the conscientious, the before stage may begin days, even weeks before departure. The first item on the beauty agenda is hair. Doctors and beauty counselors say that an overexposure to sun or extreme cold encourages hair loss. But even if exposure does not precipitate fallout, it dries hair to the point of brittleness and eventual breakage. Some conditioning is essential before you set forth. Mary Ann Crenshaw, in *The Natural Way to Super Beauty,* claims it is possible to condition hair from the inside out. If you long for healthier, thicker, more lustrous hair, she recommends getting hooked on wheat germ oil. Friends who have faithfully downed a tablespoonful a day report that within two months they are receiving daily raves about their thick, shiny hair. (Because there is no medical evidence to support this, however, dermatologists contend that the principal beneficiaries of this treatment are those selling the wheat germ oil.)

External conditioning is important too. Just before departure, wash your hair with a protein/acid balanced shampoo. Next condition it. Jhirmack's MOISTURpHLEX is specially created to add moisture and pliability and to fight the effects of the elements. If this is not available, go heavy on your favorite conditioner.

Next comes skin. Because there is so much of it (the surface area covers about 19 square feet), and because all of it is sensitive, skin can be a troublemaker on the trail. Its primary enemy is sun. Any amount of sun damages skin slightly, but an overexposure to its ultraviolet rays destroys elastic fibers in the skin and causes it to dry and wrinkle. Beyond that, there is the more immediate and painful matter of sunburn. The skin pigment melanin helps filter out harmful sun rays. Brown-eyed people have a higher percentage of melanin. As a result they burn less. Blue-eyed blondes, redheads and women who freckle easily are deficient in melanin, and must take particular care with sun.

To minimize sun damage, purchase a sunscreen containing PABA before backpacking. That is short for para-amino-benzoic acid, considered the best protection against sunburn. PABA effectively screens out between 80 and 90 per cent of rays in the ultraviolet range. Sun-Gard and Eclipse, both containing moisturizers, work well for women with normal or dry skin. For women with oily skin, pabaFilm and pabaGel, which are alcohol-based, are best.

While he endorses PABA, leading dermatologist Dr. Jerome Kirschbaum prefers sun blocks which contain Benzophenone. Because it offers a 100 per cent block, is non-greasy, requires only one application in the morning, resists removal by swimming and perspiration, and must be removed by soap, Dr. Kirschbaum's favorite is Total Eclipse 15. He also names Piz Buin #6, another total block; this contains peanut oil and acts as a lubricant as well. This, however, does rub off, and requires repeated applications to remain totally effective.

The second step you can take to minimize skin problems before leaving is to find yourself a soap substitute. Erica Fielder heads a growing list of women who avoid soap in the backcountry. "I never wash with soap when I'm out," she says. "It's terribly drying and so are the elements. Also, soap can be dangerous, particularly at high altitude. It can dry your skin so thoroughly it causes it to crack, which makes you susceptible to infection. If you're backpacking for any length of time above five thousand feet, avoid it at all costs!"

If you absolutely cannot do without soap, Dr. Kirschbaum recommends a specially fatted soap such as Basis, or Neutrogena Unscented. People with very dry skin might use Aveenobar. The beauty of these soaps, Dr. Kirschbaum says, is you can use them to wash your face *and* do your laundry in.

Frequently in wilderness one's eyes require as much protection as one's skin. In snow, sand and high altitude the intensity of rays can sunburn the eyeball, and can, in extreme cases, cause temporary blindness. One friend has permanently red eye whites because she failed to protect her eyes when backpacking in snow. The single source of protection for eyes, besides Vitamin A, is sunglasses. The pair which accompanies you backpacking should not be the tinted trendsetters one wears on top of the head, but should be snug-fitting polarized, dark-tinted glasses which preferably curve around the side of the head to totally shield eyes from harmful reflection. For snow and glaciers select a pair with an extra-dark tint.

The day before leaving, trim finger- and toenails. Long, manicured nails have their place, but the backcountry is not it. Unless they start out short, something will shorten them for you—a jagged, sometimes painful process. I faithfully remove nail polish, but other women contend that it strengthens and protects their nails from breakage.

The final beauty preliminary, which relates to deodorant, is a purely personal choice. Some women prefer leaving theirs behind and letting nature take its course for a change. For the weight they save, and the liberating sense it gives, the idea has genuine merit. Yet, Dr. Kirschbaum challenges this practice. "Body odor," he says, "results not from excretions, but from bacteria acting upon them." Deodorant is useful if it kills the bacteria, rather than simply masking body odors. "In the backcountry you do not have the option of washing your clothes—which is all the more reason to use deodorant." If his advice is traditional, his suggestion regarding deodorant is anything but. Instead of the high-priced, heavy bottle and spray variety, he recommends Neosporin ointment, available in a tube from your drugstore without a prescription. "This is the best deodorant you can buy," Kirschbaum claims. "Besides that, it also is a great antiseptic cream for the first-aid kit." Rather than using deodorant in the morning, he recommends applying it at night. When sleeping you are not perspiring, so the deodorant has the opportunity to kill bacteria. This leaves you, throughout the next day, fresh and odor free.

During the trip, the less complicated the beauty regime, the better. An early morning splash of icy water on face, hands and teeth, followed by a liberal dousing in moisturizer and sunscreen is as regimented as anyone need be. Makeup? Who needs it? The natural glow from adequate exercise adds more beauty to the face than any bottled product. Besides, makeup has a bad reputation in the backcountry. Not a few women suffer puffy eyes (the combined effect of altitude, pollen and makeup), and derisive comments from trailmates who prefer the natural look in this natural environment. One exception to the no-makeup rule is lipstick—but only if you are allergic to other lip protectors.

Lips can be a real sore spot on the trail. Exertion, plus lack of moisture in the air, dries them. To replace moisture many backpackers chew, nibble and lick lips while walking, which leaves them cracked and bleeding before long. To avoid this, Dr. Kirschbaum recommends coating your lips heavily with Vaseline or Red Vet Petrolatum (his favorite), which can be purchased at any drugstore for a fraction of the price of more commonly known lip covers.

To minimize skin damage, generously apply sun block a half hour before hitting the trail. If you use Total Eclipse 15, one application will last through the day. If you use any other brand, you receive only minimal protection unless you keep replenishing it about every two hours, because perspiration or swimming removes it and clothing rubs it off. Because the sun's intensity increases 20 per cent every three thousand feet you climb, you should use more sunscreen the higher you go. When applying it, don't forget lips, nose, ears, the back of your neck and the backs of your knees—all vulnerable spots.

High altitude sun can devastate hands, too. If you travel above 5,000 feet during the sun's zenith, keep your hands covered in light cotton gloves. Both hands and feet swell from heat and usage, and your face may flush from exertion. Each time you cross a creek or stream, plunge hands (and feet if there's time) in the water. If you are wearing a neck scarf, dip it in the water, too. Hold it to the back of the neck first, then wrap it around either forehead or neck. On hot days it will make you feel human again.

Between the hours of ten and three, when the sun is its most intense, hair is best kept covered. Cotton scarves are popular, but broad-brimmed hats are more effective because they shield your face too. My favorite is an inexpensive broad-brimmed straw hat. Around the brim I braid silk cord. On windy days this serves as a chin strap; in off hours it is used to tie the hat to the outside of the pack.

Hair is ravaged not just by overexposure to sun, but by the accumulation of pollens and dust, and by exertion, which increases the output from sebaceous glands. Because of this, Dr. Kirschbaum considers it essential that you shampoo every other day, or whenever water is available. Otherwise you risk developing an itchy scalp (which for some women is a prelude to hair loss), and a secondary infection. While Dr. Kirschbaum believes any detergent shampoo is good, because of the space and weight you save he recommends a shampoo and conditioner in one.

To shampoo without doing untold damage to the waterways, carry one or two large pans of water about two hundred feet from the lake or stream—farther if possible. After wetting the hair, add shampoo and work it into a lather, making certain to carefully massage and clean the scalp. Rinse by pouring the contents of one pan over the scalp. Then repeat. It simplifies the process if you shampoo in tandem: have a friend replenish the water and pour it for your rinse, then return the favor.

The after phase of the beauty regime happens at the end of each day. With any luck you will camp near fresh water. I celebrate the fact that I made it to camp at all by paying homage to that water as soon as possible. When temperature permits I swim. Otherwise I soak feet, face and hands in it, then indulge in a brief soapless sponge bath. Then I baste myself in moisturizer and return, all smiles, to start dinner.

Dr. Vera Norhen, assistant professor of dermatology at Stanford University, considers the liberal application of ointment at day's end the most important beauty step we take. "Any ointment that contains fat helps keep your skin moist and prevents it from drying out," she says. "Once off the trail, cover any part of the body that has been exposed to sun or wind." She recommends Vaseline. Dr. Kirschbaum prefers Crisco. Having used it in his practice for twenty years on everything from children's skin to fragile, aged skin, he considers it the world's finest lubricant and moisturizer. The only reason it is not widely used, he claims, is because it is Crisco. "If some manufacturer put it in a really fancy jar, women would pay top prices for it," Kirschbaum maintains. I use it, not only for how well it works on my skin, but because in a pinch it also works for cooking. The best way to pack Crisco is in a plastic Gerry Tube, available from your outdoor shop.

After the bath, trade boots for soft shoes such as moccasins or tennis shoes. That simple gesture ranks as one of the day's great pleasures.

Nighttime seems the right time to forget about face washing. Excuses run something like this: it's dark, I'm tired, why bother? If these excuses sound familiar, you might benefit by this lazy woman's guide to enlightened face washing. Fill a cotton ball with sesame oil—a particular favorite for its high fatty content—and smooth it over your face. While the oil removes ravages of dust, sun and time, get busy doing stretching exercises designed to eliminate muscle kinks and prepare you for a sound night's sleep. Exercises should stretch taut muscles and ligaments in legs and shoulders, and should reduce tension around the spine. If you know yoga, the cobra, shoulder stand, plough and head-to-knee postures, performed on your sleeping pad, are best. (*Yoga for*

Women, by Phelan and Volin, describes and pictures these postures for the uninitiated.) Otherwise, perform these simple exercises. To stretch hamstrings and leg muscles, attempt to touch your toes from a standing position. Rather than straining, allow the weight of your arms to pull you down. Allow arms and trunk to simply hang while you count to 30 slowly. Stand erect for a minute, then repeat the stretch. For shoulders and neck, do two series of six shoulder shrugs (see Chapter 2) without weights, then allow the chin to fall to the chest. Hold for a count of ten, then let the head fall back. Hold for a count of ten. Repeat. To release tension in the back, sit on your mat with legs out straight before you. With your arms stretched forward at shoulder level, slowly begin to lean your trunk forward and attempt to touch your ankles, feet or toes. Stretch only as far as the limit of your flexibility. Now lower your head as near as possible to your knees. Hold this for a count of ten. Come out by sliding arms slowly up your legs, and gradually regaining an erect sitting position. Perform this exercise twice.

Once the stretching exercises are completed and your hair is capped, dip a corner of your towel in water from your water bottle, remove the oil from your face, brush your teeth and bid the world a weary *bonne nuit.*

For all the tangible parts we must tend to, there is one not-so-tangible element which deserves care: femininity. Backpacking is a sport which can diminish the difference between sexes if you let it. Most backpackers evolve their own subtle lightweight reminders that they are women. Erica relies on exquisite handcrafted silver hoop earrings. Some women work magic with brightly colored scarves on their head or around their throat. For the sheer delight of it, some women travel without underwear, others tote their laciest, fanciest garments. (While there has been some medical controversy about the ill effects of jogging without a bra, backpacking is less exertive and should place no undue strain on breast tissue.)

One more thing can be said about beauty in backpacking. Any woman who has walked any distance in wilderness knows that it is not how you look going up the mountain, but how you feel once you reach the top. This is not skin deep, it is soul deep. It is a beauty which resonates from your being not just when backpacking, but long after the pack has assumed its off-season place in the closet.

This brand of beauty is not something cosmetic wizards will ever capture in a bottle. Nor is there anything exclusive about it. Its special glow is available to any woman with the desire and verve to pick up a pack and go.

CHAPTER 18

Outdoor Privies and Other Private Matters

All things considered, going to the bathroom stops more women from going backpacking than any other single cause. Not the act per se, but the fact that outdoors there are no bathrooms as we know bathrooms. There are no gaily papered walls, no doors marked "W," no porcelain thrones with their intricate flushing devices. There is you. There are, if you are lucky, a few trees. And there is earth. It is the outdoor privy in its most fundamental form. For many women it is a little more (or less) than they care to cope with.

For obvious anatomical reasons, going to the bathroom outdoors is a trickier process for women than for men. Add to that centuries of modesty training and you have the makings of a dilemma. To overcome both takes a certain spunk.

Actually, the whole thing boils down to attitude. A woman either regards outdoor privies as utterly gauche and refuses to go outdoors—literally and figuratively—or, once she grows accustomed to awkward positions and no privacy, she assumes a more live-and-let-live attitude and gets on with it.

Just as there are rules for packing the pack or lacing the boots, so there are rules for taking one's toilet. There is, for starters, that old standby: when the urge overcomes you, move as far as you can from any freshwater source—at least three hundred feet, preferably farther. Otherwise you contribute to the greatest source of water contamination wilderness knows: *E. coli*—bacteria from the human stool. Because of its ability to travel, to proliferate and to foul water it is one of the heartiest organisms around. Residue from urine is little better.

Unfortunately, problems with elimination do not stop there. Many backpackers approach the matter of waste disposal with gay abandon. Either they simply don't care, or they assume that human waste magically disappears. It does not. Depending on altitude, moisture and heat, human stool may require as long as two years to decompose. There is a way to hasten the process, and that is to be conscientious in constructing the privy. In most ecological systems micro-organisms that work to eliminate matter dwell in greatest number between four and eight inches down. To speed decomposition, a six-inch-wide, six-inch-deep trench should be dug. Nancy Skinner recommends using the heel of your boot. I carry a lightweight plastic trowel instead. Once you have finished your toilet, the soil should be replaced and lightly tamped down. Do not be fooled into thinking that a shallower hole, sealed by a rock, solves the problem. Animals, attracted by the scent, remove the rock and dig up the stool, then, for want of any other option, leave it to decompose at its own slow rate.

For many women who backpack, the preceding discussion is purely academic. Their concern is not the proper dimensions of a trench, but the fact that for days at a stretch they have no need to dig a trench. The condition is called constipation. In wilderness it is quite common. Stress and the lack of private facilities, sleep, roughage and fluid all contribute to this pesky and sometimes painful problem. According to Nancy Skinner, the prime villain in the backcountry is lack of adequate fluid. When backpacking, particularly in hot climates and in the mountains, we expire massive amounts of fluid through perspiration and breath. "Nothing turns one's stomach and intestines upside down quicker than dehydration," Nancy says.

Medical specialists agree. It is claimed that more women than men are plagued by constipation simply because they drink less. To promote regularity it is recommended that you drink three quarts of fluid a day, including juice, herb tea or water. Because of the physical exertion involved, three quarts while backpacking is only a starting point. As Nancy says, "If you're not going behind a bush every two hours you're not drinking enough."

Adequate fluid intake also helps prevent one other painful

problem—cystitis. The most common cause of urinary tract infections is *E. coli* (bacteria from the stool) entering the urethra, either from improper wiping or poor sanitary habits. But, Dr. Evalyn Gendel points out that chronic cystitis also can be triggered by dehydration, by not drinking adequately or by not voiding frequently. Dr. Gendel encourages women to always wipe away from the urethra, toward the anus, to have a daily change of fresh panties, to bathe as frequently as wilderness conditions permit, and to replace fluid loss from respiration, exertion and altitude by drinking ample fluid each day. Chronic cystitis sufferers, those who experience infections every three to five weeks, should obtain medication from their doctor before backpacking, and should always travel prepared.

This leads us to touchy subject number four: toilet paper. Somebody, somewhere put out the word that toilet paper is biodegradable. Accordingly, by midsummer, trees and bushes along well-traveled trails are festooned by it, rocks are covered by it. It is hardly a pretty sight.

Actually the same rule applies to toilet paper as to any backpacking tool: If you carried it in you should, by rights, carry it out. If you don't do that, you should burn it. Either dig a shallow cat-hole—free from combustible material, and some distance from shrubs or trees—and torch it on the spot, or add it to the campfire if you have one. Even though you're going to burn it or carry it out, use only white toilet paper when backpacking, because the dyes in colored toilet paper are harmful to the environment.

To save weight and add convenience, you might follow my ritual. While packing for the trip I tear lengths of paper from the roll, then fold four lengths apiece into several small plastic Baggies. Each Baggie is expected to last a day. These tuck easily into corners of my pack and, on the trail, travel in my pants or parka pockets, thus saving me from having to rummage through the pack whenever nature calls.

A growing number of ecologically concerned women have begun viewing toilet paper as more bother than blessing. They have stopped carrying it, and are relying instead on sticks, stones, snow and leaves. It is, I must admit, not bad, though as Emmy Stonington says, "A certain degree of hygiene is lost." This is best amended, when water is plentiful, by daily sponge baths. Otherwise, use non-scented moistened cleansing wipes which, like toilet paper, must be burned or carried out.

Women must cope with one other complication in the back-country, and that is menstruation. The guidelines grow fuzzy here for the simple reason that so little conclusive information exists on the subject. After participating in a Harvard School of Public Health project wherein 400 women kept precise records of their menstrual cycle, Dr. Clayton L. Thomas, medical director of Tampax, concludes, "I have the firm belief that the only predictable thing about the menstrual cycle is . . . its unpredictability."

Yes, medical specialists concur, altitude, stress and exercise do affect the cycle, but none are able to say exactly how. Some believe exercise makes the period lighter and later, others hold out for earlier and heavier, and still others maintain that excessive exercise (as in marathon running) eliminates menses altogether.

Clearly, medical science has yet to decipher the dark mysteries of a woman's body—which might leave women in the dark about menstruation while backpacking, except for one thing. Based on the (admittedly nonscientific) opinion of many women, when they backpack for extended times—say, over a week—the period generally comes sooner and heavier. From this evolves one wise rule of thumb: always travel overprepared.

While the choice of protection is purely personal, from an ecological standpoint some forms of protection are better than others. Because of the precious resources plastic consumes and its virtual indestructibility, plastic-encased tampons should be permanently stricken from your list. Because of its small size and the fact that no applicator is needed, "o.b." is named as a favorite by women, but only those with minimal flow. Women with moderate to heavy flow complain that it does not expand and absorb. Pursettes brand tampons, which also take up little storage space because they do not require an applicator, are available in three different sizes, for light, moderate and heavy flow. Tampax tampons, which take up more space because they are used with cardboard applicators, claim the title "most versatile tampon" because they expand in three different directions when moistened.

The latest, most environmentally positive addition to the internal protection line is silk sponges. These sponges, which can be purchased at health food stores, are cut by the wearer to the appropriate size. Dental floss is affixed on one end for extraction. Throughout the period the sponge is removed, washed and reinserted. At the end of each cycle, it is boiled thoroughly to sterilize it, then stored. The sponge has but one shortcoming, and that is the lack of scientific data regarding its effect on the mucous lining and vaginal wall.

For some, sanitary napkins may work best, though because of their bulk, heat and odor most outdoor women rank them as a poor second choice.

When the cycle starts early, when supplies run out, women resort to do-it-yourself protection, the brand our foremothers used. A popular one is a white cotton sock—or half sock—rolled and inserted as a tampon, with a cotton bandanna pinned to the panties for additional protection. While not entirely sanitary, these do wash easily, dry quickly and outlive the very finest of manufactured items.

Much as manufacturers may tout their products' biodegradability, there is only one way to dispose of a used tampon or sanitary napkin: wrap it up, pack it up and carry it out. To do otherwise is an injustice to wilderness. Animals, big and small, are drawn by the odor of blood. No matter how thoroughly they are wrapped, or how deeply they are buried, within a day these unlovely discards will be dug up, batted about and left to haunt the sensibilities of everyone who follows behind you. While burning is a possibility, their moisture and bulk makes intense heat from a large fire necessary. It is really easier to pack them out.

A popular conveyance for used tampons is foil-lined soup packs—which must be packed out anyway. These eliminate odor and the possibility of seepage. My favorite carry-out container is a mini stuff sack (appropriately colored red), into which I place the foil-lined soup pack.

Because of animals' reputed attraction to blood there has been some concern among women about the safety of backpacking while menstruating. They worry that animals, and bears in particular, will be drawn by the odor and will attack. According to biologists and doctors, absolutely no medical or scientific evidence exists to support this fear.

David Graber, the University of California's renowned bear biologist, believes that the myth springs from an incident in Glacier

National Park in 1968, when in one night two young women were attacked and killed by grizzlies. The press blithely attributed the tragedies to the fact that each woman was having her period. Graber considers this "a quick concoction by the Park Service's front office when they were looking for some way to avoid charges of negligence. Somebody, not a biologist, dreamed it up to stave off the press."

As far as Graber is concerned, the explanation makes no biological sense whatsoever. "Look at it from the bear's point of view," he says. "Bears are not carnivorous. When they do eat meat it is from dead animals. They do not use their sense of smell to locate prey. The minute they smell people they run. Blood is going to smell like people. It will drive bears away rather than attract them."

Dr. Clayton Thomas of Tampax also is unable to cite any data regarding animals' reaction to women during menses. To diminish the possibility of encounter, however, he recommends that women make every effort to reduce the output of odor. "This can best be done," Thomas suggests, "by using an internal form of menstrual protection rather than an external pad. In addition, the woman should be certain to clean the perineal area and her hands as carefully as possible after changing tampons."

A third opinion comes from Dr. Gendel, an enthusiastic backpacker herself. Menstrual blood, she points out, is dead tissue, serum and broken-off capillaries. It produces a different odor than fresh blood. Being a decidedly human odor, theoretically it should repel rather than attract mammals. And yet the question remains: if animals seek out and dig up used tampons, is menstrual blood not a proven attractant? I, for one, will not shelve my concerns on this issue until specific scientific studies are conducted. And, while menstruation will not stop me from backpacking it will, while I am backpacking in bear country, keep me conscientious in my sanitary habits and, when I am alone, keep me on edge.

Individualistic as menstruation is, women suffer more or less from premenstrual blues and first-day blahs. Many women fear that with cramps and weakness they will not be able to perform up to par. There is social pressure to contend with, too. Women worry that others will accuse them of using their period as an excuse not to exert themselves. Outward Bound leader Leslie Emerson has found that despite apprehensions, women generally do fine. Still, she advises, "If you feel like cooling it the first day of your cycle, do it. The beauty of that environment is that you can't really afford to do anything but listen to your body and act accordingly. The feedback, the outcomes in wilderness are such that you can't get by fudging."

Menstruation sensitizes a woman to the rhythms and messages of her body. Beyond this, it connects her to larger rhythms which order the universe. I first grew sensitive to this two years ago when researching and writing an article on the effect of the moon on the human body. When I completed the two-week project I donned my pack and started off on an 180-mile trek down the mighty spine of the Sierra. On the eve of the full moon, six days before it was scheduled to arrive, my period began. For whatever mystical or physiological reasons, my cycle maintained near-perfect synchrony with the full moon for one year after that. I felt one and in rhythm with the universe—and that felt good.

There is yet one more thing to be said about outdoor privies and you. The more often you use the facilities the more comfortable you become. Outdoors may never rank as the most luxurious, private or commodious commode around. But, all things considered, it beats lugging a Porta Pottie along.

CHAPTER 19

Fear

I was backpacking alone in a remote valley in Washington's North Cascades when drum rolls of thunder announced the approach of a storm. The tarp was raised, my bag placed under it. There would be but a short time to collect and store dry wood before sheets of lightning and rain moved in. I began collecting wood within a hundred-foot radius of my shelter. In the process I noticed something I had not before. Bear fur. It hung on wood snags; it carpeted patches of ground. Unknowingly I had occupied space where bears came to scratch, roll and shed. The storm was here now. It was too late to pack up and move on.

I huddled under the tarp, an audience of one, observing the storm's force and watching daylight go. Between squalls I dug a small pit to contain fire. By dark the crack of lightning had faded. Leftover raindrops splattered from the drooping limbs of towering fir. The fire was set and lit. For three hours the lick of flame held back the night and staved off fear. Then, for lack of fuel, flames turned to embers, then died.

Bears would be coming now. I could feel it in the pound of my heart and the sweat of my palms. The odor of fear alone would alert them, but from my body also came the acrid odor of blood. Menstruation had begun the day before.

Night animals travel as silently as they can, but not bears. The crunch of dead limbs announced that they were near. Electric-charged nerves kept my eyes wide, staring, attempting to give shape to the creatures that moved through the dark. When the sounds came too close I relied on my only weapon: the blade of a knife pounded frantically against my Sierra cup. During one lucid moment I told myself that this night would teach me to manage fear. It did not. At sunrise, before sleep finally came, the same swift current of adrenalin coursed through me, wild and uncontained.

Fear reigned as victor that night. I vowed after that to come to know fear—to convert it, if I could, from adversary to friend.

John B. Watson, the founder of behaviorism, once said that only two fears are innate: the fear of loud noises and the fear of falling or being suddenly without support. To these must be added a host of fears which are learned. A partial list for backpackers might include wet matches, soppy down, unfordable streams, poisonous snakes, being lost . . . to name but a few.

Actually, the fears one experiences outdoors can be separated into two categories: reasonable fears, things really worth worrying about—like rattlesnakes, avalanches, the imminent possibility of death; and unreasonable fears—things that tweak primeval terrors, like darkness or the sense that some animal is about to attack.

While men are hardly immune, psychologists contend that women are more prone to fear. The reason is simple. In our upbringing we were taught to be afraid. We were schooled, for example, that it is "feminine" to be helpless. We were told that our bodies aren't very strong. Such schooling was meant to render us sexually appealing. It did little to make us feel independent or brave.

"Women are taught to be more dependent on external sources of protection than men," confirms Dr. Alan Skolnikoff, assistant clinical psychologist at UC Medical School in San Francisco. External support systems can be anything from a map to equipment to a man. Author Jan Hopson candidly admits to relying too much on her man. She and her author husband, Michael Rogers, backpack as a vacation from writing. On their last trip to Yosemite Jan discovered one inherent risk in such reliance. As always, Mike took the lead and assured her that he would watch for snakes. "There I was just spacing along," Jan recalls, "when all of a sudden this diamondback pattern was crossing my path two feet ahead. Mike had walked right over it without seeing it. Talk about an adrenalin jolt! I felt like I'd been electrocuted. The first thing I heard was my own scream. Then I just turned and ran."

Women are at a disadvantage, too, Skolnikoff claims, because they are conditioned to think that they don't know where they are going, that they will lose themselves on the trail, that they won't be able to follow a map. The fear of getting lost, then, looms larger in women than it does in men.

One positive factor is that women have the freedom to express fear. They have no stereotypical image to uphold. Most males, on the other hand, are bound by the he-man mold. They experience fear, but they can't let it show without violating the image they are expected to present.

How women—and men—handle fear is an intriguing study. Usually the fight-or-flight response comes into play. Outdoor writer Lynn Ferrin awoke one dawn to the scratch and scrabble of two cubs coming down a tree. "Nothing to worry about," her male friend coolly assured her. But when, from the other side of their bags, momma made her presence known, in a single motion they both were up, out and away from the scene.

Erica Fielder spent two weeks alone on Mount Baldy, outside Los Angeles. Every night near dusk she began hearing voices issuing from a nearby stream. Reading Thoreau as she was at the time, she knew that streams can produce every sound humans ever have heard or will hear. Still, these sounds possessed unsettling clarity. She heard children playing in a school yard, and the recess bell that brought their play to an end. She heard people in a monastery chanting what sounded like Latin. Erica tended her fear in what seemed a most logical way. Every night after dinner she would jump into her sleeping bag, pull it over her head and stuff earplugs in. By morning both the voices and the fear would be gone.

Erica's example raises the point that imagination serves as a fertile playfield for fear. The more a woman has, the more vulnerable she may be to fear.

Veteran backpacker Colin Fletcher devised his own solution for overcoming fear. For years he harbored a morbid dread of rattlesnakes, which seemed only to grow with time. Offended at being ruled by fear, he set out to take control. First he earned an assignment to write an article on rattlers. In the next year he read everything on the subject he could find. The education process granted him such incredible cool that, while sunbathing in the Grand Canyon, he allowed one rattler to stretch, curl and snooze within striking distance of his bare hip!

Fear is a sensation most people strive to avoid. We don't know how to handle or control it, so it usually controls us. One way to avoid this, Dr. Skolnikoff maintains, is to consciously identify your fears, then overcome them one step at a time. Professionals call this gradual desensitization. You take a small part of the task and gradually increase the amount you can perform until you are able to do the whole thing.

It sounds fine in principle, but who, when backpacking, has such leisurely time to prepare? The river or chasm crossing faces you immediately. Either you cross it or head out the way you came in.

Another method for taking fear in hand is to locate a role model, someone with more experience or competence than you. Once a successful example is set the task may seem easier. Such is the procedure practiced by Outward Bound. The instructor takes the lead and demonstrates in agile fashion how easy it is to do. Students merely follow in her or his footsteps as best they can.

If you're short of a role model there is yet one more way to cope. "First get all the information you possibly can in terms of the intellectual aspects of it," Dr. Skolnikoff says. "Knowing as much as you can about what's involved will reduce your anxiety." Is the log steady, will your boots grip, is there something to grab onto should you fall? Answering these and other considerations brings your brain back into control.

"There's a theory that you must suppress fear in order to perform," Skolnikoff says. "To a certain extent that's true *if* you're completely overwhelmed. But, if you're anything other than hysterical, in the midst of a crying attack, talking about it will reduce it."

Leslie Emerson sees fear in wilderness as a friend, a guardian emotion which protects her from ineptness. "My fear is not so much a loose boulder field or a stove that might blow up. It is a fear of not staying physically and mentally centered and in touch so I react appropriately. In that environment, with its God-willed factors such as avalanches and lightning, you have to stay your sharpest. I guess I wouldn't be drawn there if I weren't still making mistakes and learning . . ."—if she didn't, in other words, still have fear. Perhaps that is the ultimate answer with fear: to see it as a positive force rather than something to avoid; to move toward it instead of backing away.

Long before explorers discovered that the world was round, cartographers followed a traditional pattern when depicting the earth. They would represent in great detail every continent and body of water they knew. When they reached boundaries of the unknown they drew dragons—fire-spitting, fork-tailed dragons. In a poignant essay, John Lipton borrows on this metaphor to examine fear. Rather than dodging it—as most of us do—Lipton encourages us to go where dragons lie, for only by confronting and pushing back barriers of fear and the unknown does awareness and capability and the size of our world grow.

The very act of choosing to backpack says you seek more from life than a safety guarantee. How much more you receive depends largely on how you face the dragons, on how you handle fear.

※※※※※※※※※※※※※※※※※※※※※※※※※※※

WILDERNESS FEARS AND WAYS TO COPE

In wilderness women worry most about: encounters with poisonous snakes or aggressive animals (principally bears); getting lost; being raped or robbed; and being injured. Such fears are not unfounded. Each year a small percentage of wilderness travelers die or are seriously injured. In some cases trauma might have been avoided if the individual had been better informed.

••• On Snakes

Poisonous snakes are no laughing matter. Neither are they an extreme threat to those who backpack with caution. There are four types of venomous snakes in America. Various members of the rattlesnake family are found throughout the nation. The coral snake inhabits a section of the Southwest; the water moccasin lives in the wetlands of the South. The copperhead ranges widely throughout the East. As many as fifteen hundred persons are bitten in the United States each year. About one in every hundred die, many of these small children.

Snakes are as eager to avoid humans as most humans are to avoid snakes. The best way to avoid snakes (besides staying out of snake country) is to warn them of your presence by walking noisily, and by periodically thumping the ground with a walking stick. Beyond this you must be observant. Watch the path and be wary of stepping over logs or rocks without first checking the other side. Stacked logs, rocks or boulder fields, crevasses, dry gullies and thick underbrush are preferred hangouts for snakes. Exercise particular caution when traveling in and around these areas.

Before entering any wilderness area, consult guidebooks or resident rangers to ascertain if poisonous snakes are present and where you are likely to find them. Before backpacking where poisonous snakes live, learn to use a snakebite kit. The Red Cross recommends the "cut and suck" method. Immobilize the bitten body part. If the bite is on an arm or a leg, immediately tie a snug constricting band two to four inches above the bite (between it and the heart) to slow the circulation of poison through the system. After sterilizing a blade with flame, make one shallow vertical incision over each fang mark, then suck the venom from the incision and spit it out; continue this effort for thirty to sixty minutes. The victim should remain immobile and should try to stay calm. Under no circumstance should she be permitted to walk out.

••• On Wildlife in General, Bears in Particular

Wildlife, when you are lucky enough to observe it, is to be enjoyed, not feared. Still, there are certain animals and situations which you should assiduously avoid. These include skunks and porcupines (for obvious reasons), elk and moose in rutting season, bears at all times, any mother with young, any young temporarily without mother (when she returns you're in trouble), and any animal that seems ill or behaves oddly. Such behavior may indicate rabies or plague—both transferrable to humans, both potentially fatal. Under no circumstance should wild animals be fed.

Because of their unpredictable nature, bears are to be feared, not enjoyed—except when observing them from considerable distance. Bears which are indigenous to national parks and more popular backpacking areas include black bears (whose fur usually is brown), brown bears (which outweigh blacks by 700 pounds) and grizzly bears (whose reputation precedes them).

Bears of any make, model or color are to be avoided. There are at least two ways to do this. When hiking in bear country, always warn inhabitants of your presence by tying bells on your pack or boots. Always bear-proof your food (see Chapter 5). If a bear approaches while you are cooking or eating, gather up what looks edible and back off steadily. If the bear continues approaching, begin yelling and throwing rocks. As a last resort, abandon food and continue backing off. Finally, never take any food into your tent or the area in which you sleep. My one close encounter with a bear happened because it wanted the two M&M's which were stashed in my parka pocket. The parka happened to be serving as my pillow at the time. Because I remained perfectly still, the bear got the M&M's and I got to keep my head.

If a bear attacks, do not scream or resist. Instead, if you are able to, go perfectly limp after covering your head and the back of your neck with your arms. If you remain passive the bear usually will lose interest and leave.

••• On Rape. See Chapter 21 for a discussion on self-protection.

••• On Getting Lost. See "If You Are Lost," in Chapter 12.

••• Physical Injury

Because injury in wilderness is always a possibility, a course in advanced first aid or mountaineering medicine should be mandatory, as should the carrying of a first-aid kit. This kit should be tailored to your individual needs. In addition to your own personal prescriptions it should include bandages, antiseptic cream, water-purifying tablets, sunburn cream, insect repellant, moleskin or foam for blisters, adhesive tape, a snakebite kit if appropriate, foot powder, aspirin and safety pins. For longer trips, ask your physician to prescribe specific medication for pain, and an antibiotic to counter infection. Should an injury occur, do not attempt to evacuate the victim; instead, one person should remain to treat the injury while two others hike out for help. If you are alone or have only one companion, stay put and signal distress by blowing on your whistle three times. Continue this until help arrives.

••• On Robbery

Loss of equipment can result in loss of life for the inexperienced or for those backpacking in a cold climate. There are two ways to prevent robbery. First, keep your equipment with you if at all possible. If you must leave it, stash it in such a way that only you will find it. Before leaving your equipment, thoroughly familiarize yourself with the area, and create some point of identification (such as two small rocks on a larger boulder, or a short length of rope tied inconspicuously to a tree 200 yards beyond) so you will be able to relocate it once you return.

CHAPTER 20

The Fine Art of Not Sleeping

"No small art is it to sleep," Nietzsche once wrote. "It is necessary to keep awake all day for that purpose." Evidently Nietzsche never slept outdoors. Never heard of Bigfoot. Never knew how vulnerable and very awake one can feel when abandoning a familiar mattress for a slice of hard ground and a canopy of stars.

Anyone who has ever tried sleeping in wilderness knows that there are as many reasons for staying awake outdoors as there are people staying awake outdoors. There is, for starters, the phenomenon of first nightitis—in simpler terms, culture shock. Your brain and body simply are not accustomed to the silence, the stars, the exercise or the earth. You may think you are going to sleep, but these conspire jointly to keep you awake. The best part about first nightitis is second nightitis. After two days of strenuous activity with no sleep in between, you're bound to sleep during the second night.

Then there is the nightly matter of being too hot or too cold. Far from the dial-a-heat environment back home, temperature control outdoors is achieved by sleeping bag zipper and clothes. You awaken to find yourself either half out of the bag in an attempt to keep cool, or totally snarled in every piece of clothing you own in a valiant effort to keep warm. Surviving that without frostbite or heat prostration, you still must endure the perils of turning over. Each time you do, you are reminded that your hipbone is indeed connected to your backbone, etc.

Meanwhile, fear supplies a first-class ticket to the inner sanctum of insomnia. Outdoor writer Lynn Ferrin suffers from insomnia mainly when she travels alone. "When I can't sleep outdoors it's because I have fears," she admits, "and the problem is they are *real*. There may be something that could hurt; a bear or a scorpion, or it might be people. These fears are not enough to keep me from going on trips, but they are enough to keep me awake."

If big animals (or men) don't bother you, little animals probably will. More than a few people have reported waking to find mice or chipmunks attempting to nest in their hair, or gophers burrowing holes under their tummy. One man was abruptly awakened one night when a skunk sat on his face!

Let us not forget the matter of altitude, either. Oxygen depletion in the blood, which occurs when one exercises at high altitude, can produce such symptoms as nausea, light-headedness, muscle spasms and extreme tiredness. Conversely, it also can cause sleeplessness. A victim of altitude sickness might trundle off to bed totally exhausted, only to spend a fidgety night awaiting the dawn. Such symptoms signal a lack of acclimation. If they persist, the individual should be evacuated one thousand to two thousand feet down to wait until acclimation occurs.

What keeps me awake in wilderness is a combination of all the above—plus the story of Muchalat Harry. Muchalat (or, simply, Harry), was extraordinarily wise about wilderness, as Canadian Indians tend to be. He also was brave. He'd spend months at a stretch working a trap line alone. One night he was awakened rather abruptly. Bigfoot, the nine-foot-tall furry creature who inhabits the Pacific Northwest, had decided to pay a visit. Actually he wanted Harry to visit his clan. So, he merely toted the squirming victim back to camp, then let his brethren have a go at him. Mostly they were amused by his skin—long underwear which pulled away from his body. However, when Harry spotted a pile of bones nearby, he discerned the real reason he had been kidnapped. He was to join them for lunch. In fact, he would *be* lunch.

Fortune was with Harry, though. He managed to escape. When he regained his voice three months later (*after* his hair had turned totally white), he told his story to the closest thing this world has to a Reliable Source—a man of the cloth, Father Anthony Terhaar. Needless to say, Harry never returned to the woods.

Since then the world has learned that Bigfoot basically is a vegetarian, so Harry needn't have worried. But *I* worry. I worry it's going to happen to me. But only when I sleep in the mountains.

When I sleep in the desert I worry about rattlesnakes and scorpions. Too near town I focus on unpredictable people and rainstorms.

Outdoor insomnia is not endemic to women only. After my first solo trip, I was joined on the walk out by two men who asked what I was doing traveling alone. "Not sleeping," was about all I could muster. It was instant simpatico. Both men confessed that when they backpacked alone they didn't sleep either—which was why they now were backpacking together.

From that and subsequent conversations, I conclude that preferred conditions for sleep in the wilderness are when there are no bears, during winter when everything that could harm you is hibernating, or when traveling with one or more companions. If these conditions do not exist and you are plagued by trepidations, you might engage in mind and body games. Before considering these, though, be aware of two bases for sound sleep outdoors: sleeping bag placement and food.

Where you sleep determines in part how well you sleep. Your first task should be to locate flat ground. It took just one night of skidding down a 15-degree slope and hoisting my way back up to discover that sleeping on an angle, any angle, means not sleeping at all. If there are nothing but slopes to choose from, prop yourself against a tree, preferably downed, and use your pack, braced by rocks, as a second support. To deflect wind or rain, seek out a level spot near bushes or in a grove of trees. Because meadows are fragile and trap cold, damp air, avoid them where possible. Dalma Bain, a biogeographer who has spent as long as four months at a time outdoors, urges you to be aware of animal domains. "Areas we pick first are the same ones animals are going to pick," she says. "You have to compromise if you wish to camp alone." Check your chosen site for animal tracks or droppings, holes leading to tunnels, or dirt mounds. If none are present, settle in. As for snakes, Dalma advises not to worry if camping in a frigid area or during a heat wave. Extreme temperatures immobilize snakes.

Next, scout the site for any sleep robbers—embedded boulders, surface pebbles or prickly tree droppings. This is best accomplished on hands and knees. Smooth the surface where possible, then spread your ground cloth and mat and lie down. The rest will do you good, and will give you an opportunity to notice any other problems—dead limbs in an overhead tree, an unperceived slope, another rock. If you decide to stay put, use your boot heel or trowel to dig a shallow indentation for your shoulders and a deeper one for your hips. Once your ground cloth is firmly in place, remove your bag from its stuff sack, shake it to increase its loft and set it on the ground cloth—but keep it lightly rolled to discourage any uninvited bed partners.

Scientists supply another tip regarding bag placement. For centuries the more progressive among them have used the earth's energy fields to help them sleep. Magnetic fields apparently flow north to south. Some scientists contend that by positioning your bed on the north-south axis, you benefit by allowing energy to flow through you. This trick is easy enough to accomplish outdoors. Simply take your pocket compass, align it with magnetic north, then position the portable bag you call bed accordingly.

If the night is warm, open the bag and use it as a quilt, or simply unzip the foot to permit ventilation. A T-shirt and panties constitute adequate nightwear under these conditions. When camping in a cold area, bundle into as many clothes as make you comfortable, and place any remaining clothes between you and your sleeping pad.

There is a myth afoot which claims that sleeping nude in a sleeping bag helps keep you warm. According to Jim Owens of The Smilie Company in San Francisco, that is "an old man's tale," conceived by men as a way to get even closer to their female partners. Warmth comes, he says, from the thickness of insulation surrounding you. By adding more clothes you extend the warmth ratio of your bag. If you wish to start out warm go to bed with all your clothes on. The act of removing them in a confined space sends the body temperature soaring. To avoid the binding sensation that comes from too many clothes, start the night in long underwear, socks and wool cap. If cold persist, add more socks, wrap wool sweaters or shirts around your waist and don your parka.

The second aid to a restful night's sleep is food. When food is consumed, thermogenic heat is generated within the body. Carbohydrates produce energy most quickly; because they are digested slowly, fats warm the body longest. Therefore, the more fats and carbohydrates you eat before retiring, the warmer you will be. Warm and sleepy are two different states, however. Fortunately, food also helps induce sleepiness. The brain produces a chemical, serotonin, which is characterized by some scientists as "sleep juice." Serotonin is triggered by tryptophane, an element found in such foods as milk, cheese and meat. An ordinary-size steak, for example, contains about a gram of tryptophane, which is enough to make one quite drowsy. If steaks are in short supply, as they are for most backpackers, compensate by drinking a cup of warm milk with Ovaltine just before bed. Both, studies show, are helpful in inducing sleep.

There is, of course, the easy way out—nonprescription sedatives, or a stiff swig of scotch. But as Gay Luce, who has authored books on both sleep and insomnia, maintains, "Anything chemists [as in drug manufacturers] can do the brain can do better." People who have mastered the art of mind control can sleep anywhere, anytime. "Concentrate upon one continuous sound to the exclusion of all others," Luce advises, "and the individual noises will no longer have the power to disturb."

Because the sound of running water acts as a sedative, most backpackers seem to sleep best near a stream. If a stream is not handy and the wind is not blowing, you might resort to a relaxing exercise. Lie in your sleeping bag and begin by concentrating on tightening your toes, clenching them until they almost hurt, then releasing them. Repeat this process with the whole foot, then the ankle, calves, thighs, abdomen, stomach, chest, shoulders, arms, neck, mouth, ears, nose and eyes. Finally, clench all the muscles of the body, holding them tight for as long as bearable, then slowly release them.

Then there are the shortcuts to sleep. These are best tested at home, first to see if they really do work. As a mini-relaxer and a way to convince yourself that you really *are* tired, force yourself to yawn and yawn. If that doesn't work, try wrenching your body into the most uncomfortable position possible—lying flat on your face, say. After a few minutes, of necessity you will turn over and enjoy the immense relief that comes with being comfortable again.

Beyond this, you can engage in an active round of palindromes, a game played by the world's great insomniacs. This exercise is guaranteed to drive you crazy if it doesn't drive you to sleep first. Create a sentence that is the same forward or backward. "Madam, I'm Adam," is a classic. So is "A man, a plan, a canal: Panama."

There is the possibility, however small, that you never will fall asleep—or that once falling asleep you will be jolted awake to spend the next few hours struggling to get back to sleep. In these circumstances you can either (a) suffer, or (b) learn to enjoy.

Heather McFarlane comments, "We shouldn't hurry up and go to sleep. How else are we going to know how brave we are?" When she can't sleep she whiles away the hours getting to know the stars. She studies her star chart, and claims she learns four new constellations a year. (Because of its light weight, she uses a card chart, but for something more comprehensive she recommends Peterson's *Star Guide*.)

By attuning her senses to the moment, photographer-lecturer Virginia Davidson has converted nighttime into a special time. "I never have felt so close to the universe as when in a sleeping bag at the bottom of the Grand Canyon," she says. "The cosmic sounds, the song of the river; then the infinitesimal sounds—insects, a pebble dropping, which resounds like a boulder. At that time, more than any other, do I feel at one with the earth, with the universe."

Virginia's only problem is that she is so sensitized to night happenings that after three days she has to set up a tent so she finally can get some sleep. A clear case of third nightitis.

Sleep may elude you in the outdoors, or it may be the thing you do best. No matter how you approach the night, remember this: there is as much splendor in the dark hours as there is in the day. Once you learn this, your pleasure in wilderness will expand and linger long after nature switches her glorious day lights out.

CHAPTER 21

Going Alone

.

If all else fails, do it alone.

If he can't get away for six weeks from Sunday, and she thinks backpacking means snoozing until noon, then breakfast in bed, er, bag, don't wait, don't compromise. Instead, do it now, do it alone.

I can guess what you're thinking. If you are like me you are citing and reciting all those respectable little reasons why you shouldn't, couldn't, wouldn't walk alone. I know them by heart; I rehearsed them for years. I only tucked them away a few summers ago when I found them violating one guiding philosophy. "The recipe for an interesting life," a favorite sage once prescribed, "is to do one thing a week you've never done before."

For two years—104 weeks—I eyed the possibility of backpacking alone. I kept finding reasons not to: a) I was scared; b) I was scared; c) there *had* to be some other way. Only, the some other way invariably included other people, and therein hung the boggle. For, if they couldn't go when I could, then I wouldn't go.

It's as good an excuse as any for not backpacking—if you do not want to backpack. But I did, and do. Backpacking offers things I don't find in other corners of my world. I go for answers, for perspective I can't get when brain and body are encased by roofs, relationships and daily habits. I go for health and balance—knowing that both come from silence, and that soul-mending silence only comes when you separate yourself from urban complexity. I go for men—to consolidate a relationship, to see from a distance why one is or isn't working back home. And, I go for me —to make me more. For I never roam free in wilderness with-

out choosing—or being forced—to stretch into new realms of
awareness or capability.

As week 105 approached, reasons for going clearly outnum-
bered reasons for not going—even though it meant going alone.

As solos go, my first could hardly be labeled *faux pas*-free. It
was, to begin with, hardly a wild-eyed race into wilderness. Night
One I camped four hundred yards from the car—far enough to feel
free of it, close enough to get to it before some bear got to me.
Thoughts curiously centered on one theme: Is this *really* necessary? Before anything that smacked of a sensible answer emerged,
my stove broke. Actually, it didn't break. It just wouldn't light. As
a result, dinner one was stone cold and odd: wheat germ doused
in icy milk, with a chaser of gorp.

My first evening out went to scheming how to manage four days
with no stove and no experience in fire building. The thought
flickered, however fleetingly, of chucking the whole thing and
heading back—to hide out until it was time for me to be home—but
pride and my sense of adventure intervened.

Next morning when I went to return stove to car, I couldn't find
the car. It was there. I just didn't see it, and so walked an extra
two miles in search.

My second search of the morning was for anyone, *anyone,* who
was heading out too. There he stood—blond, lanky Mr. Wonderful. I think it was me who said, "Like company on the trail
today?" I think it was he who said, "Like company in camp to-
night?" We both sought aloneness, yet the first thing we did was
find someone to keep us from being alone. He stayed through
breakfast the next afternoon (he being a late sleeper), long
enough to share his reason for coming: Should he or shouldn't he
leave his wife? Since I was there for answers to my own problems
it seemed only right that we find them on our own. So, he headed
out to leave us both with time to think.

When he left, so did his stove—which left me as instructor and
student in a three-day seminar entitled Fire Lighting 1A. I had
wood-gathering and match-striking down pat by dinnertime.

They said not to expect bears, but what did they know? Even if
they hadn't seen one in four years, it seemed good practice to
bear-proof my food. Unfortunately, night fell before I found the
right limb to hang it from, which left me up most of Night Three

perfecting bear-shoo techniques. (This, for me, consists of walking very swiftly, very silently, in the opposite direction.)

To cancel any further possibility of sleep that night, I had conveniently settled my bag square in the heart of the Indianapolis Runway for Rodents. Invariably, curtains would have just fallen in the eyelid department when some scratchy-clawed creature would manage a squealing, heart-stopping rappel from my shoulder to the earth. If not a thoroughly restful night, it was at least eventful.

Sleep missed by night was compensated for by joy experienced by day. Come dawn, little night creatures—and the imagination—turn in for much-needed naps. Following this, the solo backpacker is given a rare opportunity to play hookey from her have-to's. Your only obligation is to do exactly as you choose, exactly when you choose—unless you choose not to.

Days for me were a study in doing nothing. I ate when and as much as I chose, hardly walked at all, read a book I'd been saving for years. Mostly I sat back and let nature entertain. As I did I learned something I'd only suspected before. To walk with others means to pay attention to their needs, to hear their words, to reckon with their wishes. It means subdividing your attention into thirds: yourself, your partner, the environment. To the degree that you are open to man or woman, you are closed to nature.

Here, alone for once, I could tune in to nature's minute and magnificent happenings. I could laugh and applaud water skeeters' skittish games of tag, could chatter back to chipmunks, could get eyeball to eyeball with stirrings down a mousehole. There were quiet times and times of hilarity. And, always, there was music. The birds, wind and leaves staged a nonstop concert for this audience of one. Time by myself turned me in on myself and taught me how it feels to synchronize my pulse with the natural world. In being free to flow with the current of the days I learned one of what must be a score of significant values that come from going alone.

Backpacking alone is something a woman does in her own good time, for her own good reasons. If it seems right for you, before heading out, heed these lessons gathered by one who lived to laugh and tell about it.

Keep challenges confined to the hills you climb rather than the equipment you carry. A broken pack or an inoperative stove can convert a carefree trip to a headache. To avoid this, give your equipment a complete check before leaving home.

Don't say good-bye without first saying when to expect you back. At least one responsible friend should know where you are going and when you'll be back. Give yourself a little leeway on homecoming—a half day or so. Ask your friend to notify rangers at the appropriate locations if you're not back by then.

If bears or smaller creatures worry you, research the area you'll be traveling in to know exactly who your nocturnal visitors may be. At the trailhead, interview the ranger or the individual from whom you secure your wilderness permit to learn if there have been animal problems in the area. Finally, consult those stalwart souls who have just returned. Such hikers usually are regular Books of Knowledge. My first solo destination was an alpine lake fourteen miles from the trailhead. Four returning backpackers described the area as cold, windy and sparse in firewood—hardly heaven for one who was traveling without tent or stove. I adapted my plans accordingly.

Just because you have a wilderness permit does not mean rangers will come looking for you if you fail to return. If there are rangers at the trailhead, inform them that you are traveling alone, and either supply them with a written itinerary, or describe where you expect to be. This will speed and facilitate the search—should one be necessary.

Do not overextend yourself during your first days out. When you walk alone initially you do so with a certain trepidation. It is only natural, but as long as apprehension accompanies you it is wise to walk less and enjoy it more. Instead of fourteen miles, I walked eight and barely budged for the rest of the time. The value came from being there rather than from getting there.

Because you do not have backup systems or support from your friends, backpacking alone is more risky. Given this, until you grow comfortable with being alone, stay on or near well-traveled trails. In this way, if you need to, you can get out, get help or get company fast. Cross-country hiking, or hiking in a remote area, should not be attempted until you feel competent with map, compass and wilderness skills.

Going alone by choice has a far different feel than going alone because no one wants to or is able to join you. It is easy, in the latter case, to feel like a social misfit. I have, and so has Jean Ketcham. This woman, who single-handedly homesteaded twenty acres of land in the Sierra foothills and who teaches university extension courses in backpacking, frequently finds prospective trips outnumbering prospective partners—so she goes alone. One summer she solo-hiked the two-hundred-mile John Muir Trail. "The loneliness I experienced was really horrible," she admits. "That first night I was overwhelmed with the feeling that something was wrong with me because I hadn't been able to find someone to go along. Once I got those feelings under control I got on a real high."

For women the sense of loneliness is heightened by the fear of being attacked by some man. Such fear is not unfounded, and is best addressed before leaving home by acquiring some skills in self-defense. (See "On Self-Protection," which follows.)

Solo backpacking is not for every woman. For those who long to experience a solo trip without actually taking one, some practical compromise is possible. First, find a friend who shares your desire and trepidations. Then stage an "alone together" trip. This can be managed in many ways, depending on how alone you want to be. You may hike alone by day and camp together at night. Or you may hike alone and camp alone, selecting sites within earshot of each other. Just having a friend close by is all the security some women need to sample a solo trip. Do not attempt such trips unless both partners are equipped with a full complement of maps and with adequate provisions to survive independently. Each morning, maps should be consulted to confirm the route, to pick a suitable lunch spot, if sharing lunch, and to determine a mutually agreed-upon terminus point for the day's hike. Some signal should be established to inform your partner if you need help or want company. For maximum value to be gained from this experience, though, spend as much time alone as possible.

Richard Katz, who conducted extensive studies on the solo experience in Outward Bound, discovered that when separated from accustomed input people either experienced a sense of timelessness or were overwhelmed by feelings of boredom and anxiety. The experience of timelessness, he believes, offers the greatest potential for personal growth. But it only occurs when one relaxes into the altered consciousness which comes from different rhythms and disrupted sleep. "Students worry about losing control and try to impose an order by establishing familiar patterns," Katz writes. "When this reaction occurs, there is less insight during the solo. Quite different were the rare instances when students accepted the order of the wilderness as unique and intrinsic to the solo. Then there were enhanced perceptions of self and environment . . . Living according to an unusual order can provide excellent opportunities to transcend yourself, to get beyond the rituals you so identify with. Moments of creative alertness, and even awareness, are then more likely."

Solo backpacking isn't something you try on your first, or even your fifth time out. It happens when you are ready, which means when you have sufficient confidence and expertise with wilderness skills to know with absolute certainty that you can make it on your own. When the desire is there, something within tells you when it is time to go.

If you heed the message, your rewards will be far more than memories. Solo backpacking allows you to graduate to a whole new level of self-awareness, for when there's no one to turn to but you, you learn how much there is within.

And that is just the beginning of a real trip!

ON SELF-PROTECTION

Wilderness once was considered a safe haven, a mending place. In some ways it still is, and yet recently the incidence of attack and rape has increased simply because more people are traveling there. In the past year occasional reports of rape in wilderness have filtered in from across the country, while in the wilderness area near my home two lone women—a hiker and a runner—were murdered.

Still, it is a fine line women walk in preparing for wilderness travel. To be overly concerned about the possibility of attack is to diminish the quality of wilderness experience. And yet to ignore risk, to travel unprepared, is to place oneself in potential jeopardy. Some form of self-protection is necessary if you are traveling alone or with women only.

Sue Verhalen is both a trained expert and an active supporter of self-defense for women. Following a nine-month training program she began conducting self-defense workshops to share her knowledge. Sue, who now serves with the Women's Protection Program of the Marin Rape Crisis Center, offers these recommendations for protecting yourself in wilderness.

Before the Trip

• MENTAL PREPARATION

The first step in self-defense is determining your limits: How much will you interact with others? How close will you allow strangers to come? Get clear on what you do not want to have happen (for example, you do not want a stranger touching you), so you will know when someone has crossed that line. Once you have identified these limits, learn to express them clearly and directly. If you have difficulty taking a firm stance, enroll in a course in assertiveness training.

Decide how far you will go to defend yourself. Are you willing to hurt somebody? How much harm are you willing to inflict? Can you kick the aggressor in the testicles? Can you tear his eyes out? You must make this distinction now, for unless you do, when faced with danger you will waste critical time and energy defining your limits.

Strengthen nonverbal communication. In a study completed in 1978, researchers Wendy McKenna and Florence Denmark showed that people place themselves in an inferior position through body language alone. Low-status people, McKenna and Denmark observed, smile and nod their head continuously, hold their arms close to their bodies, keep their legs together or crossed. The individual with higher status only smiles occasionally, moves or nods the head infrequently, and usually interacts with people in a relaxed, asymmetrical body position. Women, they observed, use low-status signals much more frequently than men. You can strengthen your position by being aware of and improving the silent messages your body sends. Practice high-status body language every chance you get.

● PHYSICAL PREPARATION

To know yourself and your capabilities you must simulate threatening situations and practice your response. With your pack on, have a friend initiate aggressive behavior. Learn the limitations of motion while standing or tussling on the ground with the pack on. Try the same experiment while in a sleeping bag. Practice getting out of the bag fast. You can only learn your range of motion and the best way to defend yourself by practicing before you leave home.

If you carry HALT! or ammonia water (one part ammonia, one part water, contained in a twist-top atomizer), equip a friend with plastic workshop goggles or any plastic goggle that totally shields the eyes, then practice with your spray container. (The spray should be washed thoroughly from the skin to prevent any possibility of burns or irritation.) How far does the spray travel, how much pressure does it have, how effective are you with it?

On the Trail

In wilderness there is nowhere to run for safety and there are no locked doors to hide behind. Compensate by familiarizing yourself with the area in which you are traveling. At the trailhead, consult with rangers or people who have just returned. Is the area heavily forested? Are there natural shelters? What is the condition of the trail?

As you walk, closely observe the surroundings. Look for hiding places. Look for obscure campsites. Keep an eye out for potential weapons—pebbles to be tossed in the eyes, rocks or sticks. Mentally rehearse what you will do if threatened.

If a group that seems friendly and harmless is camping in the area, you may want to camp nearby. Otherwise, select an inconspicuous campsite which cannot be spotted from the trail. Make certain when choosing your site that you are unobserved. Because guns seem entirely foreign to women—and to wilderness for that matter!—I cannot recommend carrying one. A less lethal alternative, which I carry when alone, is a two-ounce container of

HALT! This contains capsicum, or liquid cayenne, and may be purchased in your local pet shop. Keep a whistle handy too. Besides carrying farther, it lasts much longer than your voice. Three quick blasts on the whistle signal distress.

Pay attention to your intuitions! During her solo hike of the John Muir Trail, Jean Ketcham discovered that a lengthy stay in wilderness significantly heightened her sensitivities. She began "reading" people on the trail long before they came close enough to perceive facial expressions. She learned to respect her body's warning signals. Contact with men intuitively deemed unsafe were kept intentionally short and impersonal. As Sue Verhalen says, "Intuitions are there for a reason. Learn to listen to them. This heightens your reliance on yourself."

When a man inspires negative feelings, keep distance between you. He should be permitted to approach no closer than the length of his extended arm. Such distance gives you time to react. Do not show that you are afraid. Look the man directly in the eye, speak directly to him. Be willing to communicate your limits clearly: "You are too close to me, I want you to move back" or "I want to camp alone."

Women who clearly define their limits and recognize when they have been crossed usually get angry rather than panicked. Anger is the most effective response. It surprises the potential attacker; it plays on his fear. He does not know what to expect from you next.

If aggressive behavior is threatened, assess the situation. Is this the time to start talking calmly, to remove your pack so you will have more freedom? Are there potential weapons within your reach? If he attacks, do not pit your strength against his. You probably will lose. The effective fighter is the woman who waits for the right time to react. Use all your mental and physical resources to seek and go for the weak spot.

HALT! or ammonia water are only effective if you have them in your hand. When traveling in wilderness areas that are heavily used, attach the container to your wasitband or belt. At night store it in one of your boots near the head of your bag.

If you manage to run and hide, stay hidden until you are certain that he is gone and you are safe.

When you are attacked there are all kinds of appropriate responses, from doing nothing to taking another's life. Be willing to

THE BACKPACKING WOMAN

use your brain and your wit, Sue advises. While being attacked one of her students feigned epileptic seizure, another woman fell to the ground and began barking like a dog and eating grass. Evidently assailants find no pleasure in attacking the very sick or the very mad. Both attackers left the scene immediately. While these are not intended as recommendations, they do show the benefits of using your imagination and thinking on your feet.

Any protective device has its limitations, its positive and negative aspects. Nobody should rely on any one thing for all circumstances. Finally, Sue urges, be flexible. If a certain approach is working, stick with it. If it is not, try another tactic. The more initiative you take for acquiring knowledge and skills, the broader your range of choice will be, when and *if* the need arises.

CHAPTER 22

Going Long

For some seventeen years now, since the advent of his first book on backpacking, many people have nurtured the belief that the originator of long-distance walking was Colin Fletcher. It's an easy assumption to make. In his time, the peripatetic Welshman has walked the length of California (documented in his book, *The Thousand Mile Summer*) and forged a trail along the bottom of the Grand Canyon (detailed in *The Man Who Walked Through Time*).

By virtue of his versatile pen, Fletcher and his walks have become legend. Yet about the time he was merely *contemplating* his thousand-mile hike, another person, a woman, was *completing* a two-thousand-mile hike. Her name was Grandma Gatewood.

Grandma—who earned her name by raising eleven children on an Illinois farm—had her own reasons for walking. Basically she walked the 2,400-mile Appalachian Trail three times and the Oregon Trail once because it seemed the most efficient and economical way to see the country. In her own quaint, methodical way, Grandma Gatewood made an indelible mark on the annals of human achievement. She showed, beyond reasonable doubt, that long-distance walking is a thing women can do too.

Since Grandma's day, many women have both gotten the message, and acted upon it. At least twelve women now have walked the 2,600-mile Pacific Crest Trail—from Canada to Mexico. In Grandma's footsteps, an untallied number have walked the length of the Appalachian Trail. And, recently, two women set yet another precedent by becoming the first to walk the Continental Divide—a distance estimated roughly at 2,600 miles.

This is not to say that 2,600 miles is the magic marker which distinguishes the serious backpacker from the dilettante. Any woman who manages 200 miles back to back—or, more correctly, back to pack—certainly qualifies as a long-distance hiker.

Actually, if the truth be known, there is nothing to long-distance walking. All that's required is that you put one foot in front of the other—and keep it up eight to eighteen hours a day, one to six months a year. The challenge arises when the mind comprehends exactly what is expected of the feet. Then the resistance begins. Suddenly the brain begins ordering the body around: I'm hungry; I'm tired; I hurt; I want to go home!

Compelling as these commands may seem, most long-distance hikers ignore them. For there is another side to it, a side which motivates women to go, and to keep going. There is pride in setting a goal and achieving it. There is the chance to grow in understanding of self and appreciation of nature. There is the satisfaction of improving one's body and one's outdoor skills. And there is something far more moving and less intentional than all of these. There is the thrill of simply being there and doing it.

Women I know who have taken long-distance walks differ from others only in their eagerness to be outdoors. Before she solo-hiked the Pacific Crest Trail, Teddi Boston, a forty-nine-year-old mother of four, graduated from two mountaineering courses, led a troop of Girl Scouts through the Grand Canyon, walked the 200-mile John Muir Trail and, as a volunteer forest ranger, covered on foot an average of 25 miles every weekend for more than a year. Stephanie Atwood, who at age twenty-five walked 500 miles in 40 days, was a graduate of Outward Bound, and had worked a year as a staff member with this wilderness skills teaching group.

Besides desire and experience, one needs certain knowledge to succeed at long-distance walking. This is best gained either by doing it, or by picking the brains of those who have. For those who contemplate distance hiking in the future, the following guidelines are offered by women who have managed it in the past.

The most vital aspect of a successful long-distance walk is thoughtful planning. In Stephanie's words, adequate planning "reduces variables to things you find on the trail. That feels pretty good." Expect to spend at least six months writing letters, reading maps, gathering guidebooks, scheduling, shopping and packing.

Finding someone else who has made the trip is a little like finding
lost money. This individual can identify the most convenient post
offices for possible food drops, can warn of potential trouble
spots, and can recommend favorite little-known campsites. If your
list of long-distance walkers is nonexistent, check with a local
backpacking store. People there are most likely either to have
made such a trip, or to know others who have.

To keep from running out of time before you run out of trail,
precise scheduling is a must. Teddi's carefully typed itineraries are
divided into days between food drops. Each day is then broken
into the four to six points on the map she plans to pass. Mileage
between these points, and the day's total mileage, is indicated right
down to the last tenth. Jeannie Smith, the only woman to walk
both the Pacific Crest and the Continental Divide, is equally ada-
mant about scheduling. "You need a schedule to keep to or you'll
end up getting behind," she says. Jeannie and her PCT partner,
Cynthia Stockwell, scheduled one day off each week. Although
they were delayed by sickness and injuries, they were able to stay
on schedule because of that extra day.

Health needs are essential to consider before departure. If you
have chronic health problems, such as sinus, migraine or urinary
infections, understand the cause and know the steps you must take
to effect a cure. Aware of the fact that IUD's cause cramping and
bleeding even among inactive women, one woman had hers removed before the trip.

Kathy Kipping, who walked 500 miles in 30 days, believes that
a course in advanced first aid is essential before undertaking such
walks. "Anything can happen—heatstroke, broken bones, concus-
sions. It's better to come prepared." When Cynthia fell, cut open
her head and had to be evacuated, Jeannie found her first-aid
training invaluable. In addition, before leaving she had read everything she could find on survival.

Another education essential, in Jeannie's opinion, is a course in
navigation. A good facility with map and compass will save you
time and will diminish deep-seated fears of getting lost.

After more than 5,000 miles of long-distance walking Jeannie
has established her own firm rule about food drops. "Use every
possible post office near the route," she says. "By carrying as little

weight as possible you are more comfortable, the trip is more enjoyable, and you are more apt to stick with it."

To spare the expense of shopping at remote stores along the route, Jeannie recommends including in the boxes which serve as your food drops such replacement items as flashlight batteries and small bottles of hand lotion. She also advises including a cup of detergent to save you from having to buy some at each laundromat.

The Walk seldom begins in a blaze of glory—more likely, it starts with a cloudburst or the beginning of a snowstorm. Teddi Boston trudged in deep snow for three solid weeks before once setting foot on the trail. About two days out, under these conditions, mental resistance begins. "Especially," Teddi confirms, "when you're fighting as many things as I was—snow, no clearly defined trail, a 65-pound pack and my mental attitude. It would have been so easy to sit down in a heap and say, 'Ahhh, this is too hard.'" But she didn't.

The body protests the stress of heavy pack and long miles in many ways. Sore muscles and blisters are standard. More than one woman has been forced to discontinue the trip due to blood poisoning from infected blisters. Stephanie's complaints were more subtle: though she started out in perfect condition and always completed the planned daily mileage, she remembers always feeling tired.

Jeannie has developed her own method for reducing physical complaint. Months in advance she begins running five to six miles a day. Despite such diligence, at the start of each trip she purposely travels slowly. During the first week on the Pacific Crest Trail she walked only six miles a day. In the next few weeks she upped mileage to eight, ten, then twelve miles. By the end of the third week she was covering fifteen miles daily with ease and without injury.

One commodity that long-distance hiking gives you is time to think. Kathy Kipping describes the experience as "One long meditation. You really get to know yourself well." In her thirty-day trek to the base camp of Mount Everest and back, Lynn Ferrin lost all desire to communicate with her companions while walking. "I just wanted to be inside myself, to figure some things out. What I discovered for the first time was that the only men I was attracted to were real headaches. Having that time to think was the one thing I needed to begin changing that pattern."

Those who have walked alone recite, chapter and verse, adventures in loneliness. One nineteen-year-old who hiked the Pacific Crest Trail last year confessed to spending hours at a stretch crying because she felt so lonely. Teddi combated loneliness by repeating a phrase which fast became her motto: "Wow, I'm glad I'm me and where I want to be!"

For Teddi, time alone resulted in changed values: "I realized out there that material things aren't worth a hoot and a holler. All that really matters is your health and your outlook on life. Other things aren't really all that important." Too, the trip revived her sense of wonder. "I had never been aware of how darkness comes," she says. "But on the walk I'd always try to get real high for sunsets. I'd watch the navy blue of night sneak up from the valley and overtake the gold of the west. I also became very aware of animal sounds. I'd snuggle into my tent and wait for the first hoot of owl at night . . . or the howl of a coyote . . . that was music!"

After weeks of powdered, compressed and freeze-dried everything, food fantasies take hold. Immersed though you are in geologic and botanic splendor, at times all you can see is the precise outlines of a cold, crisp head of lettuce. Salads and a chilled glass of fresh milk top the list of most-missed foods. Teddi quelled her fantasies by harvesting miner's lettuce and wild onions, blueberries and thimbleberries, which she found along the way.

The most common food problem is that there's never enough to eat. Teddi always felt hungry. Stephanie attributed her constant tiredness to too-little food and insufficient vitamins and iron in what she was eating. Kathy resolved the vitamin shortage by carrying Vitamin C in powdered form, while Teddi kept her energy up with Tiger's Milk candy bars. She ordered a case of these high-protein bars—360 of them—then happily consumed two a day, though she warns, "If you ate them in town you'd weigh three hundred and fifty pounds."

Food fantasies take a vacation when you reach your food drops. Because most food caches take the form of general delivery packages in small-town post offices, it means brief encounters with restaurants and real food and different people. "You look forward to seeing somebody else besides the person you're with," Stephanie admits, "so going out to a city is sort of like going to a party." To enhance the occasion she always added something special to food boxes, such as homemade banana bread. Teddi, who had sixteen food drops, anticipated them for a different reason. It meant she could use the laundromat. "Every time you go to town, if you really wash things, really clean up all your equipment, and have a new food box, it's just like starting a new trip. It was a morale boost not to have anything dirty."

Always in long-distance walks, you deal with undependable factors. Heading the list is weather. "The only time the trip began to lose its humor," Teddi recalls, "was one thirty-one-mile and one thirty-four-mile stretch between Shasta and Lassen." California was enduring a drought then, which left her crossing beds of black lava in 103- to 107-degree heat with no water. A series of dry stream beds forced her to do without dinner and breakfast. "Nothing to cook with," she explained. What kept saliva flowing, and she thinks saved her, were Life Savers and chewing gum. She experienced the opposite extreme later. Because of the drought, she approached the Mojave desert with certain trepidation. Yet she was greeted there by the first tropical rainstorm in thirty-nine years. It took three days in a motel for her equipment to dry out.

You take your chances with nature, and sometimes you take your chances with man-made products. In selecting the site for their only two-day layover, Kathy and her trail partners followed the recommendation of her favorite guidebook. Evidently others had too, for in place of beauty they found trees stripped bare, piles of garbage, foul water and smog so bad they couldn't see across the canyon. They left early the next morning.

Maps, too, have their unfortunate incongruities. Some maps are old, some trails are new, and some cartographers should have made their living in some other way. The result is that, at some point, most long-distance hikers get lost. "The first time it happened I panicked," Teddi recalls. But her response was pure British: she merely took out her stove, boiled up a cup of tea and carefully thought things out. Getting lost, she soon discovered, assumed certain patterns. Either she got lost ten times a day, or she'd get really lost just once. After one major flub in Oregon, she began traveling with four different maps. She now recommends that everyone do the same.

Odds are, though, that no matter how many times you get lost, you will reach your destination. Your homecoming committee may not be as large as Teddi's—twenty-three friends (including one husband and four proud children) and fourteen bottles of pink champagne—but you are certain to be met by one thing: a new you. Stephanie has found that since she returned, "I can do anything I want to do. From the trip I learned how to take charge, follow through and actually do everything I want. That lesson has stayed with me."

Teddi simply says, "I came back a whole different person. Things don't bother me like they used to. I once had a low boiling point, but no more. When you're out there by yourself for so long your whole being becomes very calm. I've held on to this pretty much. I like the new me much better than the old me!"

The desire to walk long varies according to age and the stage of life through which a woman is passing. The experience is similar to religious retreat. A woman walks alone with her thoughts. She discovers new facets of courage and strength and self. She returns renewed.

There may be easier ways to achieve these ends, but for those women who have walked long there are no better ways.

CHAPTER 23

The Story of Two Who Did

To walk 2,600 miles—to be the first women on record to course the trackless spine of a continent—is not an opportunity most women would jump at. To do so one would need to be either slightly mad or singularly committed to concerns larger than comfort, security and safety. Jeannie Smith and Lynn Wisehart were so committed—Jeannie to the symbolic statement such a trip would make to all women, Lynn to the opportunity the trip offered to advance a burgeoning photographic career.

And, so, one sparkling spring day in 1978, under packs which would on occasion weigh up to seventy-five pounds, two young women set forth to hike the Continental Divide, border to border.

To look at them, one would hardly think them capable of such an undertaking. Both stand five feet three inches tall, neither weighs more than 120 pounds. There is in each inherent softness—in Jeannie's imp face, fair skin and gentle Texas drawl, in Lynn's Mia Farrow prettiness. But size and essence seemed no impediment. If anything it added magnitude and meaning. It stood as wordless confirmation of what Jeannie hoped to say by making the trip—that size and sex and spiritual qualities need not hinder women as they adventure and achieve.

Besides commitment, they had another quality going for them: experience. Two years before, Jeannie had walked the 2,600-mile Pacific Crest Trail. With skills mastered there she taught navigation at Outward Bound. Lynn was a skilled mountaineer, a graduate of Northwest Outward Bound, a proficient runner and cross-country skier. Such physical competence generated a bond of mutual trust and respect between the two women.

They began, actually, as a group of four. Through the conception and planning stages, through the first days on the trail, Jeannie and Lynn joined together with Nancy Gardner and Rosemary Stevens as the Rocky Mountain Women's Expedition. Printed T-shirts made it official. Under this aegis they sought and gained needed backing for the expedition. Northface, Kelty, Galibier Boots and Wigwam Socks contributed equipment; National Geographic donated film.

Because no trail existed, because no four-color guidebooks or neatly printed maps pointed the way, to plot the route Nancy flew to Alaska to consult with one of the small handful of men who have ever walked the Divide. The advice and dog-eared maps he supplied served as the vital axis around which the trip was planned.

After more than a year of plotting, conditioning, purchasing, packing and dreaming, they made their anxious way to the bleak, windswept Mexican border. After one day of hiking Nancy complained of knee pain. After one week, by whatever processes change human relations, the Rocky Mountain Women's Expedition had inalterably split. There existed no group consciousness, no desire to walk together or be together. "We could see right off it was going to be emotionally wearing," Jeannie says. "I wasn't into that." An early decision was made to part. Nancy and Rosemary would take the low route, Lynn and Jeannie would walk high.

New Mexico. Dusty, low-level road walking. Endless lanes of asphalt; Indian hogans; sheep and free-ranging cattle. To residents, two women with backpacks were curiosities, something to point and whistle at, something to laugh at. They walked short miles at first, until their bodies grew accustomed to hefty packs. Gradually mileage increased to an easy fifteen miles per day.

Southern Colorado. Near the gradually sloped base of the San Juan Mountains they abandoned roads to commence enervating snow walking. Although it was spring now, the worst winter in recorded history was far from spent. On the shaved-edge spine of the Rockies lay a mantle of snow 150 per cent its normal depth. They started off on snowshoes, slogging up, over or around peaks as high as 14,000 feet. They could not wait out unrelenting storms, so they learned to walk with them. They walked at times with five to seven inches of fresh snow bedecking heads and shoul-

ders. Stiff 30- to 40-mile-an-hour winds reduced the chill factor to
a point where they had to wrap their faces in wool in order to continue. It was too cold to pause for lunch. They allotted 15 minutes
at most to hunch together and jam down what food they could before body warmth began to dissipate. One whiteout lasted four
days. With map and compass as their only guides, they picked precarious routes around crevasses and massive ice cornices. They
were forced to rely on muscle relaxants to enable them to sleep
through the sounds of fierce winds and flapping tent walls.

The cold finally got them—Lynn with mild hypothermia, Jeannie with severe frostnip to both feet. They were forced to seek a
lower route, but first Jeannie needed medical help and time to
mend.

The doctor in South Fork who examined her feet asked her to
distinguish between the stroke of a butter knife and multiple
needle pricks. She could not. He advised that she rest until feeling
returned. For eleven days she languished on the living room couch
of Lynn's brother. As time passed and Jeannie's feet failed to improve, tension between the partners grew. Finally, despite persistent foot pain, Jeannie made the decision to proceed.

Because of the weather conditions, they abandoned their
planned straight-arrow march from south to north. They would
hike the second half of Colorado when storms diminished. For
now they moved north to the flatlands and warmer weather of
Wyoming's Great Divide Basin. Their first day back, as if in welcome, a fierce storm, with sufficient power to incapacitate Mid-
western states, struck. They survived it, then continued on. They
moved in relative silence now, allowing bodies and senses to
orient to a gentler land. Once the storm dissipated they were
greeted by May heat. They walked to the pervasive fragrance of
sage, to melodic coyote song. It was a recuperative time, exactly
what was needed to prepare them for what was to follow.

The Wind River Range received them in silence. No one had
penetrated its boundaries yet that year. With 180 per cent normal
precipitation, no one had dared. This remote range, they knew,
would be more physically taxing than the chain-linked Colorado
peaks. Added to the challenge was a dangerously low food supply.
They carried only eleven days' sustenance. The wilderness would

make no compromise. If they failed to cover the distance before food ran out, they faced the imminent possibility of death.

Fourteen- to sixteen-hour days commenced at midnight, when freezing temperatures had resolidified the snow. They walked in silence and pervasive darkness, deprived even of starlight by a persistent, sulky overcast. Using ice axes as their only brace, they stumbled over fields tattooed in knee-high snow pockets. They trod unstable paths across ice bridges, around gaping crevasses. They walked until dawn, then lunched, then walked until sun warmth converted the snow to slush. Then they slept, but restlessly. With hibernation now over, bears, they knew, were aggressive and hungry. They traveled without weapons. Their sole protection was knowledge and meticulous care taken in bear-proofing the food.

The harder the sun worked by day, the more treacherous travel was by night. Each night snow bridges and ice-choked lakes became less stable and more perilous to cross. Midway across a lake one night they heard the guttural moan of tons of protesting ice. They retreated hastily to begin the long walk around the lake. They were traveling in single-file togetherness when suddenly, without warning, Lynn's leg penetrated the snow crust to the top of her thigh. She screamed, then held herself motionless over what seemed a bottomless crevasse. Pleading with Jeannie to stay away, she carefully removed her pack, then extricated herself from the hole. They changed her immediately into dry pants and socks. A mile later it happened again—this time to the other leg. "About then," Lynn says, "I decided I should have checked my biorhythms before taking this trip." An hour later they forded a potentially treacherous stream—without incident. Next they passed into an area where all trees were snow-ghosted. By now, unknowingly, Lynn had slipped into a state of aftershock. "I started feeling very very small and really quite insane to be out there. I started seeing the trees move. I thought I was seeing snow leopards. I began asking insane questions like 'What's a bear's range?' I decided to stop, took my pack off, began getting my bag out. Jeannie was poised immediately at my side, explaining with great tact how imperative it was that we continue. I said I would only under the condition that she held my hand. She agreed. We held hands and walked awhile, and then daylight was there."

They covered in eleven days what maps and experts in the region had told them would take at least twenty. This, their most stressful time, is what they refer to most frequently now. "An incredible sense of strength and well-being infused our spirit as a result of facing our fears and succeeding," Jeannie says. "We were the first people to cross the Wind Rivers that year. It was a glorious feeling."

They kept walking north then, into Yellowstone. While fording the Heart River, which borders the national park, they had their closest brush with death. They crossed sideways, as always, clutching each other's wrists. They progressed crablike, playing strength and balance against powerful waters swollen and chilled by spring snowmelt. In one step, without warning, Jeannie plunged waist-deep into a hole. Both women lost their balance. To right themselves, they instinctively released their grip on each other's arms. With the bond broken the river assaulted them individually. Both felt their footing going. Shouted instructions were drowned out by the roar of the river. Adrenalin pumped strength through them. They grabbed each other, and with charged energy retreated to their starting point. They traced miles of river forks that day until they found a safe crossing.

Trail routine varied little: get up early, walk long and, when time permitted, photograph, write, identify birds, plants and wildlife. It was four and a half months before they encountered another person on the trail. In nearly seven months, days off totaled five: two days near the Wind River due to an impassable storm, another two days in Montana when Lynn's arches fell, one day simply to relax. The remaining six months and nineteen days found them covering fifteen miles a day. By so doing Lynn was left, she says, with a feeling that she'd been scoured from the inside out. "I remember having total body daydreams where scenes from my past were revived and reenacted. I viewed them with emotional detachment—as if they'd happened to someone else. The walk connected me to the elements of heat and wind, snow and cold, rain and thunder. But the main connection was the one made to elements of myself—pain and fear, exhaustion and boredom, as well as deep spiritual joy, laughter and song and finally the peaceful calm from success."

News of their former partners filtered to them at each resupply point. Rosemary had traveled as far as the Colorado-New Mexico border and quit. Nancy had continued on alone. Knee problems persisted and grew worse. She took two weeks off at one point to return home for orthopedic consultation. She returned to walk the length of two states in knee braces. By the time she approached Montana she needed help each morning to get out of her sleeping bag. Nancy eventually was forced to abandon her dream within two weeks' walk from the Canadian border.

The trials from weather began again. Mid-August storms closed Yellowstone and Glacier national parks. Weather experts predicted an early, hard winter. Fall approached. Time was running out. "The journey began to center on the race against winter and, for myself, an emotional endurance," Jeannie says. "There were days my heart and soul cried out for my family and loved ones." To help finance the trip, Jeannie had sold a series of newspaper articles, which she wrote along the way. Unexpectedly, her writing income went to financing the hours of long-distance calls that she placed to maintain contact with those she loved.

From Wyoming they jumped to the Canadian border to walk south through Montana. Bob Marshall Wilderness, a 2.5-million-acre lobe in northeast Montana, introduced them to the monotony of lodgepole pines and the electric shock of fear that accompanies one on a walk through moose and grizzly habitat.

They traveled at a precarious time. Bull moose heralded in the annual rutting season with defiant bugling. They were most dangerous. But, in this pre-hibernation period, grizzlies also were their testiest. Their threatening presence was everywhere—in scat, in tracks longer and broader than the span of Lynn's boot, in trees whose bark hung in threads following mauling by the mighty claws. They stayed on ridges when they could. Jeannie tied bells to her pack and mastered her yodeling. Lynn played softly on her harmonica. One moose was inspired to join her in chorus. At a distance considered safe by them both, these unlikely musical partners staged a duet, intermittently serenading each other until the moose retreated uncertainly to her forest domain.

They traveled the last five days from Montana's Madison Mountains to Mammoth, Wyoming. They traversed 11,000-foot peaks, camped by cirque-held alpine lakes, called on their senses to savor sights and sounds so familiar to them now. They remained uncertain, as they approached their terminus, exactly how far they had walked. *National Geographic* estimated 3,200 miles. Other sources guessed 2,400 to 2,600 miles. To foot-weary Lynn they were all wrong. "I'd say it's closer to four thousand," she pronounced then—and continues, in wry moments, to hold to now.

The trip came to a quiet end. "There were no crowds amassed at the end of the trail," Jeannie recalls, "no movie cameras trained to catch our exit from the woods." Instead, their greeting committee consisted only of a cool breeze and the sound of automobiles passing on the paved road.

A magnificent statement of achievement had been made. It stood as a symbolic gain for all women. But there was personal gain in it, too. "I had always known I could do anything I wanted," Lynn said. "This simply confirmed it." For Jeannie the trip deepened her commitment to radical feminism. "I was just awed by how much we could accomplish without strength and power," Jeannie says. "I came out of the trip with the awareness that we are a very strong sex—capable and self-reliant—and that we have been told things that are not true. We are conditioned, I believe, to be passive and weak, to be not actors but observers, to be dependent upon men. We are rewarded for these qualities. The more dependent we are upon a male, the more social reinforcement we get. I no longer support this conditioning. I came off the trail really committed to women. I want them to know you can do it, you *can* . . . just try!"

Part of the overflowing scrapbook of memories which will accompany these two through life—and perhaps the finest tribute to the quality of the experience—is this recognition, which came to Lynn after nearly seven months of absolute physical and mental commitment: "I didn't wish once," she said, "that I was doing anything else."

Section Four
WHAT IT GIVES

Profile / NANCY SKINNER

Wilderness works its way into women's lives in its own sweet time, for its own sweet reasons. Many times those reasons don't become apparent for years. One day, as you sit giving mental order to your past, it dawns that specific value or new direction came from what seemed at the time an insignificant happening, a trivial little meeting.

Nancy Skinner was thirty-seven when, for Christmas, a friend presented her with tickets for a series of guided nature walks. There was, she claims, absolutely no reason for it. Since birth she had diligently maintained the image of an indoor woman—a wealthy one at that. Young years had been spent reading and studying to become a concert pianist. During college she decided to pursue marriage instead of music. Throughout the birth and childhood of her three sons she remained a boisterous participant in the good life. Her clothes wore designer labels, her habits wore the standard touch of class: fashionable luncheons, cocktail parties, a reliance on nicotine and hard liquor, a commitment to opera, ballet, and such esoteric pursuits as Elizabethan England.

Her body in those days served as little more than a glamorous clothes hanger. She tended to it cosmetically and otherwise ignored it. It protested this mild-mannered abuse. In her twenties she played victim to recurrent colds. By her mid-thirties her two-pack-a-day habit had caused her to develop the early stages of emphysema. There were other chinks appearing in her perfectly coiffed and fashioned armor. Deep within she began feeling the vulnerability a woman knows when she overinvests in husband and children, then suddenly finds them pulling away.

No, there was absolutely nothing about her to prompt such a gift. Yet, it couldn't have come at a better time.

One sparkly spring day ten years after Nancy Skinner's first nature walk, my antique little car and I found ourselves straining mightily up the steep hill leading to her home. Even once we reached the top it was rough going. Leaning into a thirty-mile-an-hour wind, I picked my way to her front door over cobblestones studding a perfectly groomed Japanese garden.

Concern about my too-casual attire dissipated instantly. In men's Levis, well-worn running shoes and a scoop-neck cotton T-shirt, Nancy Skinner, yesteryear's fashion plate, far understated me. Her hair—medium short, salt-and-pepper coarse—served as an unruly halo for a tan, friendly face. The eyes, clear and dark, held and penetrated my gaze. She hugged me lightly in greeting and pulled me in out of the wind.

Traces of gentle affluence pervaded the sprawling hilltop home, in pastel colors, art and antique furniture, in symphonic strains of Prokofiev's *Romeo and Juliet,* which she had been enjoying when I arrived. However, Nancy herself did not call up an urge to engage in pretentious talk. She settled me on a comfortable couch, assumed a position in a chair opposite me, kicked off her shoes and put her feet up.

She had just returned, she explained with a weary grin, from leading her third hike of the week. She was hiked out and, I suspected, peopled out. It didn't show, though. She scrunched her slim, loose-jointed body deep into the chair and the questions began. She had undergone significant changes, friends had said. She did remarkable things. What was the nature of this change, I wanted to know, and what had prompted it?

"If anybody told me at twenty that I'd be the outsy-doorsy type I would have laughed," she started. "I was the most lounge-lizardy decorative kind of lady. I'd sit around and decorate sofas in pretty clothes. I lived in buildings; I never went outdoors. I drank, played all night, closed bars. I never walked down the block, I'd drive. I was that way until just ten years ago."

She might be there yet if the family budget hadn't forced her hand. When the cost of vacations at motels for a family of five soared beyond reason, in an uncharacteristic move, Nancy suggested joining the Sierra Club for Wilderness Threshold trips. Packers carried equipment and food in on mules, families came in on foot, established camp and spent a week in wilderness together. For Nancy these trips offered more sociological amusement than anything else. "We were playing our same games out there as we did at home," she recalls. "Women seemed to do more of the work, but would stay in the background saying, 'Yes, dear, yes, dear,' while men would be up there doing all the talking."

A fascination with wilderness wasn't born until she joined the nature walks. The leader, a woman, inspired and taunted her by all she did not know. It was exactly the cerebral stimulus Nancy loved. She responded by re-enrolling, and by joining other classes: ornithology, botany, geology, ecology. Within a year she became a volunteer docent at a local wildlife sanctuary.

Wilderness challenged her, too, by forcing her to use her body. At first a mile walk seemed like a marathon. When she mastered that she took up running, then swimming. Now, at age forty-eight, she runs two to five miles a day; or she joins friends for an hour of lap swimming at a local pool; or she leads eight- to ten-mile hikes. "Not exactly what you'd expect from one who flunked P.E.," she beams. But the rewards are there: "I'm healthier now than I was at twenty or twenty-five."

She was bouncing out of the chair now, heading for the kitchen phone, which was ringing. The caller wanted to join her hikes. Nancy was pleasant and patient with questions she'd answered a hundred times before. When she returned, balancing a platter of homemade poppy-seed cake, cups and a pot of herb tea, she explained, "They call for assurance. They don't even hear the answers. They just want to check out my voice, to see if I'm a nice lady." She has not forgotten how tenuous beginners feel, though she herself did not remain one long.

Nature hikes, studies in natural history, Sierra Club trips—she couldn't get enough of them. Yet, within four years, the saturation point had been reached. When she began characterizing Sierra Club hikes as "forced marches" she knew it was time for a change. To travel at a pace she enjoyed, to visit sites that intrigued her, she realized she must either walk alone or lead others. "My approach to leadership," she claims, "was pretty timid."

She started by leading friends—or *attempting* to lead friends. On her first official hike she alone showed up at the trailhead. Business picked up after that. Following a year of weekly day hikes she began offering courses through the Sierra Club, a local university and a college. With "Beginning Backpacking" she initiated beginners into the basics. For senior citizens she offered "Stately Backpacking." Middle-aged women who hiked with her became known as "The Hot Flashers." "These are women," Nancy says, "who got tired of waiting for daddy to start doing things with them. They went out and are now doing their thing. It's a real break with tradition." From day hikes, Nancy eventually branched out to lead ten-day backpack trips. She now leads two longer trips a year.

Nancy's hikes are distinguished by the inimitable *bon vivant* touch. Each year, for example, she stages potluck gourmet hikes. In some select forest clearing, delectable multi-course meals are served, complete with French wines, fine linen and crystal. "You'd be amazed what people pull out of their packs," she exclaims. "Homemade goose-liver pâté, shrimp mousse, huckleberry tarts. They are feasts in the true sense." To these gala events Nancy wears her dress jeans—the jeans she is wearing now. They differ from any old jeans by the six-inch swath of heavy cotton lace which she has affixed to the hem of each leg.

"Stunning, aren't they?" she asks, stroking the lace. I confess I had mistaken them for Courrège. Together we wonder how long it will be until dress jeans become all the rage. A rich, gravelly chuckle, which has punctuated our talk, surfaces now to accent her delight.

If trip leadership provided an outlet for inspiration and humor, it also offered two other benefits—a separate income and a sense of independence. "I'm a nurturer," Nancy admits. "I'd been putting all my eggs into one basket—with my husband and sons. I was very dependent on my husband for a validation of myself. If the house was clean and picked up I was being a good wife and mother. Once I realized I didn't have to do these things, that I didn't need to be affirmed by somebody else, then I was okay and strong."

Nancy sees an emergence of women in their forties—in her words, "a phasing-out of mommyhood." She says, "You take a lot of energy originally put toward tending the kids' needs or baking bread and put it somewhere else. Women who continue to think their teenage kids need them get into trouble. Usually these are women who don't have any other outlets." Nancy contended with this phase in her own unique fashion. With a friend, she began staging bake-offs—competitions to see who could spend less time in the kitchen each week.

Life's roller coaster took a downward curve about then. Family sickness, accidents, drug problems, marital difficulties and thoughts of divorce consumed the next two years. She grew wary for a time of answering the phone because of the unbroken stream of bad news it brought. "The crisis-of-the-week syndrome," as she labels it now, persisted until, following one final marital blow, she announced she was leaving. Conveniently this declaration came two days before she was scheduled to depart for Outward Bound. The course emerged as a perfectly timed turning point.

Patrolmates in this Women Over 30 course in Utah's Canyonlands National Park ranged in age from the early thirties to fifty-three. Nancy, then forty-six, quickly emerged as one of the strongest. "I gained a sense of my strength then," she says. "By carrying heavy packs, by climbing, by running a marathon, I saw I have great physical power. It made me realize I can do anything I want —that the only thing that holds me back is mental." Nancy gained emotional and spiritual sustenance from women she traveled with, but the ultimate rewards came during her three-day solo.

"The first day was like a spiral going down, down into myself," she says. "The next two days I was deeply centered within myself, yet I also could perceive every little grain of sand on the narrow ledge where I camped. I was on many planes at once."

She paused now, covering her eyes with loosely clasped fingers.

"Ahhh," she said, "I'll tell you the real value that comes from wilderness." There was silence between us. "I am certain Someone was there with me. I spoke in tongues—and I am not that type. There was a presence there which never left me. I came out of that experience with a new covenant, a new relationship to God. I realized I would pull my personal religious dogma from many sources instead of just one. As a result I left formal Christianity." Today she describes herself as a "laid-back Christian—a Zen Christian."

Spiritual insight came, and so did emotional strength. The patterns in the marriage were no longer acceptable. While she had at one time feared the loss of her family and home, now she was willing to face that loss. "I left as a wife-dependent-subordinate," she recognizes now. "I came back with strength, knowing I had to do it alone. I decided to take a chance on the future."

This decision alone altered the tone of her marriage. "I saw I no longer needed my husband as a big protector. I have a lot of skills and I can survive. Knowing this has shifted the balance of power in our relationship. Now it is a marriage between equals. Now I remain here by choice."

Nancy gained yet another awareness during her time alone: "I learned that the worst thing in life is not to try at all. The best thing is to try and succeed. The next best thing is to try and fail. I take chances today where I played it safe two years ago. Now I'm willing to live dangerously, to live closer to the edge."

She moves toward challenge these days rather than backing away. Because she thought it would be difficult to do, she ran a six-mile stretch of beach barefooted. She pulled a tendon in the process, but the satisfaction that came from the achievement more than compensated for the pain. During rock-climbing classes now she asks for help when she's stuck. "That's a big step forward," she says. "I never used to be able to ask for help—even when I needed it."

Her willingness to be vulnerable connects me to this woman. I feel exhilarated. I feel less alone. How, I want to know, can she risk being so open? "It has to do with finding my personal power," she says. "There is no change without opening. Besides, I learned long ago that if you make walls around yourself to keep people away you also keep yourself in. If you are going to make a meaningful connection with others you must be open and free to be vulnerable. You must be willing to take chances—like a little kid on a skateboard."

Nancy is no longer able to recite verbatim the names of top dress designers. Nor does she care that her closet is no longer packed with the latest. "I'm becoming a little less pretentious," she admits. She has, she claims, shed those "heavy femininity tapes that control indoor women." This is not to imply that her femaleness is ignored. There is, instead, a fine balancing act going on. Underneath the heavy boots and scratchy Levis and long-tailed men's shirts are the laciest underclothes. "I love the pretties," she says, "and it's got to be French perfume. All the beautiful lace never shows, but I know it's there."

Wilderness offered Nancy new direction and values, and it continues to do so. "I go for the solitude. I can't get enough of it," she says. "When I'm here at home the needs of the world are very strong. The inner voice is saying, 'Okay, time to go to work, time to clean the house.' There's a certain quality of passing through, of leaving the dailiness when I drive up to a certain place. There's a quality of taking off outer layers, of stripping away civilization. Sometimes the farther away I go the more intense my experience is."

Nancy was exasperated at one time by her husband not backpacking with her, but now she prefers that he doesn't. The marriage is enriched, she believes, by maintaining separate hobbies. She backpacks for different reasons—for exercise, to get in touch with herself, to be still. In one trip with a woman friend she never wandered farther than a hundred feet from her sleeping bag. She spent an entire morning studying a caddis fly larvae. Pebbles in a stream were good for another few hours. Cloud passage easily consumed the rest of the day. They ate little and talked little. They emerged from the experience totally refreshed.

Wilderness provides a perfect foil for measuring her own growth. She began with a need to catalog, to know the Latin name for everything. This compulsion has left her. In its place is the ability to appreciate the swoop of bird wings, the iridescence of a beetle's back. The wind will carry the waft of an unknown scent. Rather than separating leaf from limb to key it, she is satisfied merely being tantalized. She has moved to a present-moment appreciation of nature.

"I had an absolute inspiration while swimming the other day," Nancy says. "I almost drowned, I was so excited by it! I realized that how I respond to and perceive nature is how I respond to and perceive life. It is not something apart from the rest of me. Now in all areas of my life I find myself not needing to catalog. I just experience and allow things to happen and people to be. I just accept them."

She has changed, yes. But in her mind the transformation is not complete. There are lessons yet to glean from wilderness. There are fears to be overcome. She is moving toward the time when she will backpack alone. What stops her is the fear of sleeping outdoors by herself. She is giving herself two years to overcome it.

At that point, on the eve of her fiftieth birthday, she and her pack will begin a solo pilgrimage. She will hike the two-hundred-mile length of the John Muir Trail, from Yosemite National Park to Mount Whitney. Already her costume is planned. Across the front of her T-shirt, in bold print, will appear the proud declaration, "NANCY IS 50!!!"

"Join me for champagne and pâté at Whitney Portal," she said as we braced ourselves against the wind on the brief walk back to my car.

I can see it now. Nancy striding in under the weight of her pack —sporting, naturally, her dress jeans. A card table will be spread with fine linen, silver, crystal. In the background will come the sound of popping corks from bottles of French champagne. From nowhere a tray of delicate canapés will appear. We will be there to celebrate a woman's long walk and, more than that, her victory over fear and inertia and age and an upbringing which never encouraged her to do such things.

CHAPTER 24

Universal Gifts

Wilderness works on that old principle: the more you give, the more you receive. From you wilderness expects a certain preparedness—in body, in spirit, in what you bring along. Those who abide by these demands, who approach wilderness with anticipation and openness, are usually rewarded by abundant gifts.

There are, for starters, grandeur and silence, pure water and clean air. These are things people speak of when they encourage others to go. But there are less obvious gifts, things not seen but felt. There is, for one, the gift of distance. Wilderness grants one the chance to stand away from relationships and daily ritual—to appreciate them more, or to see areas that need change.

There is the gift of energy. Wilderness infuses us with its own special brand. It is everywhere; in natural light and color, in invisible fields which emanate from rocks and rushing water and trees. I remember lying by the Snake River in Idaho once and becoming aware that I could not sleep. There was a simple explanation. Nature's forces had me in hand. I was engulfed by a dance of ions and atoms. My body was responding to the pervasive pull of the moon. I did not begrudge my night awake. Had I sheltered myself by roofs and walls, had I cut myself off, I might not have greeted the dawn so energized and thoroughly refreshed.

Experiences like this inspire women to characterize wilderness as a healer. "In the business environment the elements are tearing you down," Pookie Baird Godvin maintains. "In wilderness it is just the opposite. The elements there feed you, heal you."

Given inherent sensitivity, many women feel wilderness feeding not just the body, but also the soul. Women in the Wilderness cofounder Randi Du Bois describes herself as a nuts-and-bolts person, yet in wilderness a certain pantheism unfolds, and a reverence. "I feel a lot of spirit around me that is ill-defined," Randi says. "I just feel presence. I do not feel anxious, usually because I've done a pretty thorough brainwashing on myself that no evil spirit would waste its time on me. I've been in two canyons in my life where I felt embraced by them, not by the flowers or leaves, but by the canyons themselves. I was just overwhelmed by a sense of containment, a sense of connectedness." The earth sends out messages which some are receptive enough to hear.

Perhaps the most fundamental gift is the ability of wilderness to make one feel good—physically, mentally. This is no here-today-gone-tomorrow good, but one that lingers and penetrates and sometimes changes the way a woman sees herself and lives.

SENSE OF SELF

When traveling with a backpack in wilderness we walk in two directions at once: we walk inward, and we walk away. We leave behind urban complexity and mechanization. We abandon the labor savers. We are placed, for a change, on a one-and-one with the body. If we want to go somewhere or do something we do so entirely under our own steam. In the process we discover what may, for some, be a whole new facet: physical capability. We begin to discover not what the body isn't, but all that it is. "There is physical exhilaration," Annie Ketchin says. "There is a recognition that the body is an amazing miracle that is vastly underrated."

Suddenly the fact that our breasts are too small, or our waist too large, or wrinkles too plentiful becomes secondary. The negative orientation, implanted by a society stuck on appearance, gives way gradually to positive orientation. Our attention is diverted from physical beauty to the beauty in performance. This shift in focus, for many, triggers a domino topple of new awareness and change.

Kathy Evans, a wife and mother of three small children, was asked on her first all-women backpack trip to evaluate her own strength. In a group of twelve women she placed herself next-to-last in line. "I saw myself as one of the weakest and most dependent in the group," Kathy explains. "Yet on so many occasions I surprised myself—carrying the climbing ropes, getting to tops of mountains second or third. In the end I learned I have more inner and physical strength than I thought I had. From knowing my strengths are much more I gained a sense of self-worth."

The sense of self is enhanced and so, it seems, are mental capabilities. "Since I've gotten a higher awareness of my physical self," Marlene Simonson says, "I've been able to look at decisions that were facing me in a much more complete way."

Strengthen the body and you strengthen the brain. It is a one-way street to which women have only recently gained access. But this is merely the threshold of rewards that await. In the shift from passive to active many women experience a deepening. They begin subtly separating themselves from society's dictates and symbols. They begin forging their own values instead of subscribing to the ready-made brand. Take the concept of femininity as a case in point.

Concerns about relinquishing one's femininity prevail until the woman connects with the deeper wisdom wilderness holds. To hasten this process, Outward Bound insists that women leave all makeup behind. Participants' standard reaction, Leslie Emerson reports, is "God, I'm so scared I'm going to come back as a man." "They're afraid," Leslie says, "that by losing these social symbols of femininity they won't be feminine anymore. But what they realize through the wilderness experience is their femininity is deeper than makeup or not shaving their legs or having a dirty face for a few days. It's a much deeper kind of energy and power." As Leslie concurs, "Wilderness doesn't make you into a man. It makes you into more of the woman you already are."

AGE

Nowhere is the attitudinal schism between indoor and outdoor women more apparent than on the subject of age. I participated in a cameo scene recently which subsequently has come to symbolize the indoor woman's attitude toward age. My seatmate on a cross country flight was a beauty in a classic sense: flawless skin, smooth thick hair, eyes the color of oiled walnut. She was a newly promoted computer programmer returning from a seminar on the west coast. Her husband and young daughter accompanied her. We spoke, as strangers sometimes do, more openly than if we were friends. She talked mostly of the past. Looking toward the future, she was fearful. She wasn't sure the promotion was taking her in a desired direction. She wasn't where she wanted to be— either in her job or in her personal life. She wanted to explore other avenues, but she couldn't because it was too late. She was past her prime.

How old was she, I wanted to know.

She had just turned thirty-one.

Did she ever go outdoors?

No, there wasn't time. Besides, sun wasn't good for her skin.

This scene might not have impressed me so deeply had I not once felt exactly the same way, and had I not, two days later, met Pat Kielsmeier. Pat co-directs Colorado Outward Bound courses for women over thirty. She has led hundreds of women, up to age sixty-six, on ten-day wilderness sojourns. "These women have a different perspective about age and time," Pat claims. "I've never heard an outdoor woman say she's too old, or that her age is limiting her." Because of their example, Pat's own attitude about age has changed. "It's opened up another whole twenty years in my life," she says. "There's no reason to ever get old."

Wilderness offers women the opportunity to put to rest the grim myths about age. The woman who actively exerts her body discovers she can direct and control physiological processes. She can shape and firm her body and control her weight. Best of all, as medical science now concurs, she can slow the inevitable tick of time. In the past twenty years, Margot Patterson Doss, America's first National Curator of Walking, has covered more than sixty thousand miles on foot. This newspaper columnist, author of four books, wife and mother of four, parries questions about her age in this way: "Take whatever age you think I am and add ten years. *That's* what exercise has done for me!"

Harriet Parsons has been backpacking and mountain climbing since her twenties. Her last official climb, in Wyoming's Grand Tetons, occurred when she was fifty-nine. Now, at age seventy-six, she considers distance walking a vital part of her daily regimen. Rewards, in her opinion, are a certain mental resiliency and, as important, excellent health.

Age is one part physiological, one part attitudinal. In this latter realm, too, outdoor women shine. Marjorie Farquar distinguished herself in the 1930s by becoming the first woman to climb the east face of Mount Whitney and, later, Cathedral Spire in Yosemite. Marjorie, whose husband, Francis, served as president of the Sierra Club, kept pace with his climbing and backpacking even while raising their four children. She is a grandmother now, though hardly a traditional one. "I'm not too good at reading," she confesses, "so I teach my grandchildren rock climbing instead." At age seventy-five, Marjorie still climbs, still hikes, still downhill and cross-country skis. She is more active than many women half her age. "I wear everybody out—all my contemporaries," she confides. "My friends are getting to be old people now, but I don't have time to be old."

Women who remain active in wilderness have this in common: they grow older, but not old. They breathe meaning into the wisdom Renee Taylor writes: "The keynote of life is growth, not aging. The life that flows through us at eighty is the same that energized us in infancy. It does not get old or weak. So-called age is the deterioration of enthusiasm, faith to live, and the will to progress." I wish I had been able to quote that to my companion on the plane.

PERSPECTIVE

We walk inward when backpacking, and we walk away. We stage a literal and figurative leavetaking from all we are accustomed to. From noise and distraction. From speed. From the jangle of the telephone and the drone of TV. From civic and personal obligations.

We move into a realm which, on the surface at least, seems simpler. Wilderness components are numbered: animals, birds, trees, earth, weather, water, sky. And, they are engaged in a dance of their own. You can participate in the dance, if you choose, or you can stand apart. Actually, the latter is hard to do, for nature seldom lets you alone. A mere wildflower, for example, has the power to bombard you with new awareness. By its very nature and design it speaks of many things: of beauty—of the concentrated energy required to produce it, of how short-lived it is; of fragility; of miracles, of some entity with the creative capacity to mastermind a flower, something humans have never managed to do.

So it is with all components of wilderness. We had no hand in their original design. We take no credit for them. We can merely stand in awe. And we can, if given to such thought, take our measure from them.

Wilderness is the land of little and large. You might fool yourself into believing you stand somewhere in between, but that delusion seldom lasts. Eventually you see that you are smaller and less powerful and more temporal than many forces and beings that live there. Few face such recognition without in some way being altered, being humbled.

Rather than feeling diminished, however, one emerges feeling infinitely connected. A certain solace comes from this. Avon Mattison, a rich-voiced, striking-looking woman, recently endured her life's most trying time. At the outset of her divorce her husband confiscated all the furniture and money. This left her homeless and living on welfare. The stress from these combined events produced what tests showed to be breast cancer. While she waited for surgery (which proved the lumps nonmalignant), Avon made a daily habit of donning her backpack and taking to the hills. "From this I gained the perspective that I was not all there was in this world. As long as there was a flower to look at, as long as there was sunshine, as long as there was a tree to greet me on my way, I knew I could make it."

Many who spend time in wilderness share this perspective. "It's important to recognize life as a process that doesn't begin and end with the individual," says Allison Clough. "Once immersed in wilderness you see yourself as just part of a huge living, seething process. It has given me a sense of philosophy," she says. "Whatever happens I can accept. At the moment I'm not afraid of dying. It's partly because of my sense of being part of a larger order."

Wilderness embellishes the philosophical outlook—the thoughts you bring home—and it lifts the immediate mood. "There usually is something there that just draws me up short in the midst of my ponderous feelings," Avon says. "A butterfly often has a way of swooping in front of my nose as if to say, 'Hello, you can be this way too.' I put my cross down for about two seconds, and all of a sudden I can find a moment of laughter."

If wilderness imparts certain lessons, the backpack imparts others. We live in a society that advocates acquiring multiple everything—cars, televisions, dresses, husbands. It makes its living that way. There are, as a result, inordinate pressures on us to consume. There is an advertising industry that spends more than $25 billion a year convincing us to buy. Many things are lost in this process, not the least of which is a solid sense of what matters in life. The backpack functions on a principle exactly the reverse. According to its rules (or, in this case, dimensions), the less you acquire and carry, the better off you are. By paring us down to basics it coaxes us to examine what is a necessity and what is purely a frill. It shows us exactly how little we need to be happy and to survive.

This doing without—if you can call it that—promotes a change of values. It encourages one to look a little closer at the glittery "buy products" and ask if they really are necessary. It leads some to a simplification, to a gradual detachment from materialism. This serves both the environment and the individual well.

INTIMACY

Invest in things, the consumer society urges, and you will be happy. This is proving to be a false message. Divorces, suicides, mental illness and aberrant behavior are on the upswing. Suicide is the number three cause of death among teenagers. Never, according to these statistics, have so many people with so many things been so unhappy. Granted, happiness springs from different sources for different people. Most agree, however, that two sources are health and meaningful contact—or intimacy—with other people. These the backpack and wilderness promote.

In wilderness the props are gone, the stresses are unfamiliar, the limits of endurance and cheerfulness are tested. "The nice-lady veneer drops off after about three days," Nancy Skinner maintains. Randi Du Bois gives it a couple of hours to a couple of days. "When you're tired, sweaty, you've got two thousand more feet to climb and storm clouds are moving in, you can't hide much," Randi says. "When you're in a tight spot there's a real opportunity to see yourself and the person you travel with. It's a real 'Oh, I see you' experience. In wilderness there's nothing to cushion it."

So, there you are peering into the depths of someone's soul, and all of a sudden something magical happens. A rainbow arcs overhead, or a hawk dives. You tug at your partner's sleeve and point, then stand together in silence and wonder. When two people share a vision no one else has had, they grow somehow closer.

You walk inward with a backpack, and you walk away. By the very act of walking, some therapists say, you release blocks of tension in the body. This stirs deeper thoughts and feelings. To share these says to your partner, I trust you, I accept you. It is the highest compliment one can pay.

Wilderness both brings people together and holds them together. Randi volunteered once to co-lead a group of high school students on a ten-day backpack trip. Within four days with Reno Tahini, the leader, there was, Randi says, "a clicking into place. It didn't have so much to do with romance as a shared attitude toward preparedness, thoroughness, an appreciation of esthetics. There were a lot of unspoken words when shooting stars were popping. To share those experiences is very moving. It set the stage."

Married now, Reno and Randi share a small farm on the outskirts of San Francisco. If it were not for wilderness, Randi claims, they would not be together, and if they did not actively pursue wilderness experience in their relationship they would get in trouble because it is so nourishing to them.

"To get through a grueling day, to get over a pass, to experience a sunset that's breathtaking, to curl up in your sleeping bag, snuggling with your sweetheart, watching the stars and sharing your thoughts and dreams," Randi says, "you can't put a price on those kinds of experiences. That's the cement that can easily be built upon for the hard times all of us go through." Randi threatens to knock the ceiling out of their bedroom because "It's just not the same here."

Unitarian minister Ann Heller considers wilderness the world's greatest facilitator. She urges women to know why they are going before they go, for that alone increases the likelihood that answers will come. Of course, some go not for answers, but for pleasure. That is there too—in abundance.

All things considered, the give-and-take scale in wilderness is totally out of whack. As a rule, wilderness gives and you take. There is one way to help set the scale straight, and that is to always walk softly and travel with care. That is the very least one can do as thanks for the gifts wilderness gives.

CHAPTER 25

First-Person Gifts

"Nature should decide what women can and cannot do. Nature should decide—not man."

CLARE BOOTH LUCE

For Laurie McCann the backpack served as merely an entry point to wilderness. Once she mastered skills and learned to lead others, she took to running wild rivers. She adventured by raft first, but soon yearned for the singular challenge of the kayak. After three years of conscientious training and practice she accepted what to her seemed the ultimate challenge. Accompanied by a support crew of friends, she journeyed to the headwaters of the Tuolumne River, a wild, thrashing waterway which had been attempted by only a few courageous kayakers. While sitting surveying the longest, most dangerous series of rapids, Laurie raised the question which comes to us all at least once during our outdoor escapades: "What the heck am I doing here?"

After completing the run the first wave of answers came. There was pride for having achieved a goal. There was self-esteem for having confronted fear. There was sheer exhilaration for having succeeded. But some answers (encased, it seems, in time capsules) came slower and have had lingering value. "There is something about achieving a physical, tangible goal," Laurie says, "that makes it easier to deal with some of the intangible things in life—like making decisions or approaching somebody that you don't feel important or smart enough to approach. I always refer back to the Tuolumne and say, 'Well, if I did that I certainly can do this.' "

Call it confidence transfer, call it anything—it happens. For women who set and achieve physical goals, it happens. Psychiatrist Alan Skolnikoff, a backpacker himself, sees particular value in it happening with a backpack. "The experience of a woman carrying her own weight in this one realm can be applied to other realms such as jobs or relationships. It has implications in terms of stereotypes that she may have applied to herself—that she could not carry enough or do enough. This can be altered."

"If I can do that," the thought goes, "I certainly can do this." By that awareness alone have women altered their lives. There have been seemingly minor changes, such as a homemaker mustering courage to apply for a job, or to reactivate a hobby. And there have been total life transformations.

At age twelve, when her gambling father first deserted the fold, Bronx-born Arlene Ustin saw life as a struggle, something that had to be gotten through. She took up smoking and started spending after-school hours and summers living by the tough rules of the street. When Arlene was midway through college her parents finally initiated divorce proceedings. To support herself, she curtailed her studies and took a job teaching. At age twenty-six—then smoking two packs a day—Arlene was invited rock climbing. Though every muscle in her body ached by the end of the day, she had sampled the thrill of physical achievement. It was an awakening. Suddenly a conditioned body became her goal. It took four weeks of daily workouts for her to run a quarter of a mile without stopping. She kept at it. She qualified eventually for Outward Bound. When she completed the course she was invited to attend the school's leadership training program. She became a full-time instructor for North Carolina Outward Bound, a position she held for six years. Today, in a private high school, Arlene leads students on runs, rock climbs and strenuous thirty-day backpack trips. If her life-style has changed, so has her attitude toward life. Now she doesn't see it as something to be gotten through, but as something she actually enjoys.

The process of cultivating physical strength is akin, for some women, to waking a sleeping giant—in this case one's inherent potential. A woman begins to perceive her life and capabilities in a whole new light. She can't help being changed by that. Positive as it may seem on the surface, though, there is danger in it. "Women who continually say 'I can't' find in the wilderness that in fact they can," says Randi Du Bois. "It's a potent and wonderful feeling. It may have been years since they felt good about themselves. It's like the rudimentary beginning of consciousness raising. They get so excited and turned on that they go home and immediately want to tear everything apart and cast people aside."

Randi labels this the "first level of clarity." When she passed through it she ended a love relationship and changed her residence. She now recognizes that she needn't have undergone such turmoil.

For Alice Herman, change commenced three years before her introduction to wilderness, when she divorced her husband, an influential bank president. She floundered in her new independent life-style until she participated in an Outward Bound course for women over thirty. "I give full credit to the backpacking experience for changing my opinion of what I thought I could not do, and for giving me positive thoughts about myself in a different vein," Alice says. "The experience produced an 'I can do *anything*' attitude and gave me confidence in myself." She returned, reinforced, to apply for and be accepted as manager of a major tennis club in Phoenix. Three years later, this onetime socialite and fashion plate applied for the Peace Corps. Assigned to Ecuador for two years, she lasted exactly three months. "I feel fortunate to have had the three months," Alice writes. "It was an incredible education, but I just found I had to have a bath, and it was very difficult accepting the lack of sanitation." As a poignant end to her note Alice admitted to having difficulty adjusting back into her old life-style with a new inner self.

These examples from Randi and Alice indicate essentially the same thing: wilderness may inspire you to make change, but don't rush into it, and don't go to extremes. There is a time to process new information, and a time to act on it. In this hurry-up society with its emphasis on now, too little time is relegated to processing. Buoyed by their new sense of strength, some women return home to make change impetuously rather than thoughtfully. They may move into new realms by such action, but these are not always better realms.

Women contemplating change would do well to consider the seed pod. Ripened slowly by a leisurely sun, the pod bursts and casts its contents at the exact moment when seeds are fully nourished and are most likely to implant, take root and eventually bear pods of their own. Much change in nature is choreographed with this same great care, and is accomplished only gradually. If change is imminent in your life, it should be implemented in the same careful, gradual way.

A more conservative and, some believe, wiser approach is to use new strengths and awarenesses to improve existing patterns or relationships. Many times it is easier to restore a familiar vessel than to shatter it and face the enervating and sometimes unsuccessful task of replacing it. There is depth, tradition and comfort in the known. There is uncertainty in the unknown—and there is no guarantee that new is synonymous with better.

"The eventual truth a woman learns out there is that she can feel good and be herself wherever she is and with whomever she is," Randi says. "The strength is within her; it cannot be violated by another person."

Sit still. Process the information. Treat the new knowledge gently. It is that old handle-with-care rider which accompanies most valuable gifts. And yet it seems a small enough price to pay for awarenesses which have in them the power to vitally improve a woman's self-perception—and life.

CHAPTER 26

What It Has Given Me

Something magical happens when you spend time in mountains. The light or the air, perhaps, taunts the senses and coaxes the blinders off. It is as if you are seeing for the first time. Meadow grasses suddenly become many shades of green, not one. Granite sparkles. Age-old swirls of glacial moraine stand out. The visual sense is not the only one affected; each sense comes alive. You cross a boggy plain and the fragrance of wild spearmint or onion reaches you. You stoop to root among the grasses to find the pungent bulb. Will it spice your soup that night, or top pink-fleshed, pan-fried trout? It is a sensory emergence that occurs when you have been long enough away from the blare of city sounds and lights, when the body has tuned down and adapted to wilderness rhythms.

I had achieved this receptive state on a trip last fall when, early one morning, I came to the edge of a high mountain meadow. The plod of my boots was soundless on the dusty path; the breeze, coming toward me as it was, kept my presence a secret. I reached the open swale with none of the inhabitants knowing it.

There were the usual carryings-on—Picas scurrying, jackrabbits munching, mountain chickadees sweetening the song of the air— but the mood was clearly frantic. First snow was about to fall; residents were hastening to prepare.

As I moved through the sunny clearing to drop my pack and rest, I heard a sound which caught my breath and held me motionless. It was the whistle-chirp of a mountain lion. There were two of them there, maybe more. Because of their stealth I knew I would not see them. It seemed privilege enough to feel their nearness and listen in on what they had to say.

By being there, by being sensitive to what was there, I received a gift of proximity to rare and wild things. No, I cannot touch this gift, nor sell it for firewood in my old age. But each time I call up the memory of that wild song my skin tingles. It has been a year now. The sensation doesn't pass.

Wilderness touches me in a way that urban experiences do not. I am temporarily thrilled by the acquisition of a slinky dress, or the chance to see a Renoir, but the feeling seldom lasts. Soon I forget the name and score of the opera I went to see, but I can't forget that wild song. Part of this results from my upbringing. I was raised on the rural edge of a city, where blackberry brambles and pine trees grew, where squirrels played and quail calls ushered in the day. Saturdays I would take my peanut butter sandwich and head off on my own. I would discover a hollow in scrub oak and sage and call it my fort. There I would lay and listen to the bees and fantasize about never being found. The connection to the earth was made then. Now when I go too far from it I feel hollow and edgy, as if some vital part of me has been left behind.

Since growing up I have polished and perfected my city ways. I avoid eyes in elevators. I cross my legs just so. I keep appointments on time. It goes along swimmingly for a while, then my insides start to squirm. My soul and body long to escape the rigid rules, to be wild and run free. It is an addiction—I realize that—but in place of drugs I crave sweet air and the feel of pliant earth beneath my feet. I thirst for sparkling mountain water and the chance to be washed by sunshine, sweat and dew.

Wilderness renews me. It brings me back from the edge of exhaustion and emptiness which come from working too hard, or giving more than I am getting back. Usually it takes at least three days of walking and looking, absorbing and being silent. Then, as if from some deep crystal spring, energy begins to seep and surge. Following this, inspiration usually comes. I remember leaving home once, thinking I would never write another line. Nine days later, while approaching the crown of a 15,000-foot peak, I was thinking on the value of backpacking for women and wondering why more weren't involved. Suddenly a swell of light occurred and the phrase "beauty and the backpack" emerged. I toyed with it for a time, then realized that a column needed to be written which would share what I had found and would invite women outdoors.

There was a rightness to the idea. One month later the column "Beauty & the Backpack," the precursor to this book, was accepted by a national magazine.

Wilderness encourages me to explore new avenues of knowledge. During my first years of backpacking, I was like a blind person passing through. I witnessed phenomena I did not understand, and so drew no value from the experience. By walking with knowledgeable friends, by reading and taking classes, I now am learning to see. My latest class was ornithology. I learned to identify many birds by sight and song. I'm still slow on Latin names, but the fact that I can recognize a plain titmouse when I see one makes me feel more connected to this feathery being.

Since studying wild birds I have joined the Audubon Society, and have been supporting birds that settle near my home with bimonthly contributions of twenty-five pounds of seed. That tells me something of the side benefits of learning. The more I know, the more I care and the more I strive to protect.

This applies to the larger scale, too. The more I have learned about wilderness, the more active have become my efforts to preserve it. This has prompted a change in values and life-style. Once I discovered how environmentally taxing consumerism is, I consciously simplified my life. I buy fewer frills now. I make most gifts. I grow my own vegetables. I walk and ride my bike more. I am no less happy or fulfilled for following the simpler path; it feels right to me.

As my appreciation for nature's emissaries has grown, so my reaction to them has changed. My first encounter with rattlesnakes happened on a camping trip some years ago. The morning we were preparing to leave, my friend and I nearly stepped on four babies rattling their way along the lake's edge. I all but ran the rest of the way to his car. This summer my second encounter occurred, right off my back porch. Because I had never heard a mature snake rattle, I mistook the high, hissing sound for a broken gas main. Leaning over to check, I found myself six feet from a coiled and clearly irked three-foot snake. I backed off, knee-jerk style, but once the adrenalin waned I experienced fascination, not fear. I sat watching the snake uncoil from its own alarm and glide a safe distance from the house. My thought was not how to kill it, but how to move it without injuring it or me.

Wilderness has given me the opportunity to redefine my limits. Actually, I have Outward Bound to thank for this. One morning, five days into the course, we arose at 4:30 A.M. After a breakfast of hot orangeade and oatmeal, we packed up and began the day's events. We started off climbing the rigid, snowy face of a mountain. After the first three hundred feet, because of steepness, we roped in and relied on ice axes for stability. Eventually the ice face angled perpendicular. Using tiny toe and finger holds, we pulled our precarious way to the top. It took four hours to make that climb. We celebrated with a few handfuls of food, then moved on to scale an easy peak. Next came cornice climbing. One at a time we backed off a mighty ice lip and rappelled to a narrow ledge a hundred feet below. Because ropes were too stiff and icy to climb, using harness and caribiners we tied ourselves into the rope, then allowed patrolmates to pull us back up to the top, like mighty fish from the deep. On my return trip the force of their pull wedged me into the cornice. There I dangled, two thousand feet up from the nearest outcropping of rock, contemplating my own mortality. When, with mittenless hands, I finally clawed my way out and achieved a stable surface again, I could only sit and laugh at the thrill of being alive. Twenty minutes later we were tied together in a running belay, a human daisy chain, and were expected to scuttle along the razor-edged, deteriorating spine of a mile-long high-altitude ridge. We were encouraged to scream loudly if we fell, so that climbing partners would not be pulled off the face too. Three hours later, when that drill concluded, we donned our packs again to start down the other side of the mountain we had climbed at dawn. Loose boulder fields, small avalanches and perilous scree kept tensions high for another few hours. Then there was a two-mile cross-country hike to the clearing which became camp. Dinner, our first bona fide meal of the day, was eaten finally at 11:30 that night.

In those nineteen enervating hours—the most taxing I ever have known—I gained a look at how profound and resilient my physical and emotional resources are.

Wilderness has put me on speaking terms with fear. Having led the careful life most urbanites do, I wasn't wild about the experience at first. However, by experiencing fear I have learned how to keep it from paralyzing me. I react more positively when afraid than I once did. There is a certain survival value in this. I was riding in a friend's car recently when smoke began billowing from the hood. We pulled off the freeway and got out fast. I ran to a nearby gas station screaming for someone to call the fire department. I tracked down the station manager and a fire extinguisher and ran back to the car. My friend, meanwhile, had moved a hundred yards away and stood there, locked and horrified. When help arrived we approached to find the motor still running. She had lacked the presence of mind even to switch the ignition off. Our reactions differed, I believe, because this woman leads a sheltered, indoor, relatively fear-free life. In crisis fear controls her.

Finally, wilderness has given me the gift of inspiring friends. Miriam Parker (known as Park) came first. We met on my first group backpack trip, a circle tour of Yosemite's High Sierra camps. The fourth night out, after we'd gone 40 miles, we celebrated her seventieth birthday. Two days later she joined us on a climb to 14,000 feet. The next morning, before dawn, I found her standing in a ring of high mountains waiting for day to begin. We were the only two up, the only two to witness the promising spectacle of a new day. We huddled on adjacent boulders in silence, celebrating the vision and a friendship that had formed despite a forty-year difference in age.

From Park, who remains a friend still, I have learned that time may slow the feet, but it does nothing to dim a capricious spirit or to strip the dazzle from life. That is good news to accompany me on the journey.

Since Park, most everyone I've adventured with has taught me something memorable, about wilderness or about themselves. I remember spending one windswept night in a stark mountain culoir with a friend reciting eerie Robert Service poems. It heightened the mood, and made me appreciate him more, for though I'd known him for years I had never known that he carried poetry in his soul.

Many times I have shared a front-row seat to nature's magic shows with a friend. I remember lying on smooth granite slabs near the high mountain headwaters of a river, watching speckled trout test their strength against the current. From deep pools they made relentless bounding attempts to return to the site of their conception. Only a few succeeded. Two people alone witnessed the futility and victory in this annual dance. We were granted this singular privilege by climbing 10,000 feet to the river's source—the only two that year who had. From such achievement and experience springs a unity which time does not diminish or change.

It is easy to conclude from this that I consider wilderness a panacea, The Answer. I do not. In some ways wilderness is but a metaphor for life. In place of walls there are trees. In place of mental pressures at work or at home, there are pressures to perform physically. In place of electronic, four-colored distraction, there is silence and there is you. It is a different pattern in the kaleidoscope, a different configuration—that is all—but from these differences I have gained new values, deeper friendships, a sense of my own potential and strength. My life is better because of these.

On the larger scale, my perception of women has changed. Because of what I have seen them accomplish in wilderness, I now know there is no such thing as a weaker sex. The woman who remains weak physically or in her life position does so purely by training—or by choice.

Wilderness offers women a higher choice. This impartial medium lets her discover beauty and meaning and personal strength she may not have known before. She may not find God or true love or a happy-ever-after life through wilderness, but she will discover more of herself. And that, according to ancient philosophers and a few modern thinkers, is one vital reason we are here.

APPENDIX

Suggested Reading

Backpacking Books

CARRA, ANDREW J. *The Complete Guide to Hiking and Backpacking.* New York: Winchester Press, 1977.

FLETCHER, COLIN. *The New Complete Walker.* New York: Alfred A. Knopf, 1974.

HART, JOHN. *Walking Softly In the Wilderness.* San Francisco: Sierra Club Books, 1978.

HARGROVE, PENNY and NOELLE LIEBRENZ. *Backpackers' Sourcebook.* Berkeley: Wilderness Press, 1979.

SAIJO, ALBERT. *The Backpacker.* San Francisco: 101 Productions, 1972.

Specific Skills

KJELLSTROM, BJÖRN. *Be Expert With Map & Compass.* New York: Charles Scribner's Sons, 1976.

Nordic World Editors. *Snow Camping.* Mountain View, California: World Publications, 1974.

General Nature Appreciation

CARRIGHER, SALLY. *One Day at Beetle Rock.* New York: Ballantine Books, 1944.

DILLARD, ANNIE. *Pilgrim at Tinker Creek.* New York: Harper's Magazine Press, 1974.

EISELEY, LOREN. *The Immense Journey.* New York: Vintage Books, 1957.

LEOPOLD, ALDO. *A Sand County Almanac.* New York: Sierra Club/Ballantine Books, 1966.

PHELAN, NANCY and MICHAEL VOLIN. *Yoga for Women*. New York: Harper & Row, 1963.

ULLYOT, JOAN. *Women's Running*. Mountain View, California: World Publications, 1976.

Medical

MITCHELL, DICK. *Mountaineering First Aid*. Seattle: The Mountaineers.

FEAR, EUGENE. *Wilderness Emergency*. Tacoma: Survival Education Association.

LATHROP, THEODORE G. *Hypothermia*. Portland: Mazamas, 1975.

WASHBURN, BRADFORD. *Frostbite*. Boston, Museum of Sciences.

Outdoor Cooking

FLEMING, JUNE. *The Well-Fed Backpacker*. Portland: Victoria House, 1976.

KINMONT, VIKKI and CLAUDIA AXCELL. *Simple Foods for the Pack*. San Francisco: Sierra Club Books, 1976.

POWLEDGE, FRED. *The Backpacker's Budget Food Book*. New York: David McKay Company, Inc., 1977.

WALLACE, AUBREY. *Natural Foods for the Trail*. Yosemite: Vogelsang Press, 1977.

General Nutrition

LAPPE, FRANCES. *Diet for a Small Planet*. New York: Ballantine Books, 1971.

ROBERTSON, LAUREL. *Laurel's Kitchen*. Berkeley, Nilgiri Press, 1976.

Specific Nature Guides

See guides to assorted subjects published by Golden Press Field Guides, Golden Press Nature Guides and Peterson Field Guide Services.

Equipment

MANUFACTURERS

These outdoor equipment manufacturers have, to a greater or lesser degree, acknowledged women's outdoor needs. If your retail outlet does not carry these brands, contact manufacturers directly for catalogs, or for the address of the nearest retail outlet.

Packs

Internal Frame

Caribou Mountaineering
P.O. Box 3696
Chico, CA 95927

Lowe Alpine Systems
P.O. Box 189
Lafayette, CO 80026

Hine/Snowbridge
P.O. Box 4059
Boulder, CO 80306

Internal and External Frame

Mountain Equipment, Inc.
1636 South Second Street
Fresno, CA 93702

Wilderness Experience
20675 Nordhoff
Chatsworth, CA 91311

External Frame

> Camp Trails
> 411 W. Clarendon Avenue
> Phoenix, AZ 85019

> Kelty Pack, Inc.
> 9281 Borden Avenue
> Sun Valley, CA 91352

Clothes

Parkas, Vests, Shorts, Knickers

> Alpine Products
> P.O. Box 403
> West Sacramento, CA 95691

> Caribou Mountaineering
> P.O. Box 3696
> Chico, CA 95927

> Sierra Designs
> 247 Fourth Street
> Oakland, CA 94607

> *Trailwise, Inc.
> 2407 Fourth Street
> Berkeley, CA 94710

Shirts

> * Coming Attractions, Ltd.
> 1524 Springhill Road
> McLean, VA 22102

> * Woolrich, Inc.
> Woolrich, PA 17779

Pants

> * C. C. Filson Company
> 205 Maritime Building
> 911 Western Avenue
> Seattle, WA 98104

*Q.P. Pants
3300 Atlantic Blvd.
Jacksonville, FL 32207

Boots

Donner Mountain Corporation
2110 Fifth Street
Berkeley, CA 94710
(Women's Model: Pivetta "Muir Trail")

Danner Shoe Manufacturing Company
P.O. Box 22204
Portland, OR 97222
(Women's Model: "Mountain Trail")

Fabiano Shoe Company, Inc.
Dept. A-7
850 Summer Street
South Boston, MA 02127
(Boots suited for women: "Padre" to size 8,
  "Madre" all sizes)

Vasque
Red Wing Shoe Company
Red Wing, MN 55006
(Women's Model: "Gretchen II")

EQUIPMENT CATALOGS TO WRITE FOR

Early Winters
110 Prefontaine Place South
Seattle, WA 98104

Eastern Mountain Sports
12408 Vose Farm Road
Peterborough, NH 03458

L. L. Bean, Inc.
Freeport, ME 04033

✳ Outdoor Gal
116 East Chestnut Street
Burlington, WI 53105

✳ Recreation Equipment Incorporated
P.O. Box C88-127
Seattle, WA 98188

Sierra Designs, Inc.
247 Fourth Street
Oakland, CA 94607

Helpful Organizations

These organizations both preserve wilderness and promote backpacking through organized trips.

The American Hiking Society
1255 Portland Place
Boulder, CO 80302

The International Backpackers Association, Inc.
P.O. Box 85
Lincoln Center, ME 04458

The National Audubon Society
950 Third Avenue
New York, NY 10022

National Wildlife Federation
1412 Sixteenth Street, NW
Washington, DC 20036

Sierra Club
530 Bush Street
San Francisco, CA 94108

The Wilderness Society
1901 Pennsylvania Avenue, NW
Washington, DC 20006

These organizations offer educational programs designed to develop outdoor skills.

National Outdoor Leadership School (NOLS)
Box AA
Lander, WY 82520

Outward Bound, Inc.
384 Field Point Road
Greenwich, CT 06830

Fitness

COOPER, KENNETH, M.D. *The New Aerobics*. New York: Bantam
    Books, 1970.

LANCE, KATHRYN. *Getting Strong*. New York: Bantam Books, 1978.

For information regarding National Parks or National Forests within
your travel range, and for topographical maps of specific wilderness
areas, write the following United States government agencies.

Office of Information
Forest Service
U. S. Department of Agriculture
Washington, DC 20250

Information Office
National Park Service
Department of Interior
Interior Building
Washington, DC 20240

For topographical maps east of the Mississippi:

Distribution Section
United States Geological Survey
Reston, VA 22092

For topographical maps west of the Mississippi:

Distribution Section
United States Geological Survey
Federal Center
Denver, CO 80225

Maps can also be procured from United States Geological Survey sub-
sidiary map distribution centers in Dallas, Salt Lake City, Spokane,
Menlo Park, San Francisco, Los Angeles, Anchorage, and Juneau.

INDEX

Index

Bears, 68–69, 139, 181, 183, 184–85,
   189
  women's menstruation and,
    176–77
Beauty, 164–71
  exercise and, 164, 167
Be Expert With Map & Compass
   (Kjellstrom), 119, 249
Behaviorism, 180
Belay lines, 121
Benzophenone, 165
Bigfoot, 188
Binoculars, 90
Bleuet stoves, 35
Blisters, 4, 76–78
Blue jeans, 50
Body heat, 123–27
  exercise and, 124–25
Body language, 199–200
Body temperature, 123, 125, 127
Bolen, Jean Shinoda, 105
Boots, 43, 44, 73–76, 78, 85–86, 87,
   121, 169, 253
  selecting, 74–76
Boredom, 6, 89–90
  from solo backpacking, 197–98
Boston, Teddi, 12, 60, 204, 206,
   207–9
Bowie, Diantha, 163
Boy Scout Handbook, 121
Boy Scouts of America, 121
Brandeis University, 61
Brown, Dee, 105
Bugs, 106, 106–7
Butane, 34, 35
"By Nature's Rules," 120

C. C. Filson Company, 47, 50, 252
Caffeine, 127
Cagoules, 54–55, 57
Calamity Jane, xiii
California, University of, 176
Calories, 59, 61, 63, 66, 124
Campbell, Dan, 133
Campbell, Sally Stapp, 133
Camp Trails, 26, 252
Candles, 118, 129
Caps, 56, 57
Carbohydrates, 61, 62–63
Cardiovascular condition, checking,
   9, 12

Caribou Mountaineering, 20, 26–27,
   46, 251, 252
Carra, Andrew J., 249
Carrigher, Sally, 249
Cartridge stoves, 35
Cashmere sweaters, 48, 57, 86
Cerebral edema, 127
Chest straps, 24
Christiansen, Jeff, 4–6
Clark, William, xiii–xiv
Clothing, 44–58, 252–53
  appearance of, 47, 53, 58
  color of, 47, 58
  cotton, 51, 55, 56–57, 76, 168
  fashion and, 44–45, 45–46, 58
  for the first trip, 86–87, 90, 92–
    93
  layers of, 48–57
  miscalculations about, 4
  nylon, 48, 50, 54–55, 55–56, 77
  pioneer women, xiv, xvi, 44
  shopping for, 47, 57
  for sleep, 190
  unisex, 45
  waterproof, 55–56, 76
  wet, 125–26, 130
  wool, 48–51, 56–57, 76–77, 126
  See also names of articles of
    clothing
Clough, Allison, 32, 42, 232
Cold climates, 125–26
Coleman Company, 37
Colorado Outward Bound, 65, 109–
   10, 113, 230
Comfort, 106
Coming Attractions, Ltd., 47, 252
Compact I and II backpacks, 26
Compass reading, 113, 115, 119–20,
   205
*Complete Guide to Hiking and Back-
   packing, The* (Carra), 249
Compressed food, 59, 60, 61, 64–65,
   87
Conditioning, 8–16
  aerobic exercise, 9–10, 12, 164
  age and, 12
  with a backpack, 11–12
  books on fitness, 249–50
  the feet, 77
  guide for, 12–16
  for long-distance walking, 206